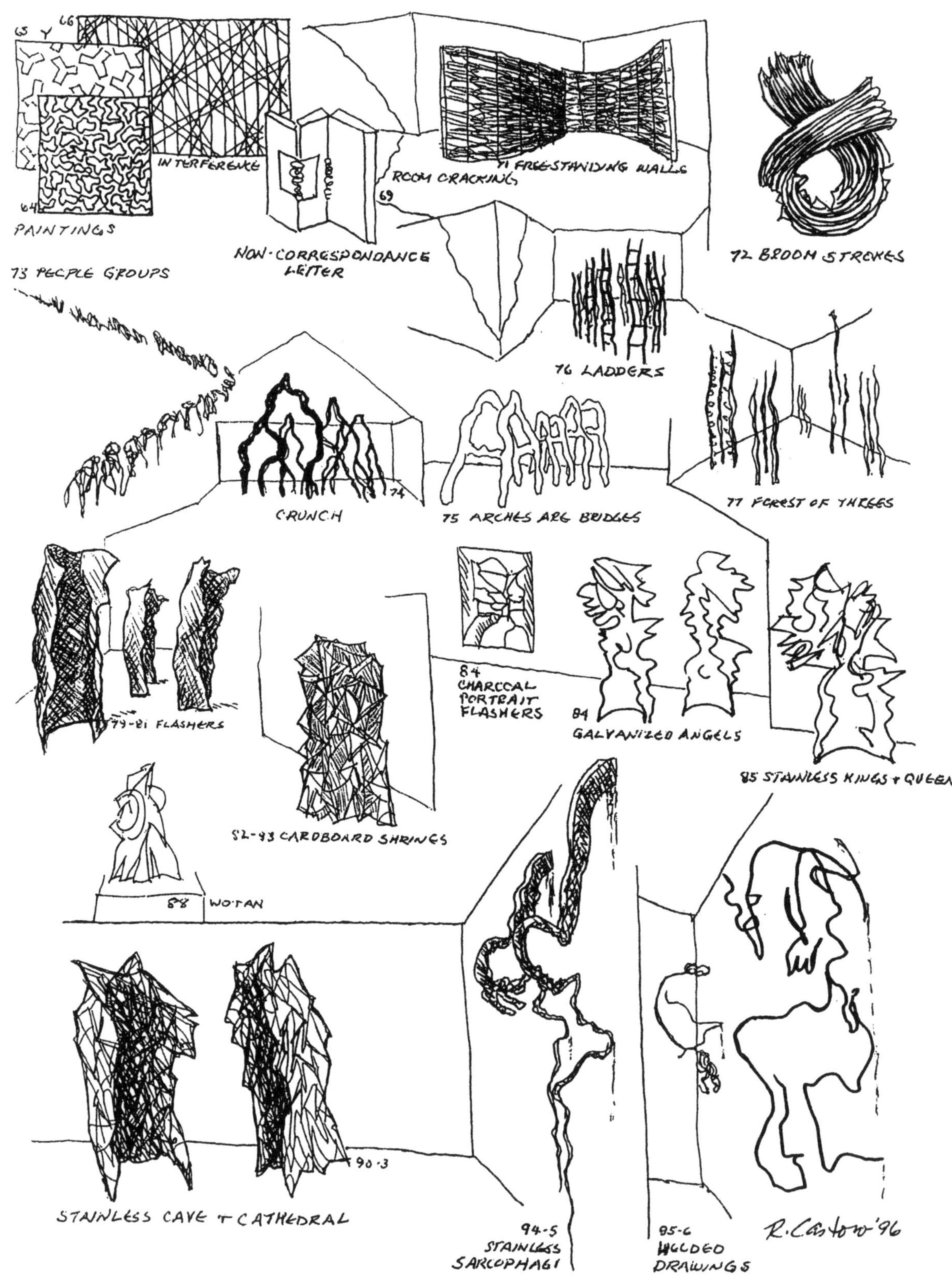

65 Y 66
INTERFERENCE
64
PAINTINGS
73 PEOPLE GROUPS
NON-CORRESPONDANCE LETTER
69
ROOM CRACKING
71 FREESTANDING WALLS
72 BROOM STROKES
76 LADDERS
77 FOREST OF THREES
CRUNCH
74
75 ARCHES ARE BRIDGES
79-81 FLASHERS
82-83 CARDBOARD SHRINES
84 CHARCOAL PORTRAIT FLASHERS
84 GALVANIZED ANGELS
85 STAINLESS KINGS + QUEEN
88 WOTAN
STAINLESS CAVE + CATHEDRAL
90-3
94-5 STAINLESS SARCOPHAGI
85-6 WELDED DRAWINGS
R. Caston '96

ROSEMARIE CASTORO

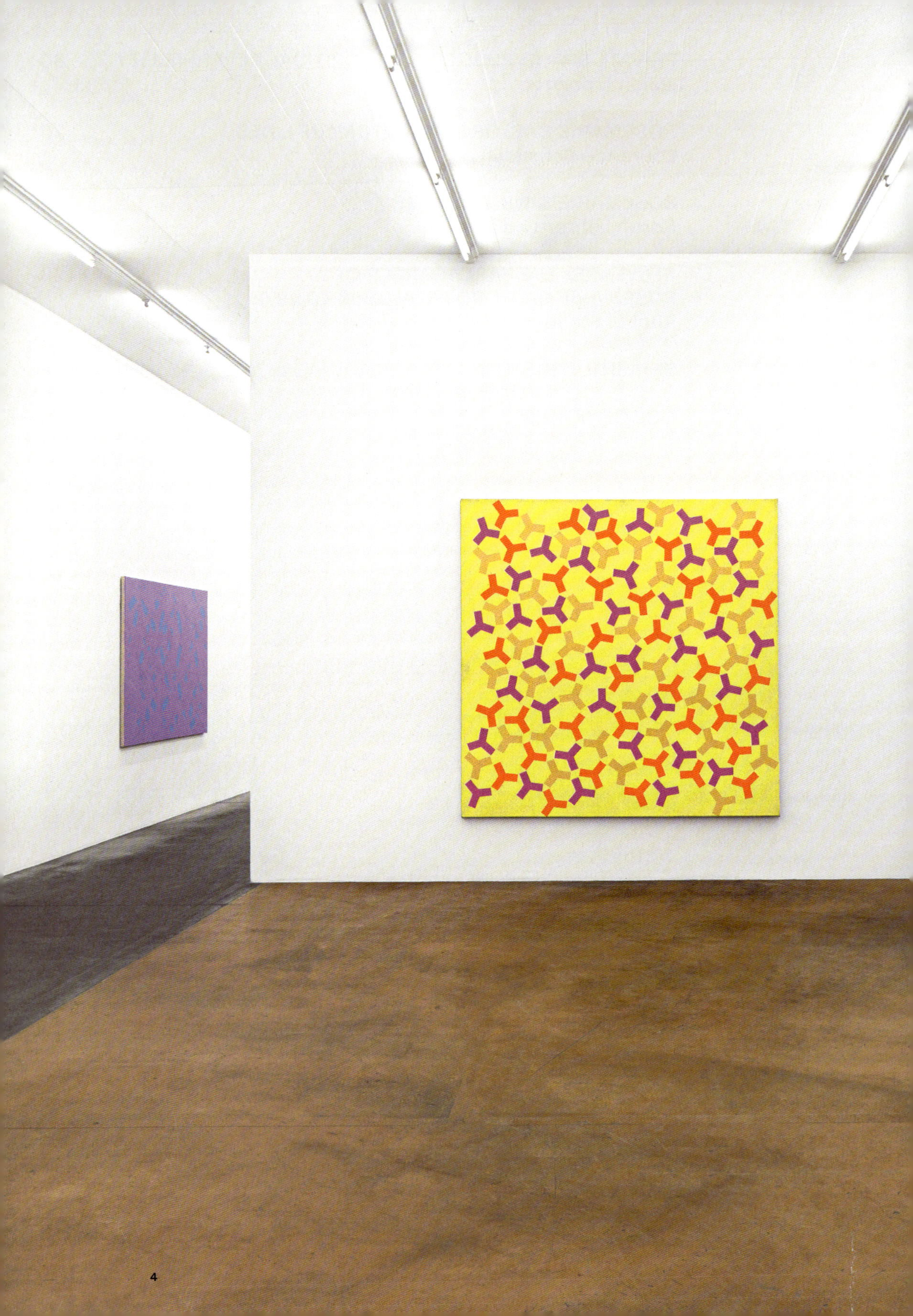

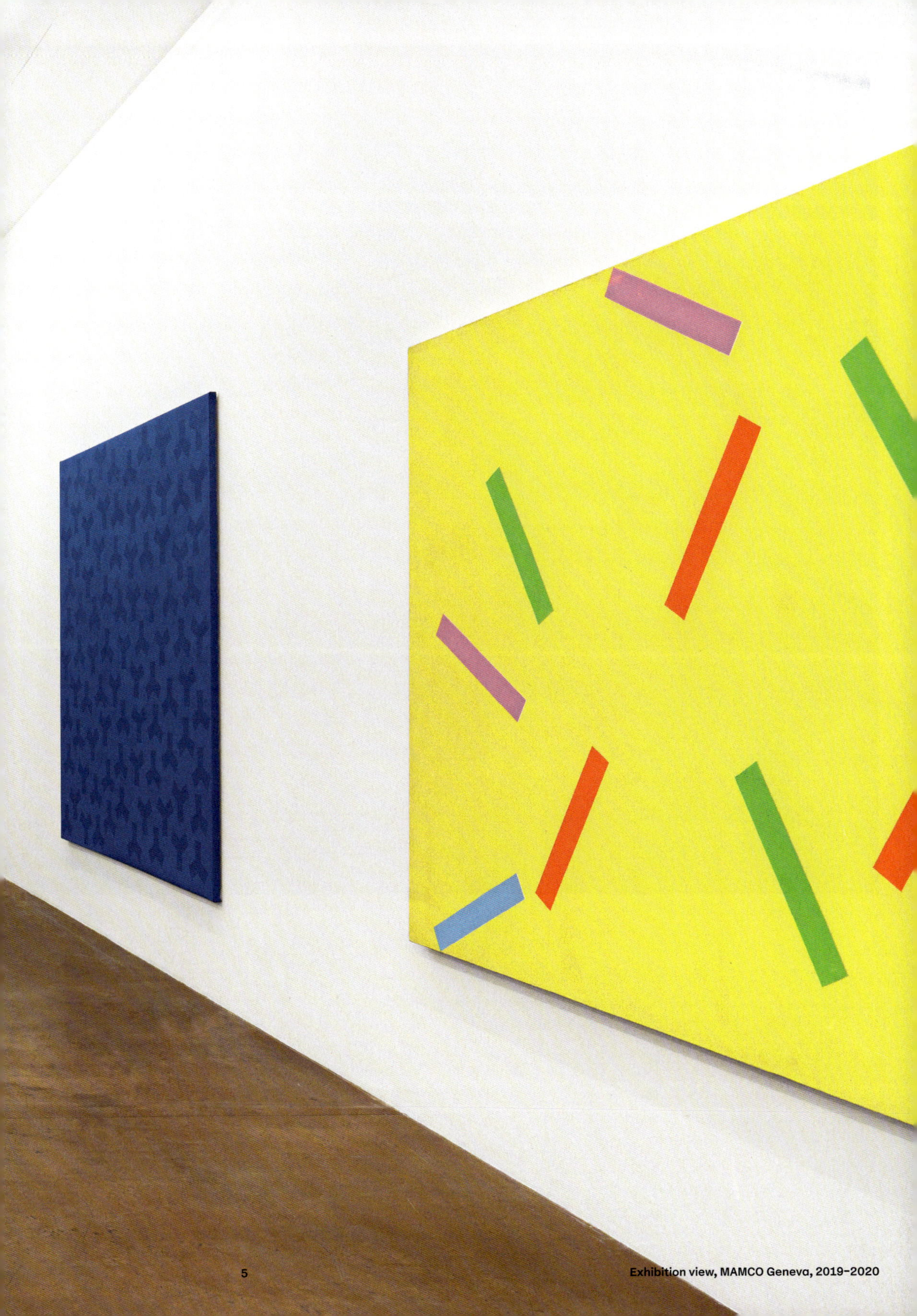

Exhibition view, MAMCO Geneva, 2019–2020

Blue Blue Y, 1965

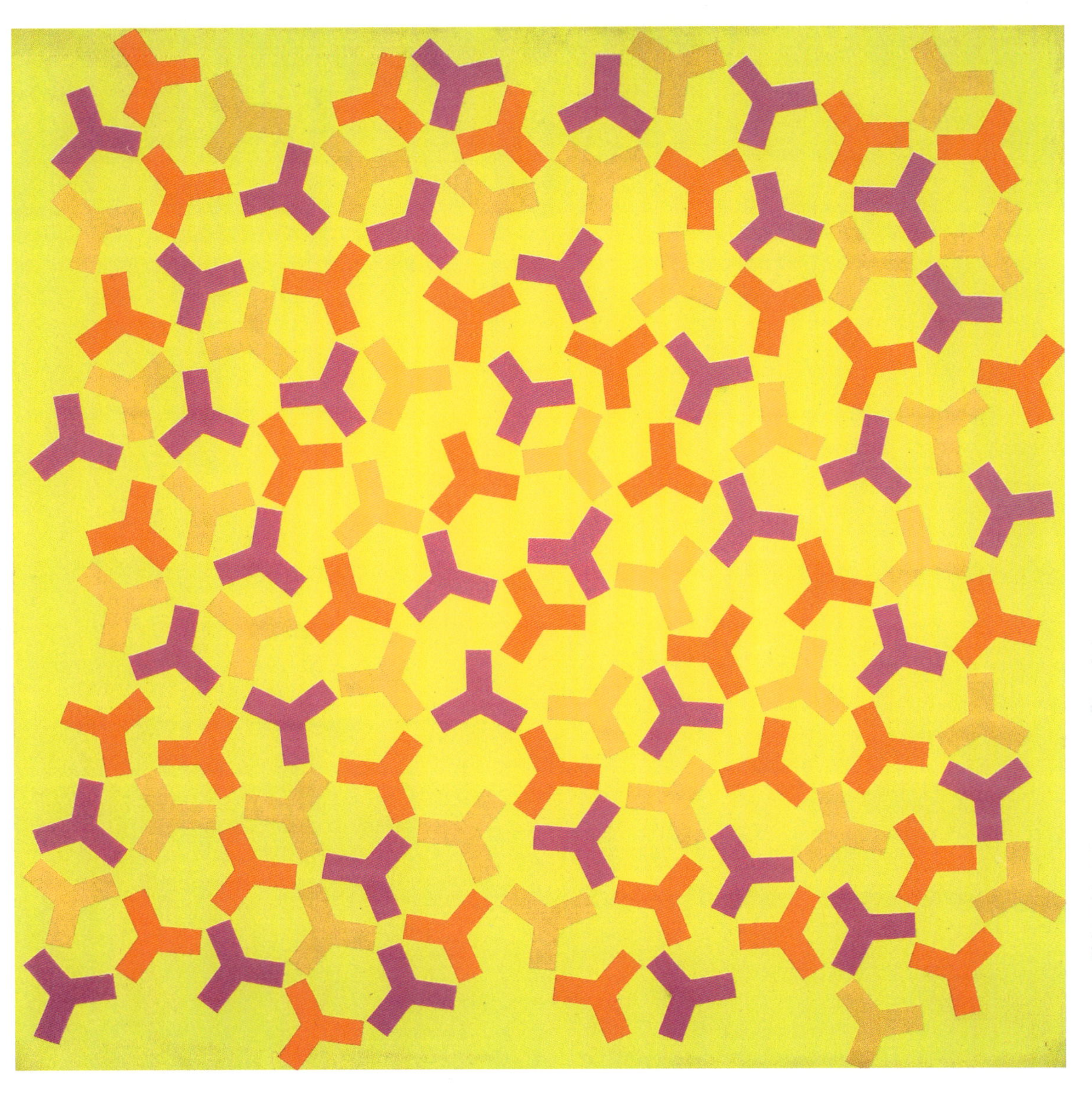

Orange Ochre Purple Yellow Y, 1965

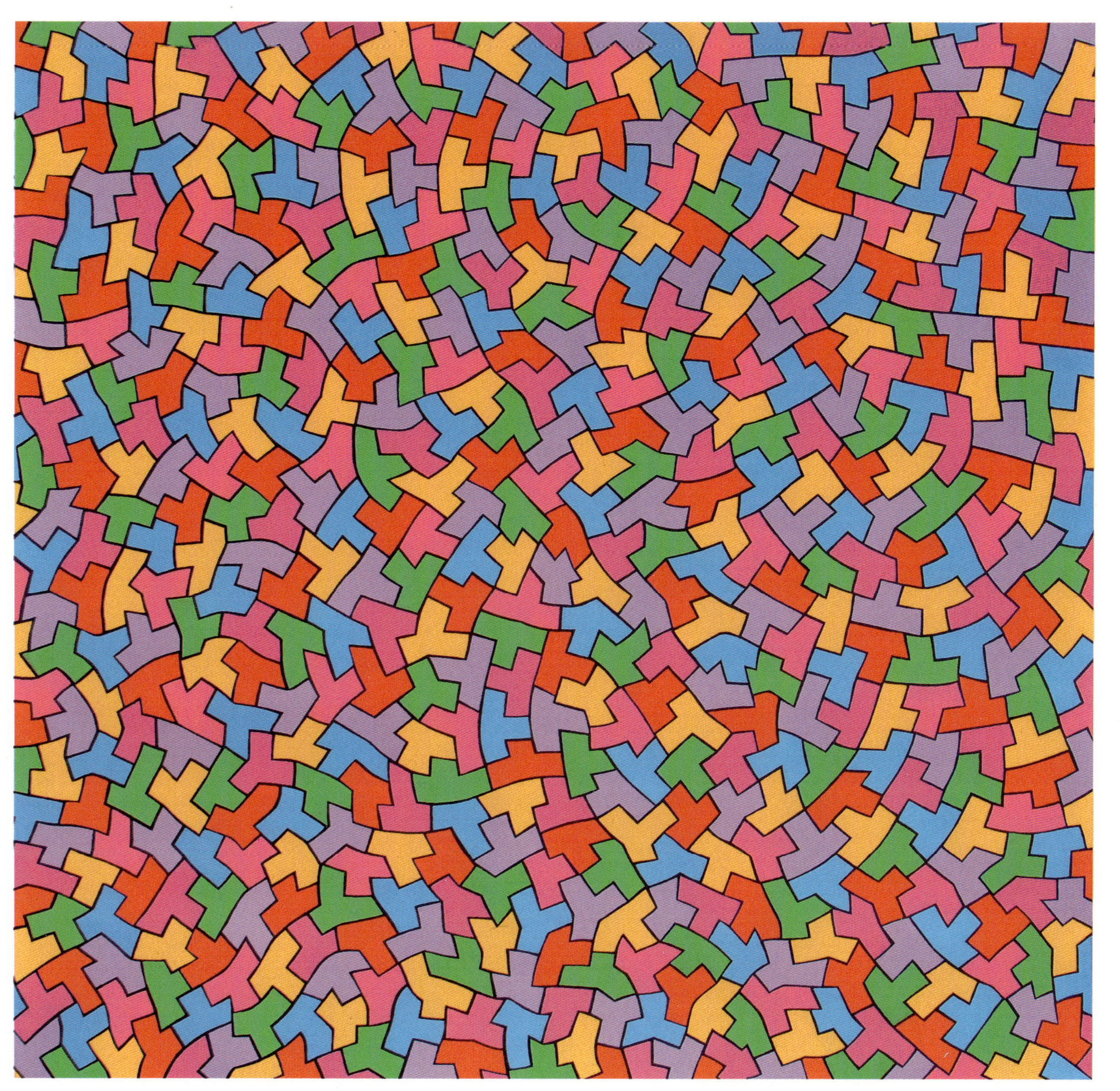

Red Pink Green Gray Blue Tan, 1964

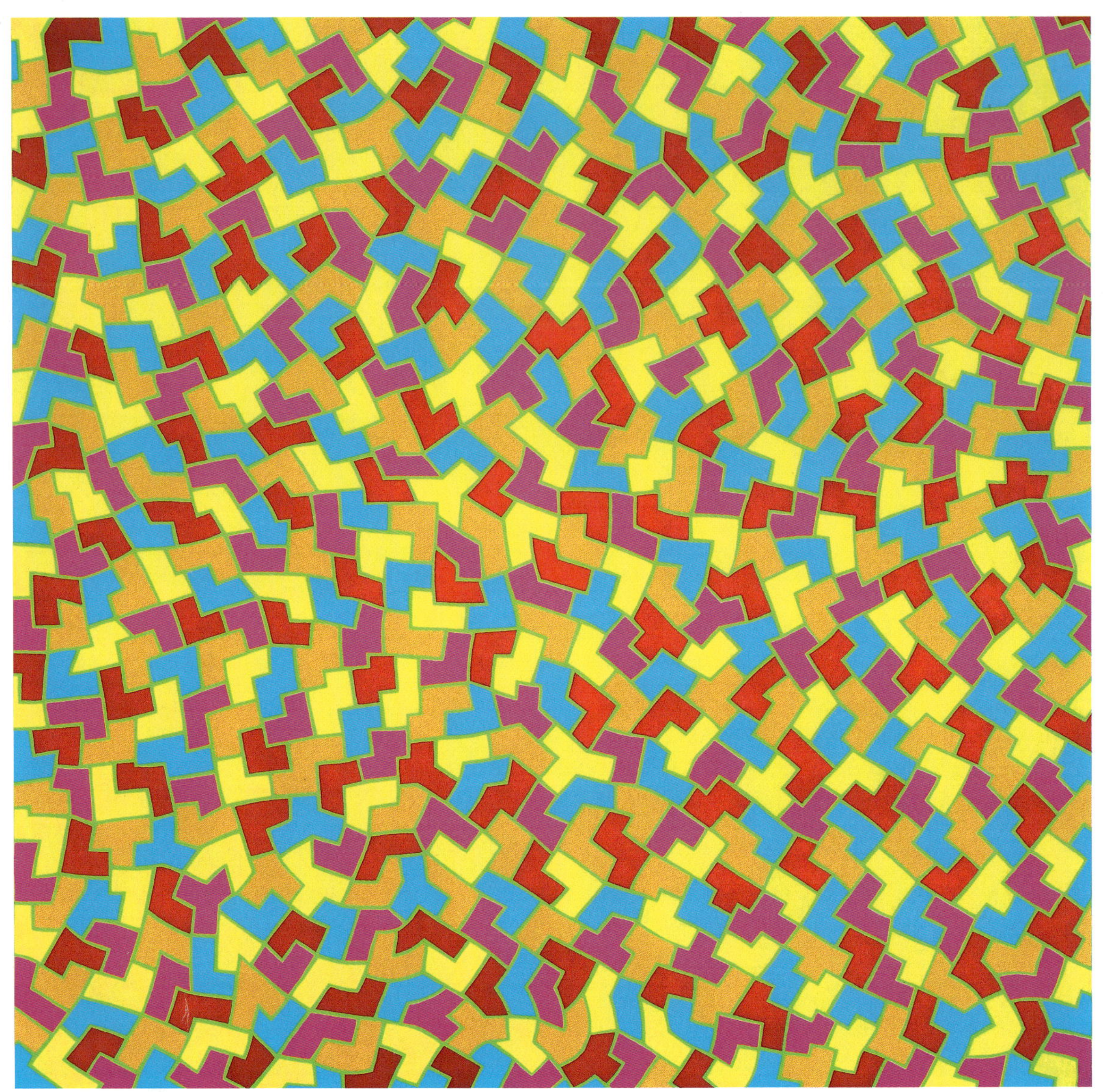

Red Yellow Blue Pink Brown, 1964

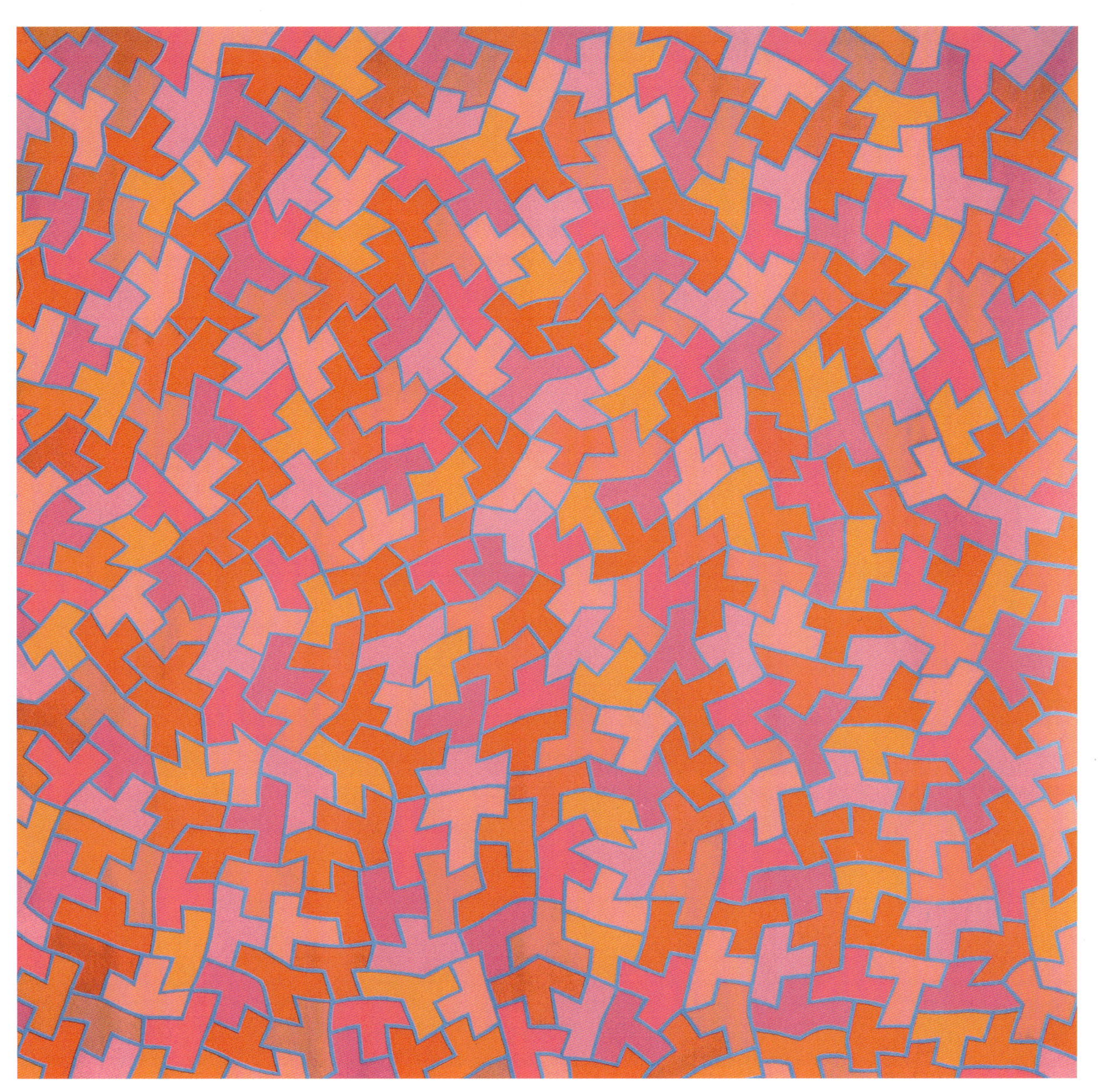

Yellow Pink Brown Blue, 1964

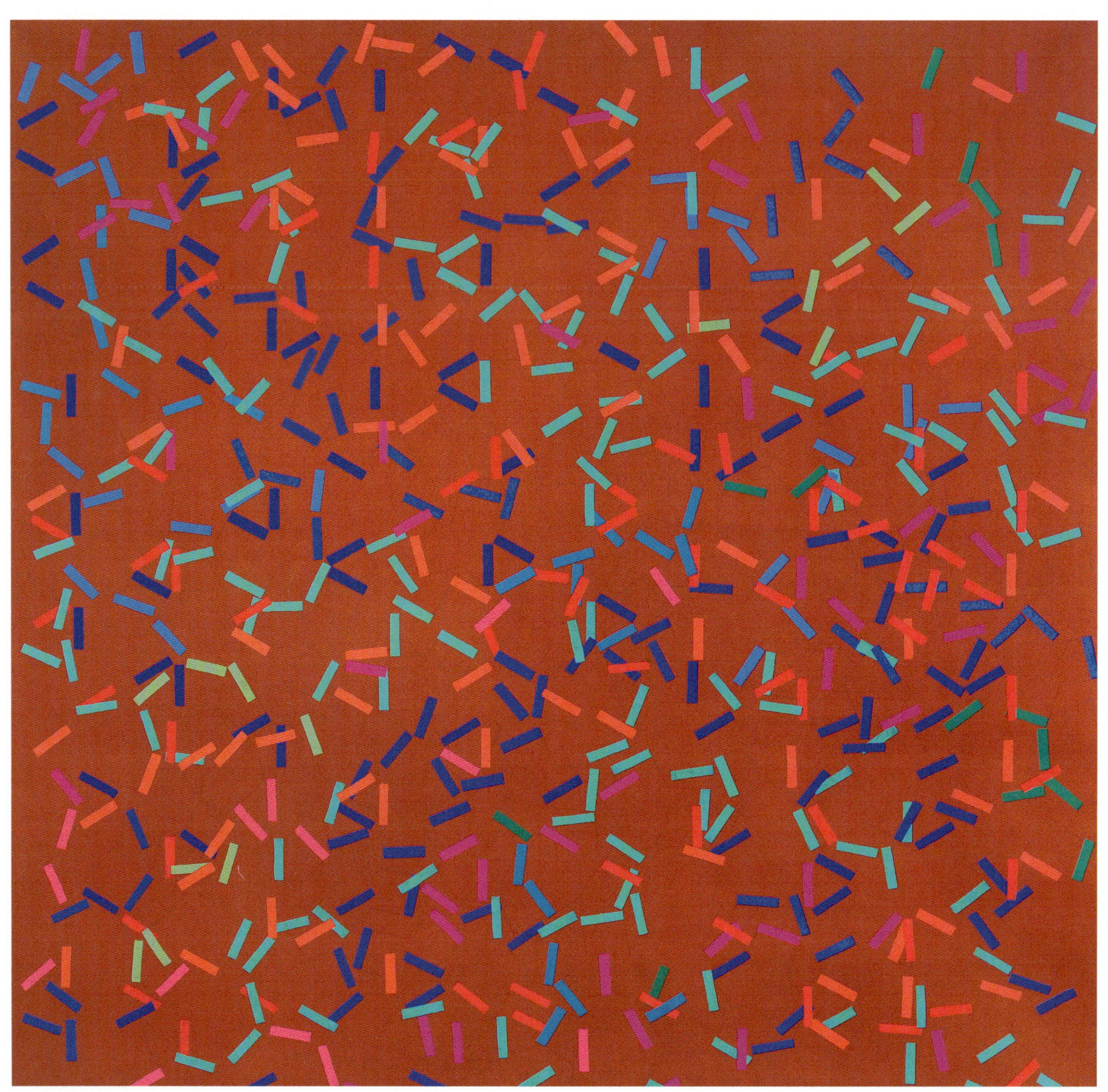

Red Pink Green Gray, 1965

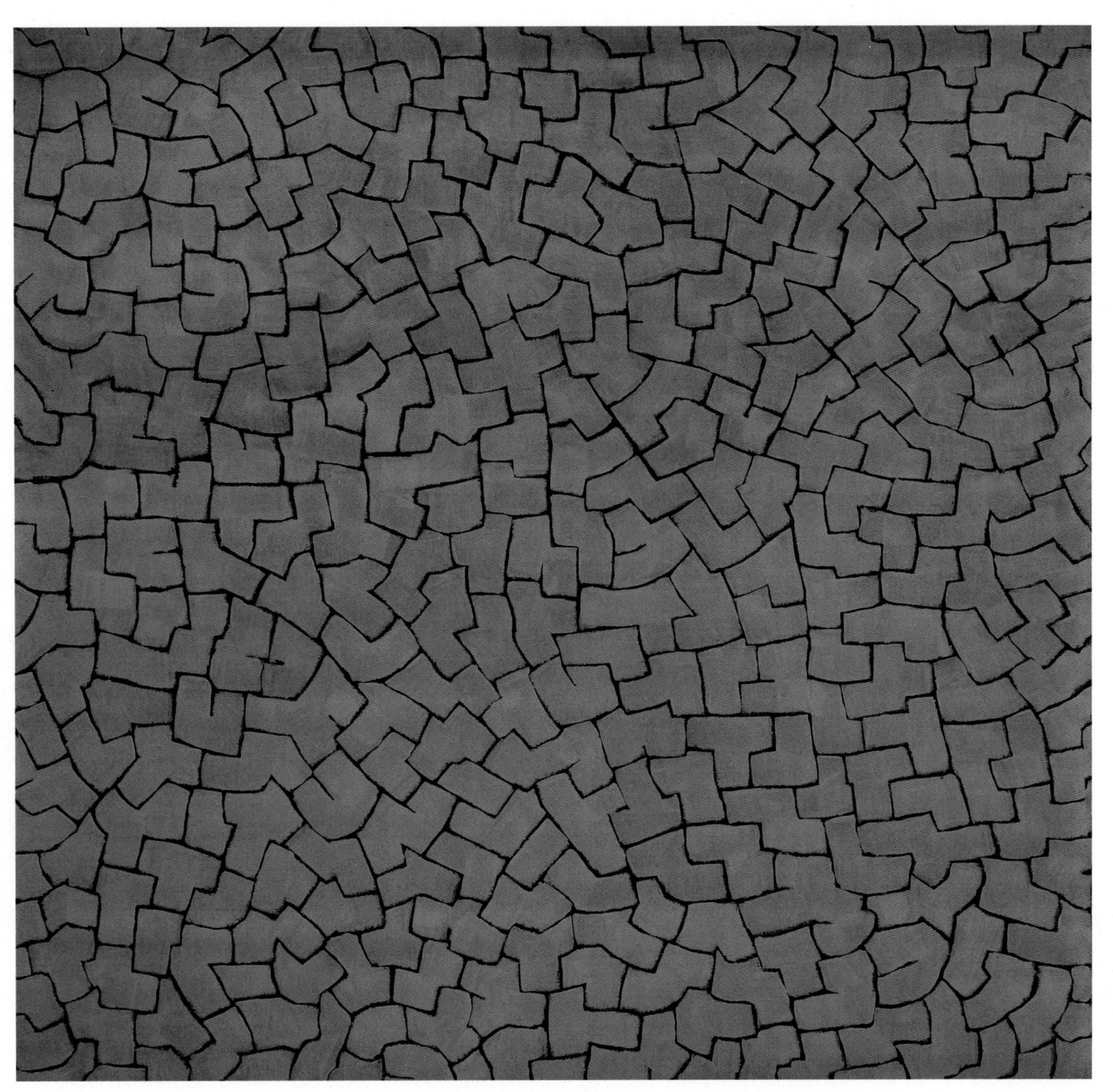

Green Black, 1964

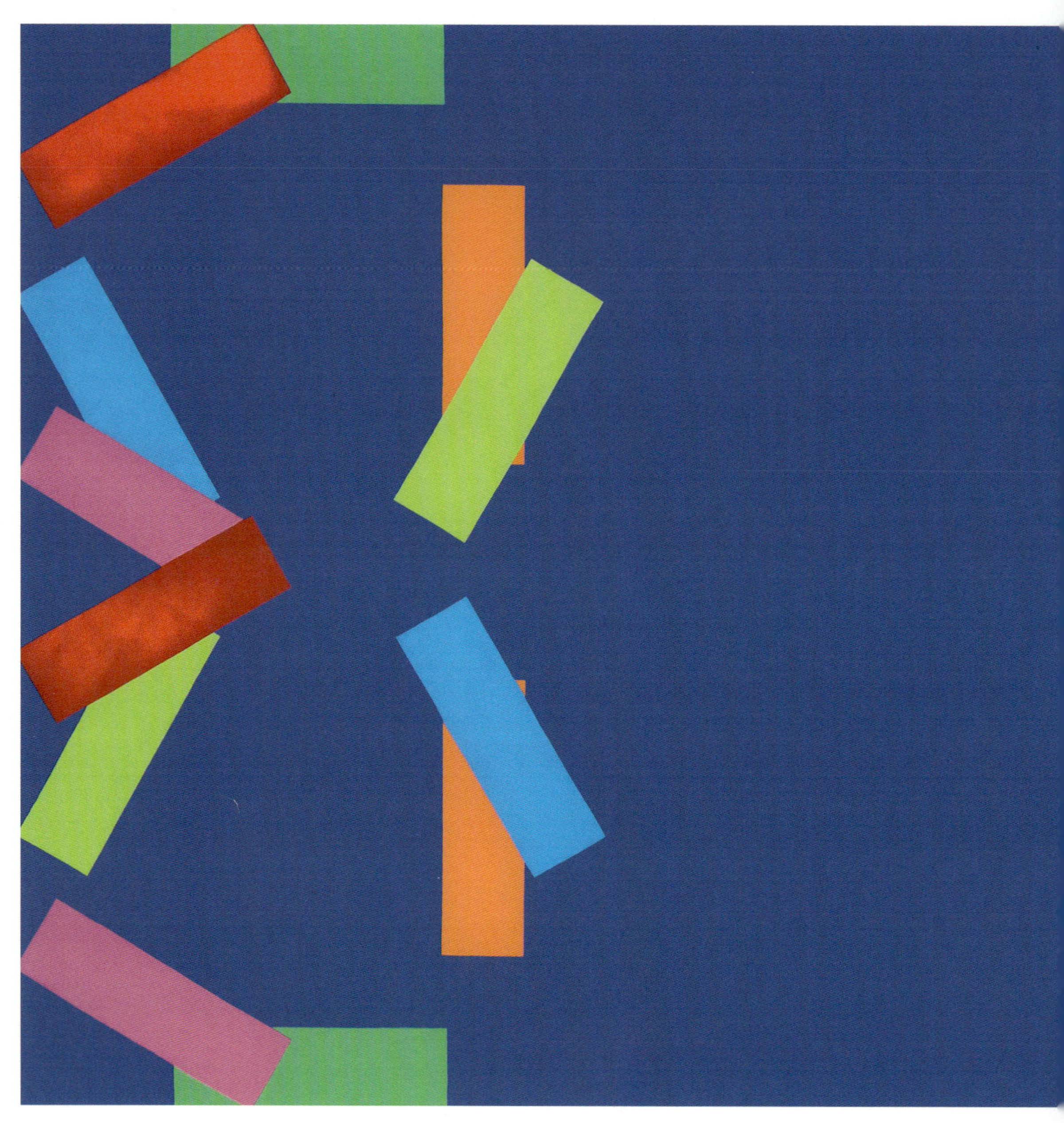

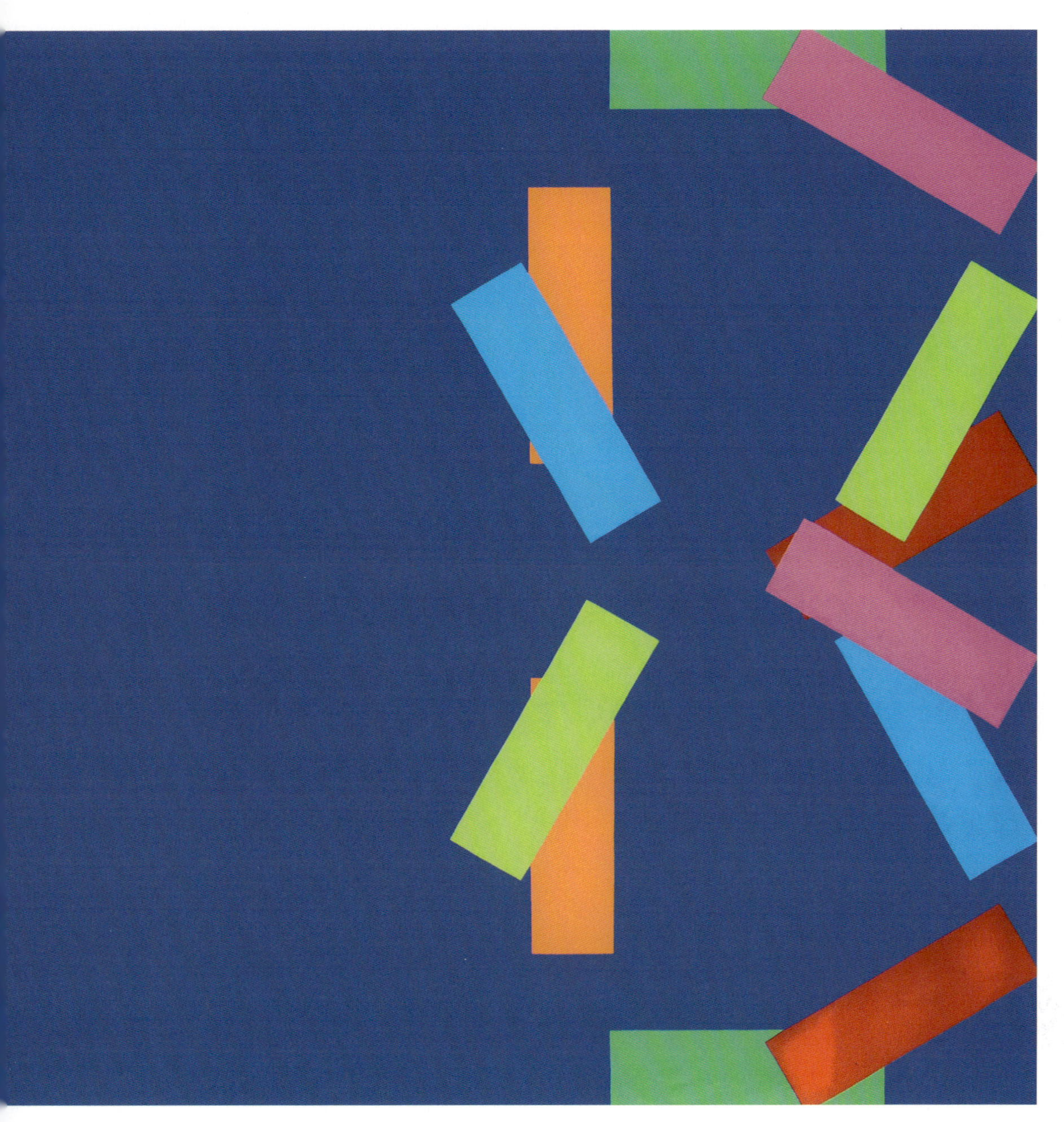

Blue Red Gold Pink Green Yellow Y Bar, 1965

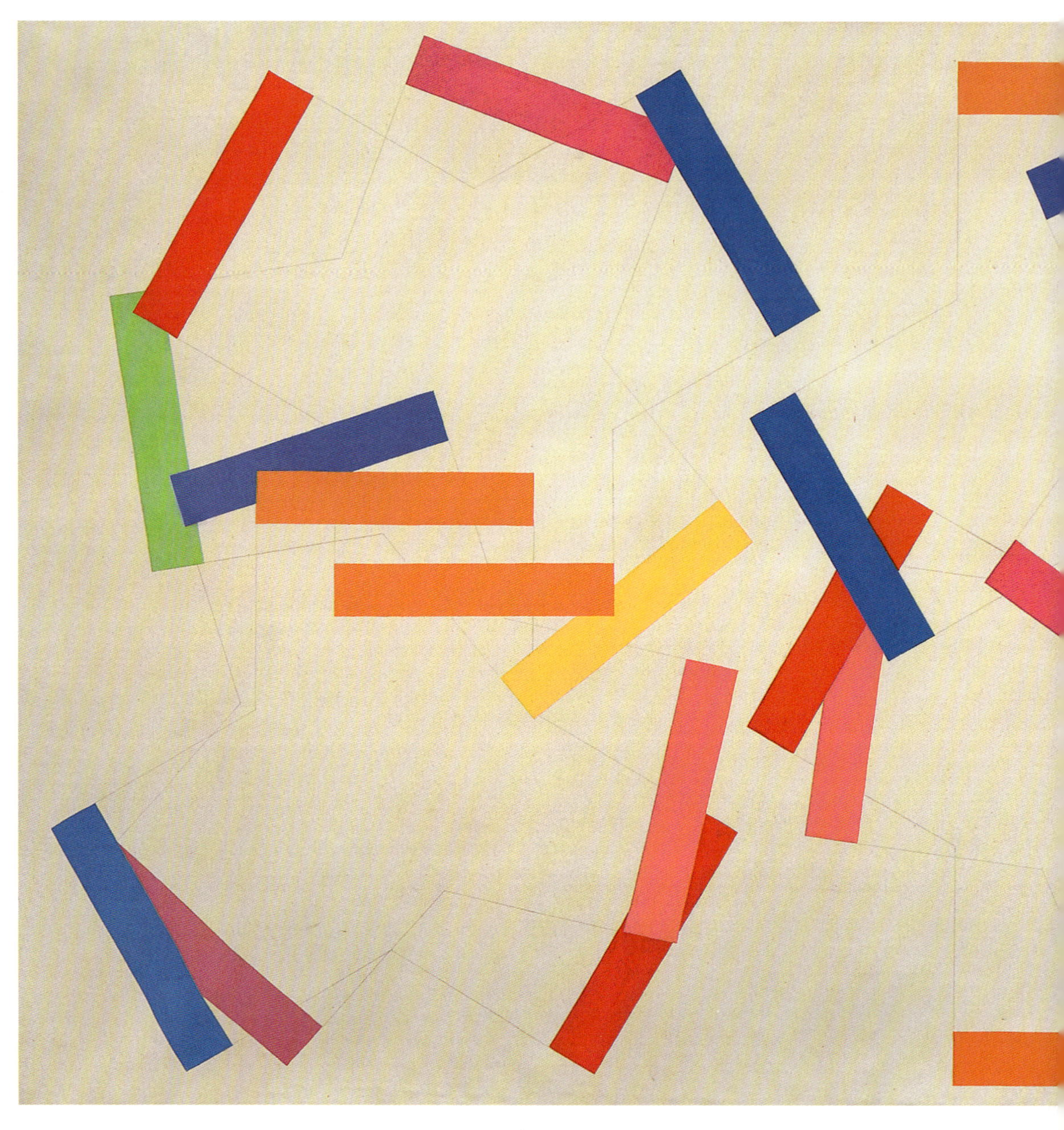

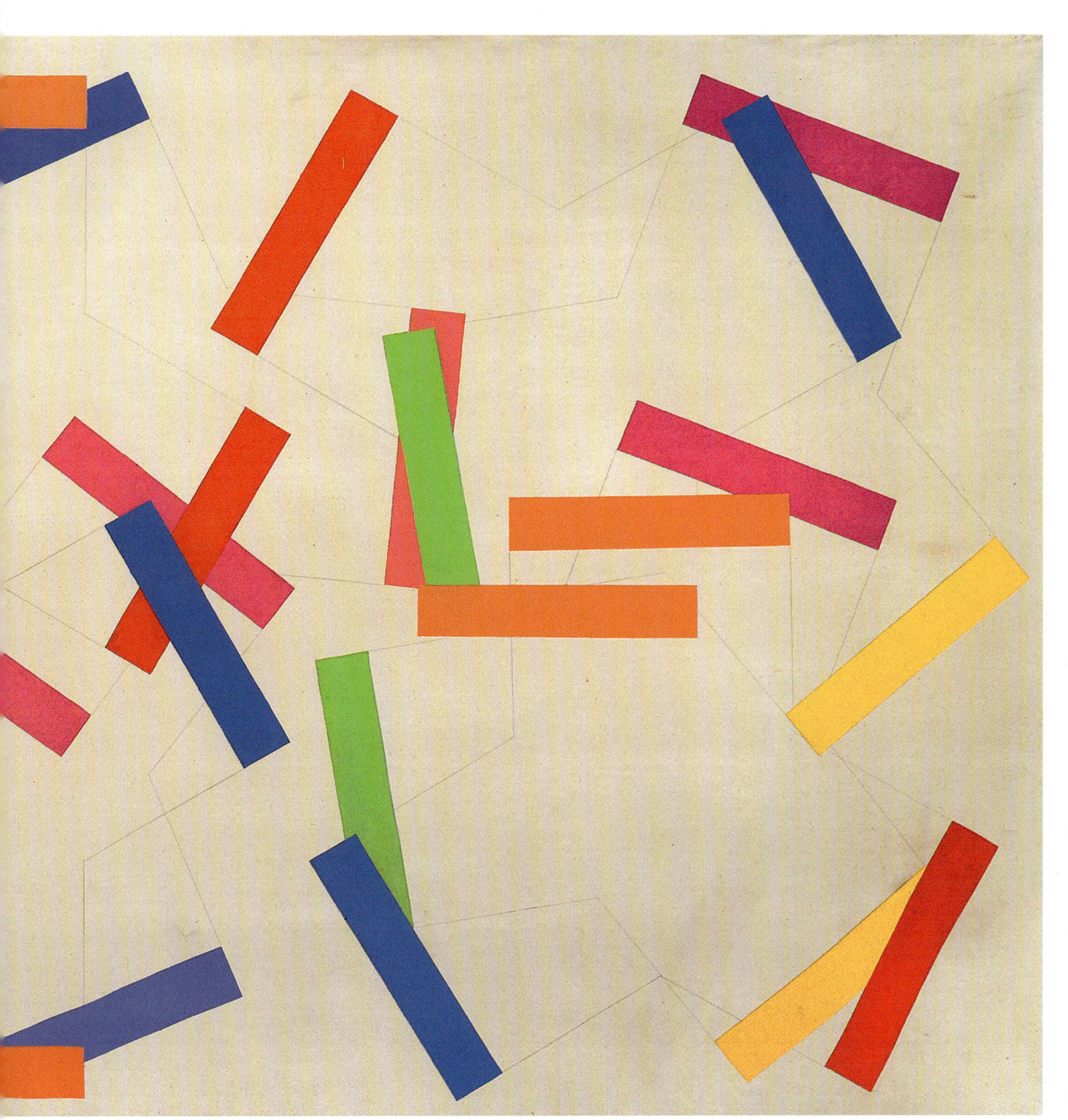

Multi Raw Bar, 1965

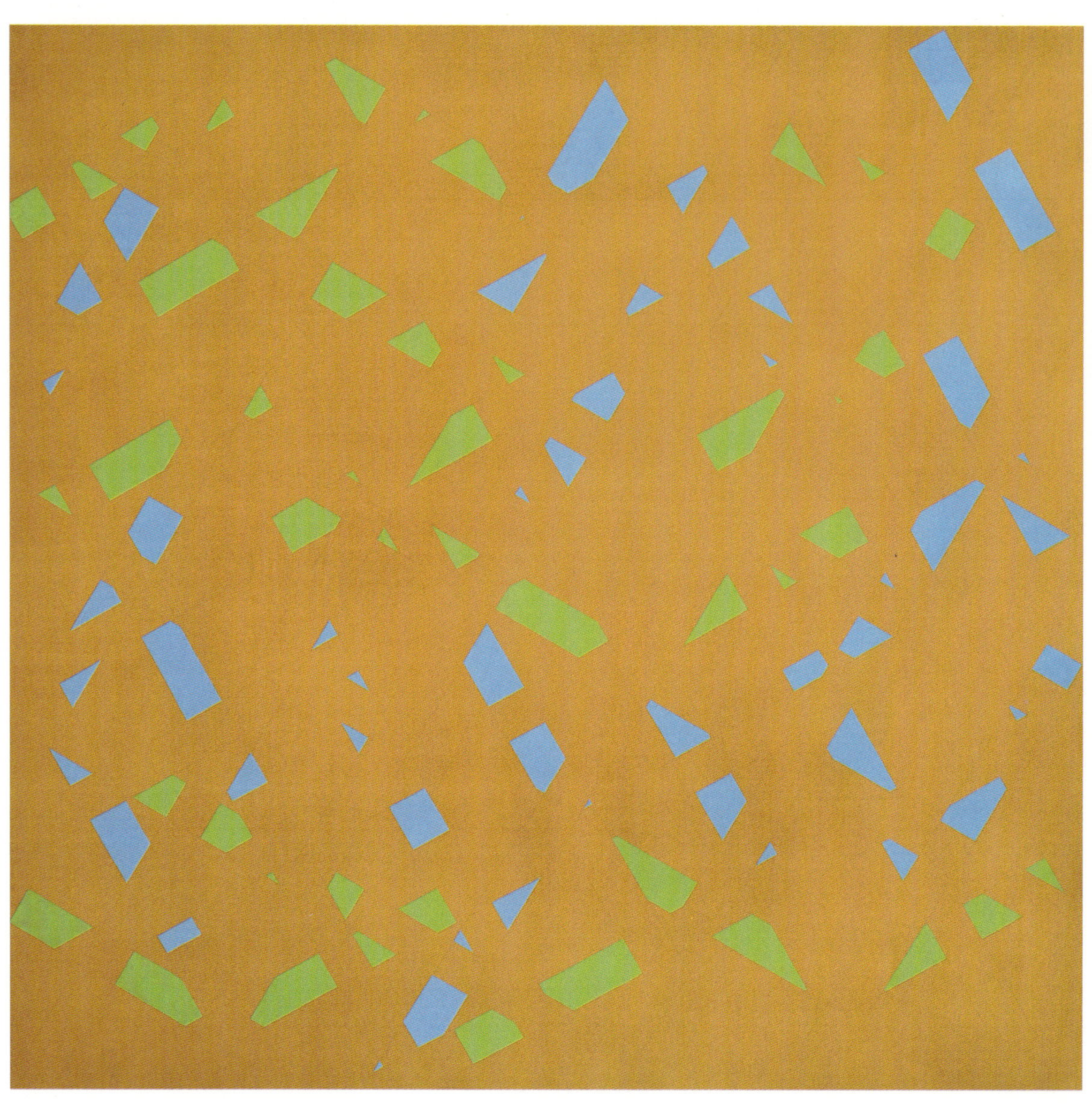

Orange Green Blue Interference, 1965

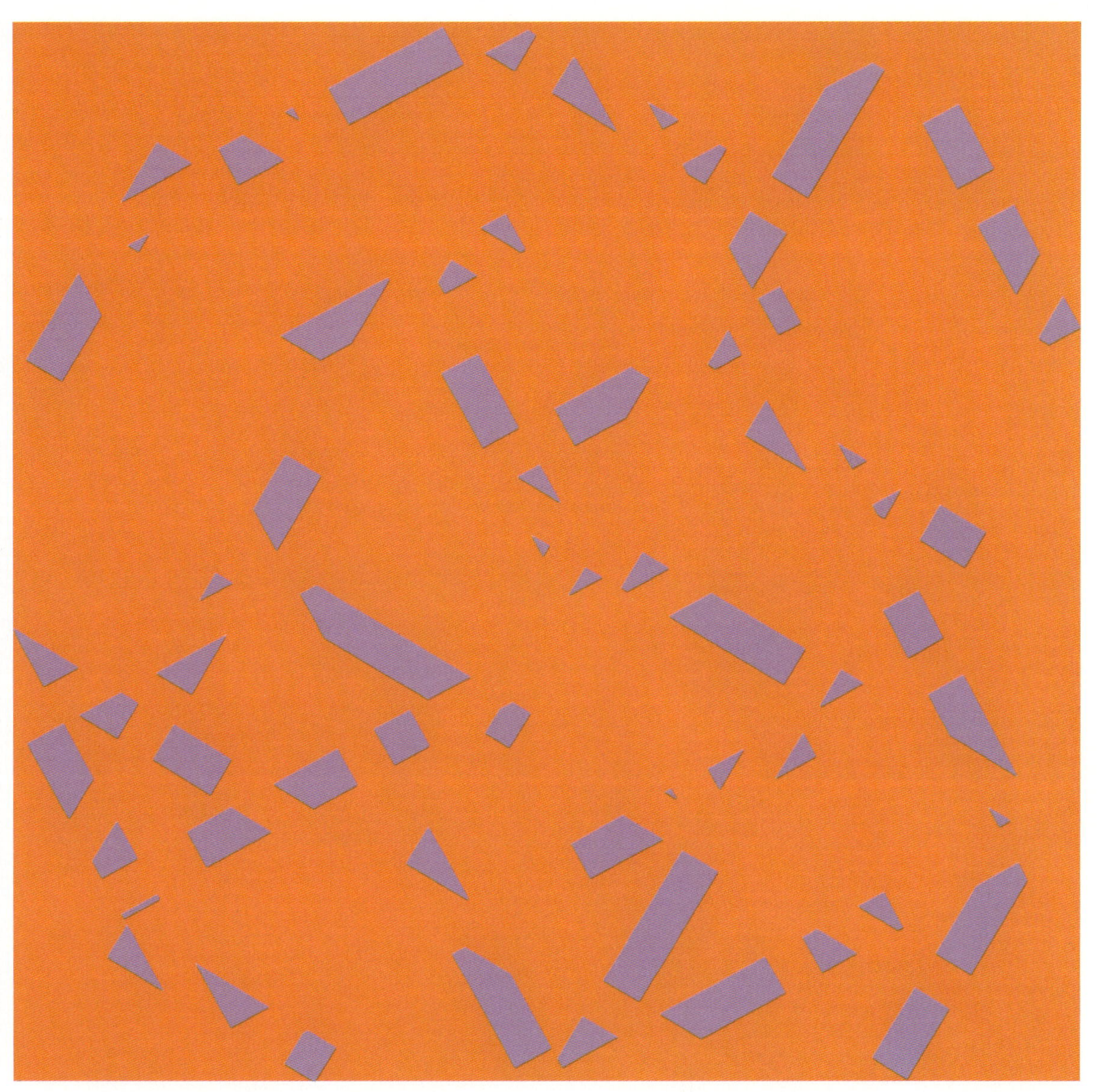

Purple Orange Bar Interference, 1965

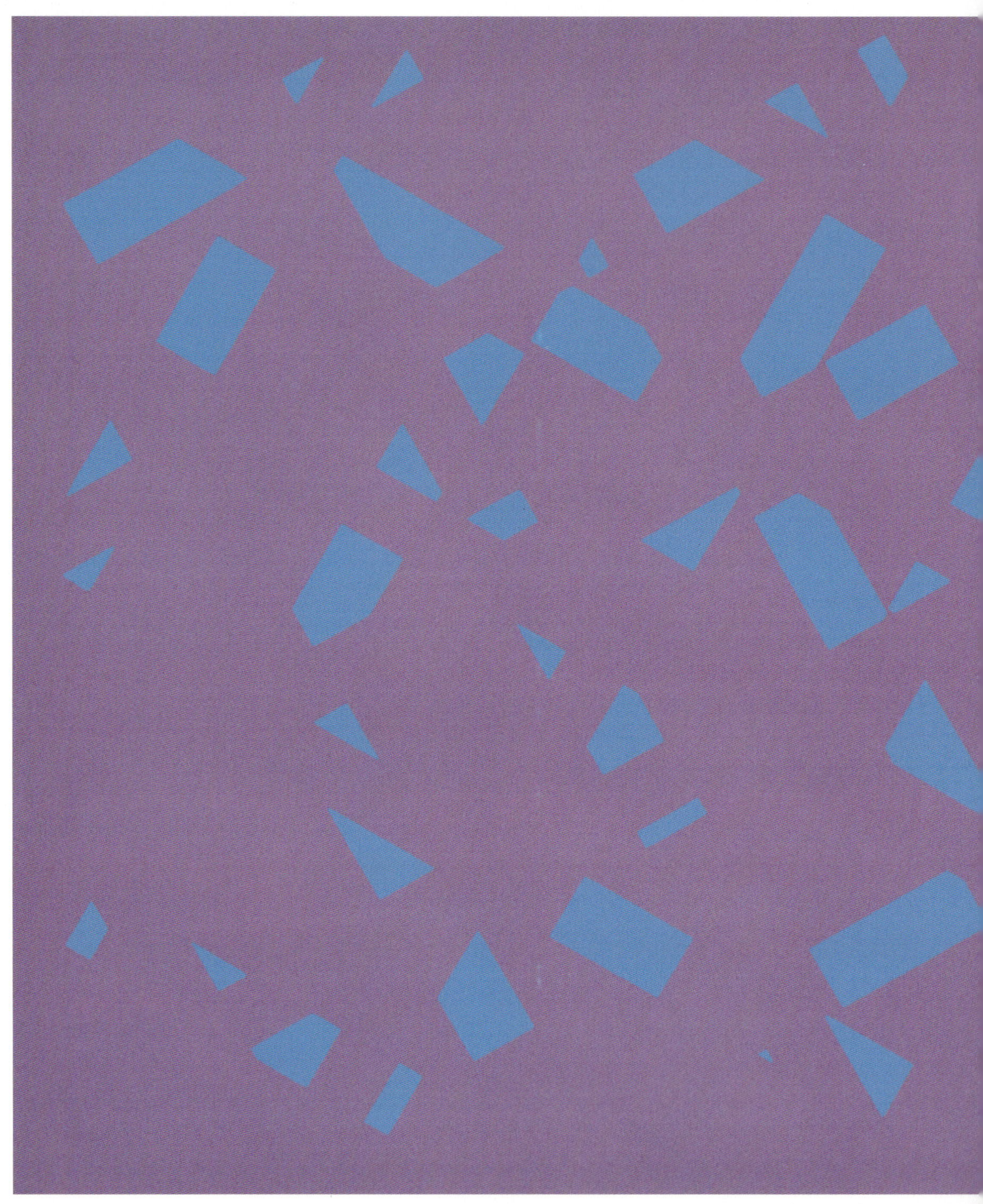

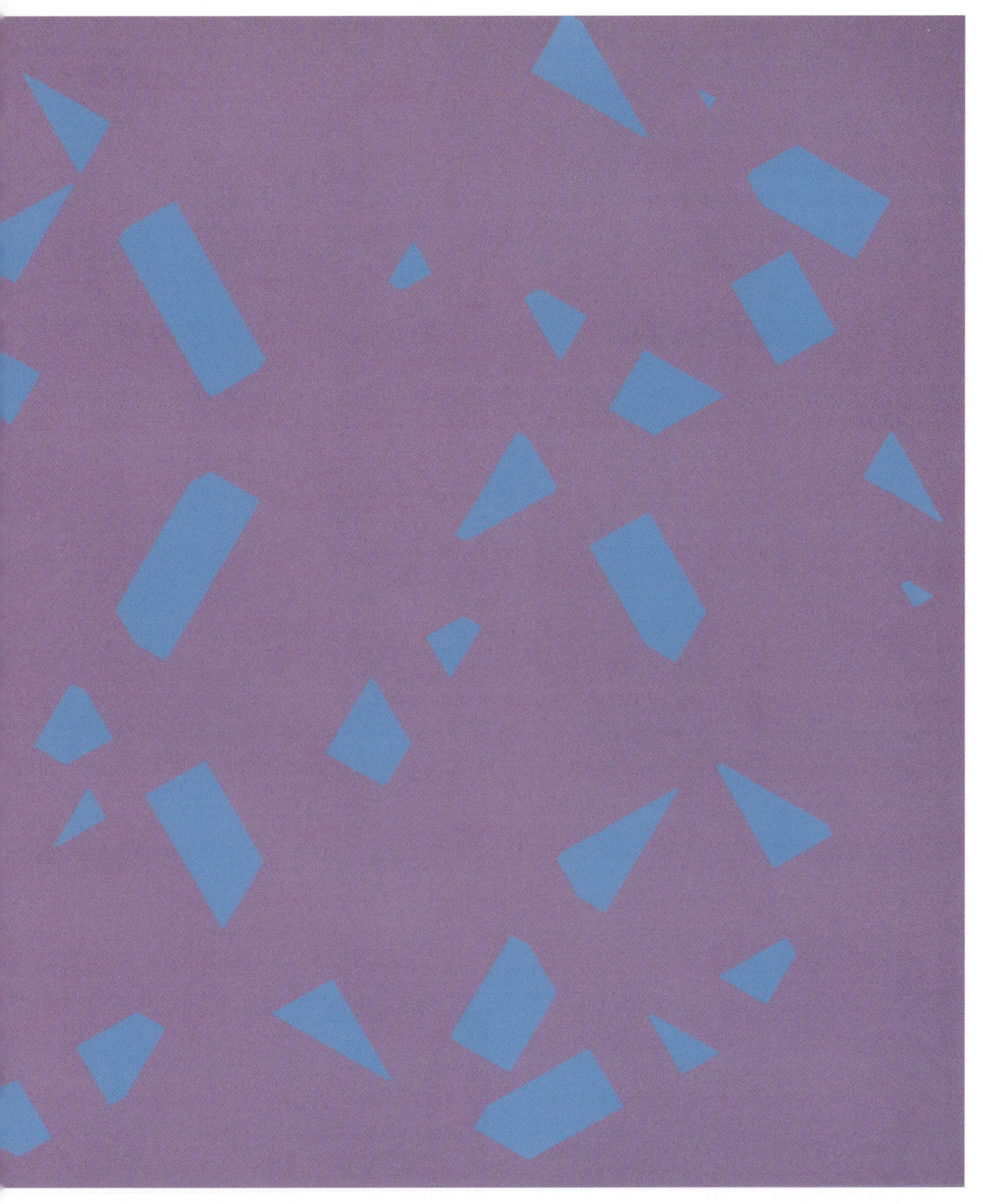

Dioxomine Cerulean, 1965

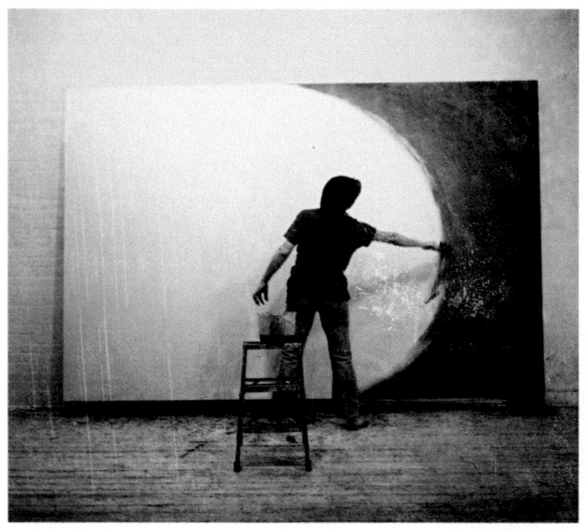
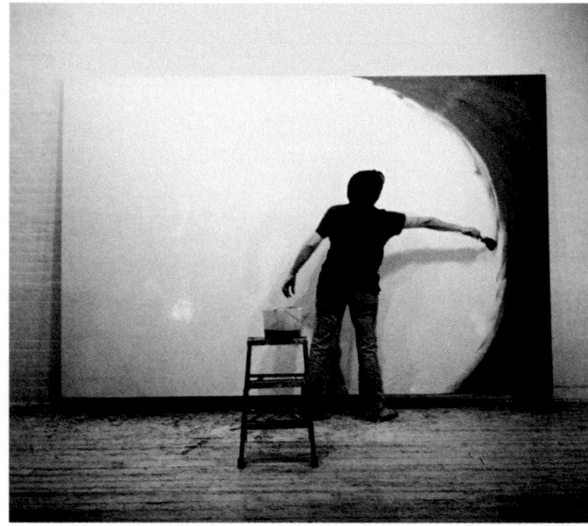
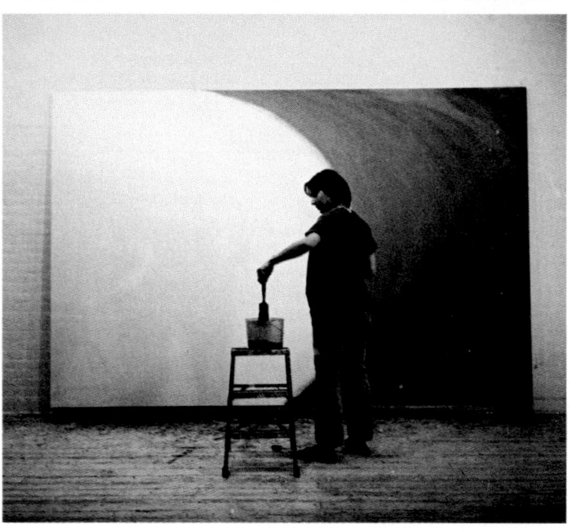
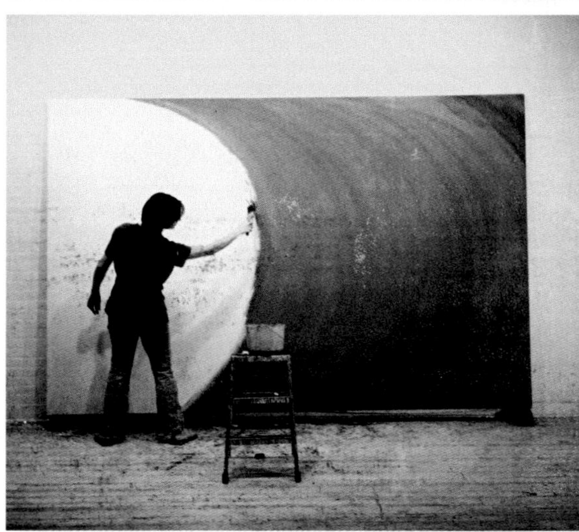
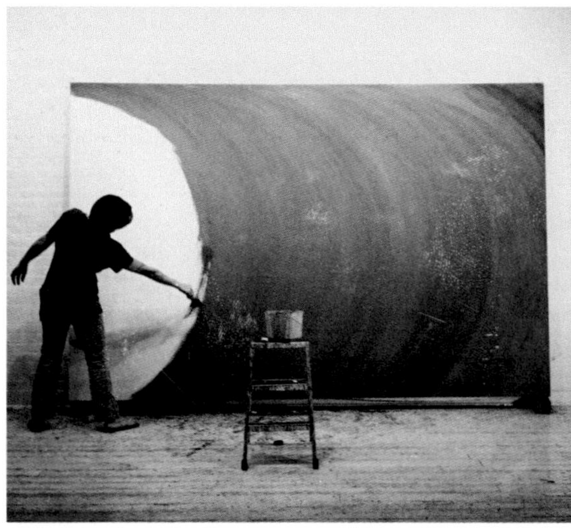
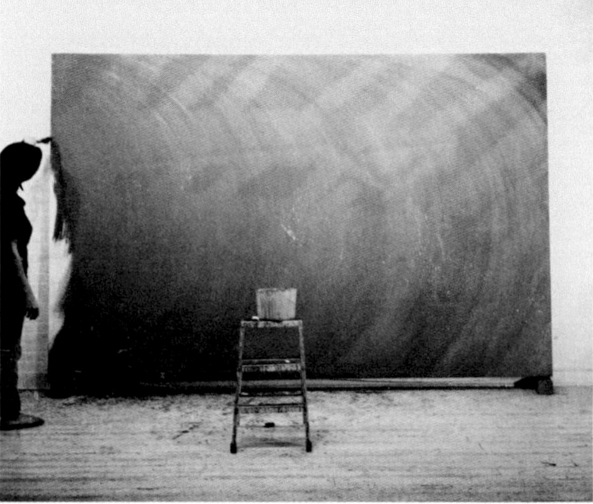

Rosemarie Castoro painting *Arm Swing Blues*

Arm Swing Blues (Pencil Paintings), 1967

Orange China Marker, 1967

   Pencil Painting Blues (Pencil Paintings), 1967

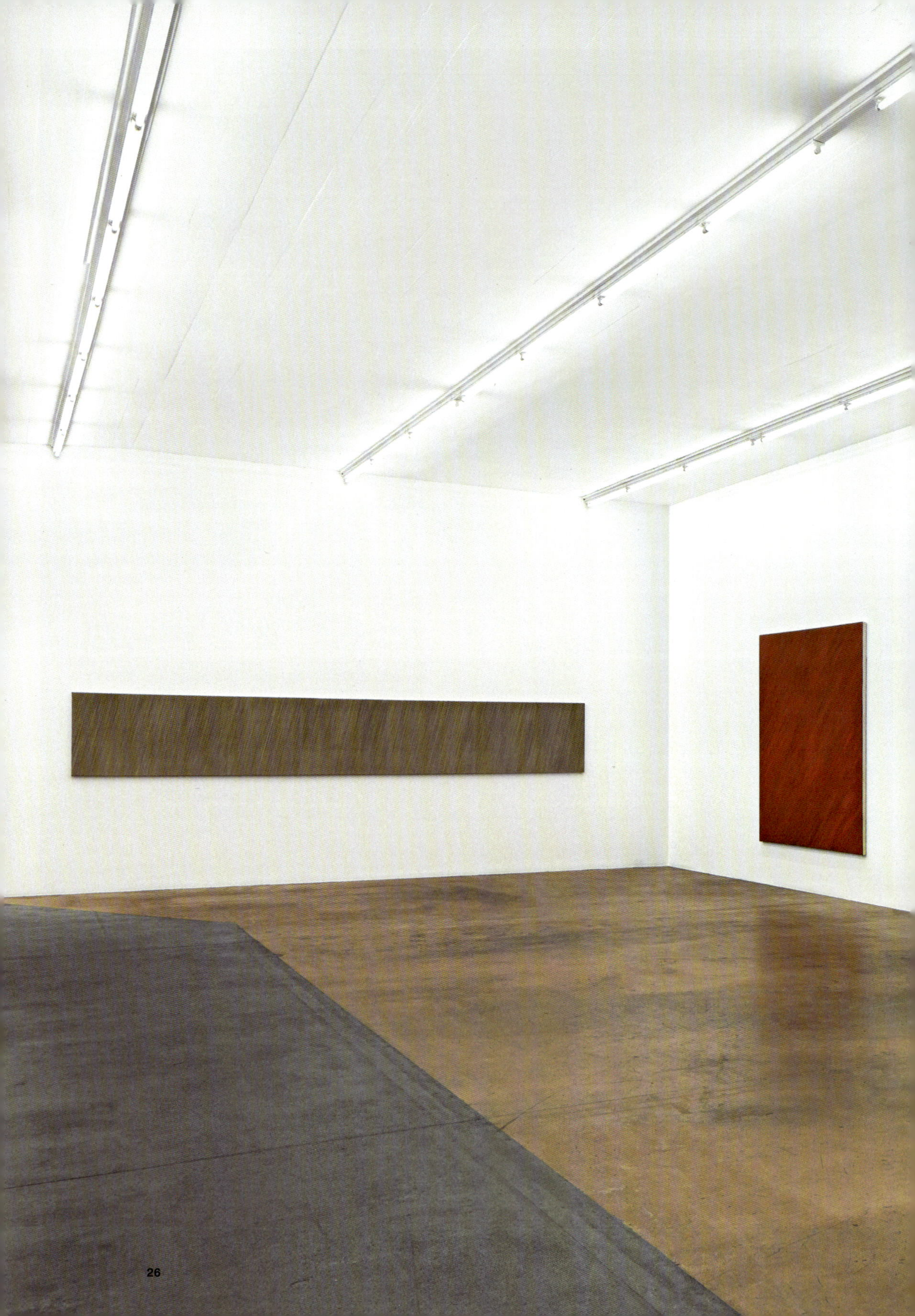

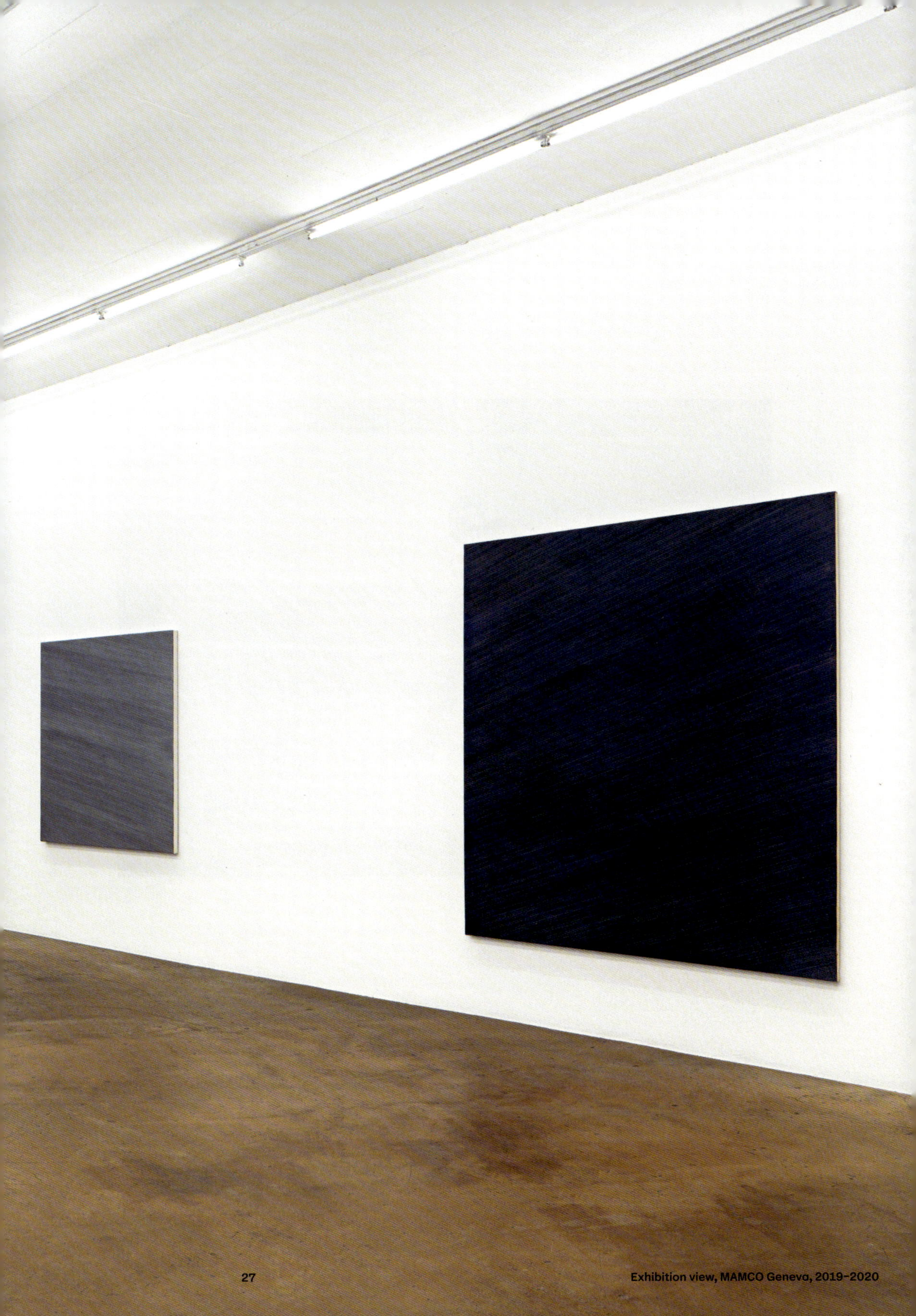

Exhibition view, MAMCO Geneva, 2019-2020

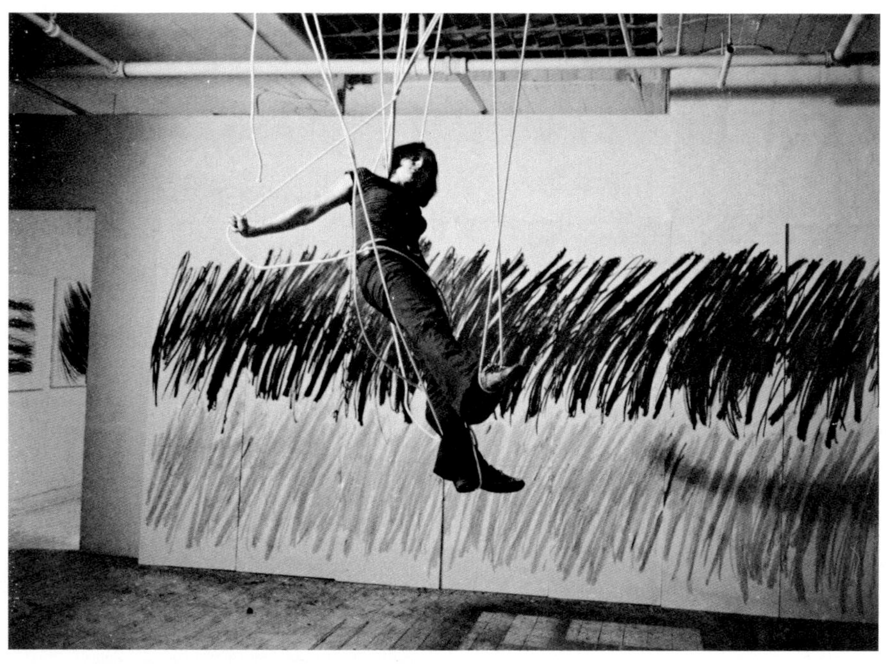

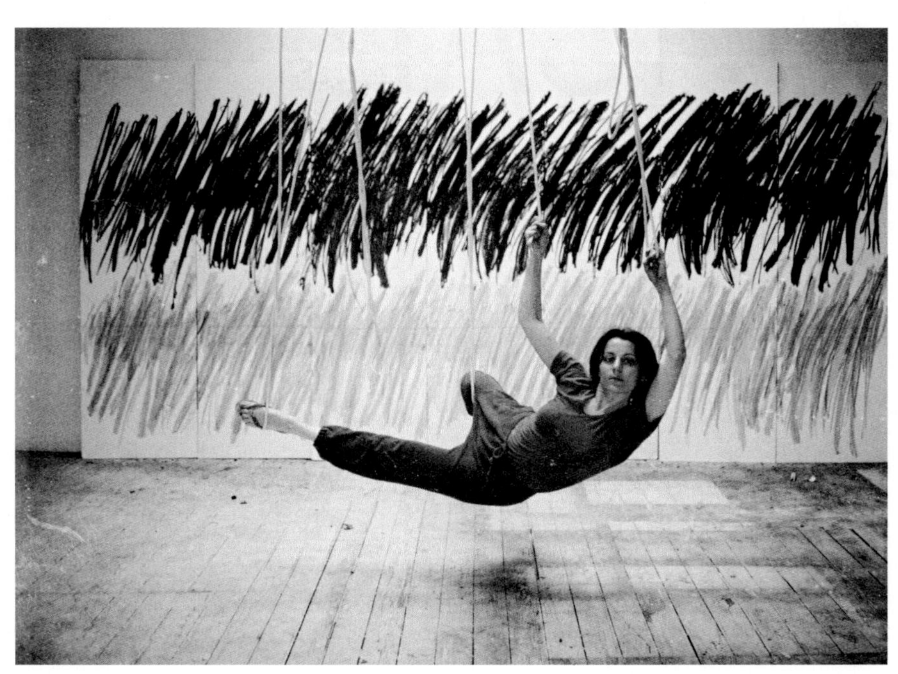

Studio Polaroids

PRIVATE SPACE, PUBLIC SPACE: CRITICAL REVERSIBILITY

Julien Fronsacq

Time = the space between the appointment and the meeting.
These few words, written (or rather, drawn) by Rosemarie Castoro
(1939–2015) on November 3, 1968, may be seen to summarize
both the artist's willfully complex practice, with its combined
emphasis on the analytical and the interpersonal, and its deeply
divided reception. At her SoHo loft in New York City, where artists
like Lawrence Weiner, Sol LeWitt, and Carl Andre met, Castoro
developed a distinctive, unclassifiable artistic approach. She
took part in *Distillation,* an exhibition organized in 1966 by art
historian Eugene Goossen, the high priest of an American school
of painting freed from external influence. Together with Christine
Kozlov and Adrian Piper, Castoro was one of the women artists
featured in Ursula Meyer's anthology of Conceptual art in the
late 1960s. Traversing the last modernist narratives—namely
Minimal and Conceptual art—Castoro's work tirelessly explores
the things that elude the latter's grasp: perspective and subjec-
tivity, of course, but also the psychological and social implications
of the body as a physical instrument. She explores the potential
of abstract and monochrome painting, then expands their sphere
and modes of operation, in formal terms, to incorporate the body,
and even the exhibition space—a conceptual extension, both
diagrammatic and linguistic. In so doing, Castoro applies a hitherto structuralist, reductionist language to poetry and distorts
elementary forms by her haptic, integrated, sexualized treatment.
As an erstwhile participant in the reflections of the Art Workers'
Coalition, she approached the modernist heritage from a social
and political perspective. Drawing on the works exhibited at MAMCO
(spanning 1965 to 2005), we will explore here how Castoro used
her art as a critical tool for blurring the lines between private and
public spaces.

Some of Castoro's earliest paintings date back to 1964. Two years
later, she took part in a number of group exhibitions. One of these
shows, *Distillation,* was organized by Eugene Goossen, an influential proponent of unorthodox Minimal art who attached great
importance to the interaction between painting and sculpture.
Between 1965 and 1968, Castoro produced *Dioxime Cerulean,*
the *Pencil Paintings,* and other series characterized by the use
of geometric patterns (Y shapes and bars). Reflecting on the
Interference series in 1968, Goossen noted that he was struck
by the way in which these rational underlying patterns subtly
revealed the sensual possibilities of blocks of plain color. The
Pencil Paintings is a series of muted monochromes in which uni-
form graphite lines appear to vibrate, almost imperceptibly.
Castoro executed most of these paintings on human-sized canvases, generally square and occasionally rectangular in shape.
Minimal art historian James Meyer emphasizes the fact that
Castoro and Carl Andre, with whom she shared a studio, both
worked on the floor.[1] Much has also been written about the links

1   James Meyer, *Minimalism:
Art and Polemics in the Sixties,*
New Haven/London, Yale University
Press, 2001.

between Castoro's art and architecture, choreography, and the human body. *Arm Swing Blues* (1967), part of the *Pencil Paintings* series, merits particular attention. The piece (which we were regrettably unable to borrow for the exhibition) is one of the few landscape-format paintings in Castoro's body of work. The title itself is linguistically interesting in its juxtaposition of the physical, the visual, and the emotional. The "arm swing" was among the phenomena documented by Eadweard Muybridge in his photographic studies of human motion. Among Castoro's numerous studio Polaroids is a series documenting, step by step, how she created the painting by repeatedly swinging her arm in a semicircular motion—hence its title. *Arm Swing Blues* is one of the first abstract paintings in which Castoro can clearly be seen engaged in the creative process itself. Here, the artist restores a sense of the human, the psychological, to the practice of modern formalism. Just as the blue color in the title gives way to melancholy, so movement opens up space for emotion.[2]

In the late 1960s, Castoro was gradually shifting away from painting. During this period, she used language as a medium of expression in several works, reflecting a wider trend, between 1965 and 1970, that placed text at the center of artistic practice. Lawrence Weiner's *Removals* series, for instance, was a deliberate exercise in the use of the written word—each piece took the form of a statement made by the artist or by another's hand. For his exhibition *Working Drawings and Other Visible Things on Paper Not Necessarily Meant to Be Viewed as Art*, Mel Bochner asked participating artists to contribute studio notes, working drawings, and diagrams to the catalogue—the only item actually exhibited in the show. The shift in the Conceptual art movement of the late 1960s can be linked to the *Information* exhibition at MoMA, a landmark event. In her pieces for Lucy Lippard's shows, Castoro explored a deconstructivist and linguistic approach to art. But there was also a social and political dimension to her specific use of language.

In 1966, Yvonne Rainer, a choreographer in the Judson Dance Theater movement, invited Castoro to take part in a one-of-a-kind choreographic performance. Although Castoro was a trained dancer through her involvement with the New Dance Group and at the Pratt Institute, this was an entirely different proposition: it involved working alongside more than a dozen artists, dancers, and critics (including Carl Andre, Julie Judd, Michael Kirby, Meredith Monk, and Steve Paxton). *Carriage Discreteness*, part of the *9 Evenings: Theater and Engineering Festival* event series, ran for two consecutive evenings in October 1966 at New York's Armory building. The dance and visual art show, which featured a star-studded cast, was a seminal moment in the history of performance art. Rainer devised a dramatic device that allowed her to explore the interplay between order and randomness. The stage, surrounded by lights and projector screens, was

2   For a fascinating discussion of Castoro's other paintings from the same period (1965–1968) featured in the exhibition, see: Tanya Barson, "Rosemarie Castoro 1964–79: An Obstacle Course for a Dancer?," in *Rosemarie Castoro: Focus at Infinity*, Barcelona, MACBA 2018, p. 21–35.

divided into a grid pattern onto which were laid various props along with beams made by Carl Andre. Rainer directed the piece in real time, communicating locations and instructions to the performers via walkie-talkies. As the people on stage moved objects, struck poses, and performed improvised dances according to these instructions, a computerized device triggered random "events"—film sequences, lighting changes, taped conversations, and moving objects. As its title suggested, the performance depended entirely on the whims of a performer-director wholly absorbed by a single task, whose isolation was accentuated by the overall effect: a series of separate yet simultaneous sequences. *Carriage Discreteness* was a piece of Conceptual performance art which, in its desynchronized structure, had much in common with John Cage's pioneering approach to randomization in music.[3]

Cage's use of simultaneity, desynchronization, and indeterminacy, subsequently adopted by Rainer for her performance, has echoes in the title of *No Connection Whatsoever* (1968), one of Castoro's last geometric works, which featured a series of diagonal yet unconnected straight lines. The piece, executed on paper, was part of a series of style drawings in which Castoro used X and Y axes as a way to visually represent the plotting of data on a chart. Here, however, the lack of connection between the elements made the chart an illusion: no data could be visualized, no trend observed. Some of the titles of the works in this series, which Castoro began in 1968, referred to phenomena that were relatively easy to quantify and correlate; others, less so. They evoked themes such as "the space between the objects" (*In Celebration of Part Time Work*), spaces between periods of painting, social relationships (*Portrait of Sol LeWitt with Donor and Friends*), and the assignment of numerical values to different moods occurring over a 24-hour period—"trickling disbelief, roaring anger, needing discipline" (*Controlled Arbitrary Statements*). Rainer's choreographed antiwar dance *WAR* (1970) has clear similarities with Castoro's concrete and political poetry series *A Day in the Life of a Conscientious Objector* (1969)—Castoro was likely sensitive to Rainer's use of dance as a Minimalist tool drawing on everyday life and the codes of cinema. In the space of just a few months, between 1968 and 1969, the written word gradually became central to Castoro's practice. She produced a series of drawings entitled *Concrete Poetry* in reference to the movement that emerged in the 1950s as a way to liberate language from the confines of print and reveal its visual and auditory properties. Employing evenly spaced capital letters arranged into blocks of the same color, Castoro's poems were very much in the American tradition, combining mundanity and intimacy to create dramatic tension:

3   Yvonne Rainer, *Work 1961–73*, Primary Information, New York, 2020, p. 305.

TIME = THE SPACE
BETWEEN THE APPOINTMENT AND
THE MEETING

In this period, Castoro was involved in the protest movements sweeping across the United States. She was part of the Art Workers' Coalition (AWC) formed on January 3, 1969, when the sculptor Takis physically removed one of his works from MoMA on moral rights grounds. On April 10, some 300 artists gathered at New York's School of Visual Arts, where the AWC unveiled a museum reform program and a list of 13 demands for MoMA to improve artists' rights.[4] Castoro's signature appears on a surviving AWC-headed document bearing the same date as the hearing. It strikes a militant tone, calling for artists to be paid a state annuity on account of their central role in society. Between May 24 and June 18, 1969, the Dwan Gallery in New York hosted *Language III*, the third installment in the *Language* series. The show included works by Castoro, Robert Newman, John Perreault, Hannah Weiner, Michael Benedikt, and John Giorno. Castoro's contributions were *Sharp Changes* (1968–69) and *A Day in the Life of a Conscientious Objector* (1969), the only slide show to feature in the exhibition. The slide show was accompanied by a voice-over recording of the artist reading the poems, each executed in capital letters and blocks of color. Its title was a subtle reference to Stefan Zweig's novella *Twenty-Four Hours in the Life of a Woman*, while its non-linear narrative structure reflected the U.S. and global political climate of the time. In 1967, media coverage of the Vietnamese resistance and the loss of human life prompted a shift in public opinion, and the antiwar protest movement gained momentum. The poem alternated between neutral and morbid instructions, with each of the 24 pages bearing the date on which it was written. Page 1 (dated February 23, 1969) contains the following words:

> HEAVE PUSH/COVER COMRADE/
> STUMBLE AROUND BEND SINKDOWN/
> RELIEVE PRESSURE/OPEN MESSAGE/
> DESTROY EVIDENCE

In its use of imperative constructions, Castoro's poem is reminiscent of Richard Serra's *Verb List* (1967). But for all their matter-of-fact delivery, these military-style commands were tinged with drama and elements of antiwar commentary:

> ROTATE HANDLES/WATER TRAP/OIL SLICK/
> SALT SPONGE/DRY HEAT
> (...)
> DON UNIFORM/SET TIMER/BURN FLESH

4   Lucy Lippard, "The Art Workers' Coalition: Not a History," *Studio International*, Vol. 180, No. 927, November 1970.

**PEEL OFF CLOTH/WASH WOUND/POWDER DRY
(…)
WRAP BODY/DESCEND TO STREET/
EMPLOY NEWSVENDOR
(…)
OPEN YOUR MOUTH AND SHOW/US YOUR BOOT**

At a time when Minimalism had reached its high-water mark and sculpture was the medium of choice, Castoro intuitively adopted a hybrid approach that combined painting and sculpture. Her disparate, performative works bore names borrowed from mythology that evoked notions of insular fortifications (*Atoll*), ruses (*Gates of Troy*), and journeys (*Ariadne's Trail*). On April 18, 1969, Castoro took part in *Street Works II*, a performance held in the area around 13th and 14th Streets and 5th and 6th Avenues in New York, alongside artists (Vito Acconci, Ben Patterson, Adrian Piper, and Lawrence Weiner), poets (John Perreault and Bernadette Mayer), a musician (Alcides Lanza), and an art critic (Gregory Battcock). For this second installment in the *Street Works* series, Castoro used aluminum tape to cut off a block of buildings. Evoking the practice of Yvonne Rainer, Castoro employed performance and movement—"Place underfoot the start (…) unroll to outstretched arms"—combined with the written word to make an atoll out of Manhattan Island. A few weeks earlier, Castoro had completed *Ariadne's Trail* (1969): she punched a hole in a tin of paint, mounted it on the back of a bicycle and rode through the streets of New York. This simple act of dripping paint onto the tarmac in the public space was both unmistakably evocative of masculine modernity and radically epic in its execution.

Castoro subsequently took part in exhibitions organized by curator and Conceptual art historian Lucy Lippard. Through her personal diaries, poems, and narrative pieces, she chronicled her work in the studio while simultaneously recording her private thoughts, conceptual ideas, and political sensitivities. In 1969, Lippard, who had previously curated the *Eccentric Abstraction* exhibition, launched her "Numbers Shows," a seminal series in the history of Conceptual art. For two of these exhibitions—*Number 7* (Paula Cooper Gallery, New York) and *557,087* (Seattle Art Museum, co-curated by Lippard and Seth Siegelaub) —Castoro produced installations from her *Cracking* series, in which she used aluminum tape to create a fault line in the exhibition space. MAMCO's collection includes a photograph of Castoro's *Cracking* for the *Number 7* show. It depicts the main exhibition room in the Paula Cooper Gallery, which appears to be empty although it contains a magnetic field by Robert Barry, a pockmark on a wall from an air-rifle shot by Lawrence Weiner, Ian Wilson's *Oral Communication*, a secret by Steve Kaltenbach, and Hans Haacke's *Air Currents* (a fan in the corner). Lippard included the work in her 1973 anthology *Six Years: The Dematerialization of the Art Object from 1966 to 1972*. Castoro's *Cracking* series of in-situ installations, deployed at different scales, also drew heavily on the bodies of her accomplices and her own face. In their structural weakening of the exhibition space, the "cracks" were a commentary on the artist's own fragility. For the last of the "Numbers Shows," held in Vancouver,[5] Castoro created *Room Revelation* (1970), a more complex in-situ installation. It consisted of a walk-in box, measuring nine cubic meters, with a light bulb on the floor in the middle. Upon entering the box, the viewer had to close the door (and keep it shut) to activate the bulb, which slowly illuminated to reveal the viewer's shadow on the wall: "Open the door onto darkness. Close it after you. A reostated 200W light bulb begins brightening within a 3½ minute cycle until intensity is reached, the bulb remains bright until the door opens. When the door closes, the cycle begins again. R Castoro, January 4, 1970."[6] The *New Oxford American Dictionary* definition of "revelation" alludes to something startling, divine or supernatural in nature. Castoro's *Room Revelation* was typical of the performative devices of the period. In this case, the performativity came not from the artist's action, but from an environment designed to bring about a transformative experience for the participant. The installation was a clear manifestation of Castoro's aesthetic, combining a dramatic, performative experience with a reference to the everyday. Later, when reflecting on *Room Revelation*, she joked that it worked like a refrigerator in reverse: the door had to be kept closed for the light to come on (as reported by Werner Pichler). Around the same time, Castoro created installations at several friends' houses, which involved her fixing four wheeled casters to the ceiling. The February 27 1969 edition of *The Village Voice* carried a small advertisement with the words "Rosemarie Castoro, mover of ceilings"—a pithy statement with an unmistakable play on words and a close resemblance to "mover of feelings."

Hollis Frampton gathered a cast of voice actors—including Castoro—for *Zorns Lemma* (1970), a film divided into three sequences: a reading of an 18th-century alphabet primer, 45 minutes of cuts of words and the four elements, and six women taking turns reading a 13th-century treatise on light and form. The film, which is named after a mathematical axiom (Zorn's lemma) and features content from Robert Grosseteste's *De Luce seu de Inchoatione Formarum* (On Light or the Beginning of Forms), explores the disconnect between image and word and the irreducible, nonverbal nature of cinema. In early 1970, Castoro produced two written-word works, each with a simple layout akin to an administrative typescript document. In *Vacation Time* and *Love's Time*, which she started on February 16 and 26 respectively, she chronicled her movements and activities. But hidden within these factual, rational accounts of everyday events were personal confessions and poetic imagery: "0–10/31 From looking at this page and bouncing on the word communication to finishing making

5   *955,000*, Vancouver Art Gallery, Vancouver, Canada, curated by Lucy R. Lippard, 1970.

6   Inscription beneath the drawing: Rosemarie Castoro, *Room Revelation*, 1969, court. Rosemarie Castoro Estate; Thaddaeus Ropac Gallery, London, Paris, Salzburg.

a phone call at 6:40 and noting at the time of around noontime that I was divorced Monday February 16, 1970 (...)." In her account of her movements around Manhattan, Castoro buried references to American poetry: "0–187/22 From Leaving 77th street station to HOW DID EMILY DICKINSON DIE." Some of her descriptions hinted at flights of fancy, as the artist imagined herself breaking the laws of physics to wrap her body around the city: "0–34/29 From stretching legs to the middle of 6th avenue."

In 1971, Castoro began creating works that transformed the exhibition space, a prime example being her contribution to that year's group show with Carl Andre and Marjorie Strider at 112 Greene Street.[7] *Art News* reported that "Castoro showed one of her heavily textured gesso and graphite panels," emphasizing the intense pictorial quality of the work. Also in 1971, Castoro produced *Eight Corners*, a series of doors in a carefully arranged pattern forming a maze. Covering over 20 square meters of the artist's studio, the installation featured a lamp, hung at a precise location, that cast shadows inside the labyrinth. The graphite applied on the top of the primer accentuated the diagonals of the shadows. Although the installation had never been seen in public before the MAMCO retrospective, it was extensively photographed by the artist. With its tight, perplexing layout, *Eight Corners* is both a theatrical space with a fixed vantage point and a tactile environment to be experienced and explored. In the 1970s, Castoro also made sculptures from black resin. She took reams of photographs in her studio, painted entirely in black and white, as she sought the ideal perspective and contrast for her pieces. One of these sculptures, *Land of Lads* (1975), was a row of slender ladders suspended from the ceiling. Its title was a play on the words "ladders" and "lads"—as if, by a sleight of metonymical hand, the pieces of equipment had come to life and transformed into a group of young men. According to the artist, the sculpture was an exercise in flipping technical convention on its head and using the tool to shape a natural, untamed landscape: "The *Land of Lads* is composed of ladders. A metaphor of time and activity, steps, and gestures, strokes. The ladder is a cultural tool; the forest a source of nourishment. I am a cultural animal who make(s) tools to build forests."[8] The following year, Castoro produced *Land of Lashes* (1976), a pendant-shaped sculpture that once again explored notions of reversibility, of progress and archaism, of desire and threat: the eyelashes multiplied and came to life, menacing the onlooker like whiplashes. Castoro played with forms and symbolism with the same consummate ease as with words. A year on from *Eight Corners*, and employing the same technique, she created *Guinness Martin* (1972), a mural executed in the fashion of an oversize brush stroke. Akin to a Freudian slip, the piece was a nod to the great Minimalist artist Agnes Martin, who at the time lived in New Mexico and had given up painting a few years earlier. In her 2010 diary, Castoro mused

7   An exhibition space opened in 1970 by artists Jeffrey Lew, Alan Saret, and Gordon Matta-Clark. It moved to Spring Street in 1978 and was renamed White Columns.

8   Rosemarie Castoro, typescript, 1975.

about their friendship and their lifestyles as independent women: "How deep is your valley? Yikes, categories again! We are all certainly individuals. When Agnes Martin exclaimed in a packed house Pasadena lecture I had the fortune to attend, (I paraphrase), 'Artists have to be lonely.' I chirped up from behind her (coming in late, I was seated on the stage) and said, 'Agnes, all you have to do is pick up the telephone.' She turned to my familiar voice, 'MaryRose (transposing my name), did you come here to bug me?'"[9]

In 1979, Castoro produced 24 pieces for the third installment of the *Artpark*[10] outdoor sculpture park program. Her contributions conveyed an ambivalent message: towering at over 2.2 meters tall, they nevertheless had the proportions of the human body and seemed to offer some sort of protection, while their titles, *Flashers*, alluded to sexual perverts (typically men) exposing themselves in public. Castoro single-handedly fashioned each sculpture from a vast sheet of rolled steel, which she laid out on a mattress, bending and hammering the material into a shape reminiscent of a crumpled piece of paper, somehow capable of standing upright without support. The *Black Flasher* pieces were a resounding success and were exhibited in public on numerous occasions. In 1984, they went on display on 3rd Avenue in New York's Midtown district, not far from the brand-new home of architecture and design firm Stephen Wang & Associates. To mark the occasion, the artist, dressed in shorts and a tank top, strolled past the sculptures with Panther, her black labrador, stopping to pose nearby in front of the word "WANG"—coincidentally, and undoubtedly amusingly for Castoro, a slang word for "penis." One of her later sculptural works, *Mountain Range* (2005), consisted of a series of modules. Together they formed a landscape, but individually they took on a bipedal quality: pairs of welded steel legs with deep, fan-like folds supported on the tips of fully extended feet. The overall effect—part ballet dancer, part landscape—reminds us that, as in geology, every protrusion is the result of often invisible tectonic folds.

Rosemarie Castoro's career began just as the second -wave feminism movement was gathering momentum in the United States: Betty Friedman published *The Feminine Mystique* in 1963, and the National Organization for Women (NOW) was founded in 1966. Within the feminist debate, there was often disagreement over the status of women and whether the struggle should take place in the private or public sphere. In the late 1970s, Monique Wittig, who also harbored an affection for mythological references (the "Trojan horse"), proposed a deconstructivist approach to categories such as class and gender. Castoro called her 1977 installation *Beaver's Trap*—a particularly ambiguous name. She could have been referring to her own last name (*castoro* is Italian for "beaver"), to Jean-Paul Sartre's pet name for Simone de Beauvoir (*castor*, French for "beaver"), or to the fact that she was a woman. In any event, the title undoubtedly

9   Rosemarie Castoro, typescript, 2010.

10   Lewiston, New York, 1979.

11   Griselda Pollock, "Modernity and the Spaces of Femininity," in *Vision and Difference: Feminism, Femininity and Histories of Art*, London, Routledge, 2003, p. 50–90.

12   Lucy Lippard, "Rosemarie Castoro, Working Out," in *From the Center: Feminist Essays on Women's Art*, Plume, New York, 1976, p. 250–256.

had feminist undertones. Griselda Pollock, writing in the 1980s, reflected on the representation of modern space since the 19th century, stressing the influence of leisure and consumerism, and of the objectification of the female body by men.[11] Castoro's practice was striking in its relationship with the great movements of the late 1960s and early 1970s, from abstract art, Minimalism, and Conceptual art to institutional critique, site-specific art, post-Minimalism, and more. Through her *Black Flasher* sculptures, for instance, she flipped Conceptual art on its head by introducing notions of intimacy, bringing private performance into the public space and setting up a kind of critical reversibility. Castoro's 1969 contributions to *Street Works II* transformed the public realm into a space that was at once mythological (*Ariadne's Trail*) and political (*Gates of Troy*). Lucy Lippard also commented on the reversibility inherent in her art when discussing *Growing*, a series of roots suspended from the ceiling which served as a metaphor for bodies buried on the roof.[12] Castoro's particular brand of feminism, if it could be described as such, emphasized the emancipation of women from institutional and patriarchal coercion— an endeavor that required the combined force of body and mind. As for Castoro's political stance, Lippard observed that "she declines to be politically classified as feminist, preferring the image of an androgynous amazon."

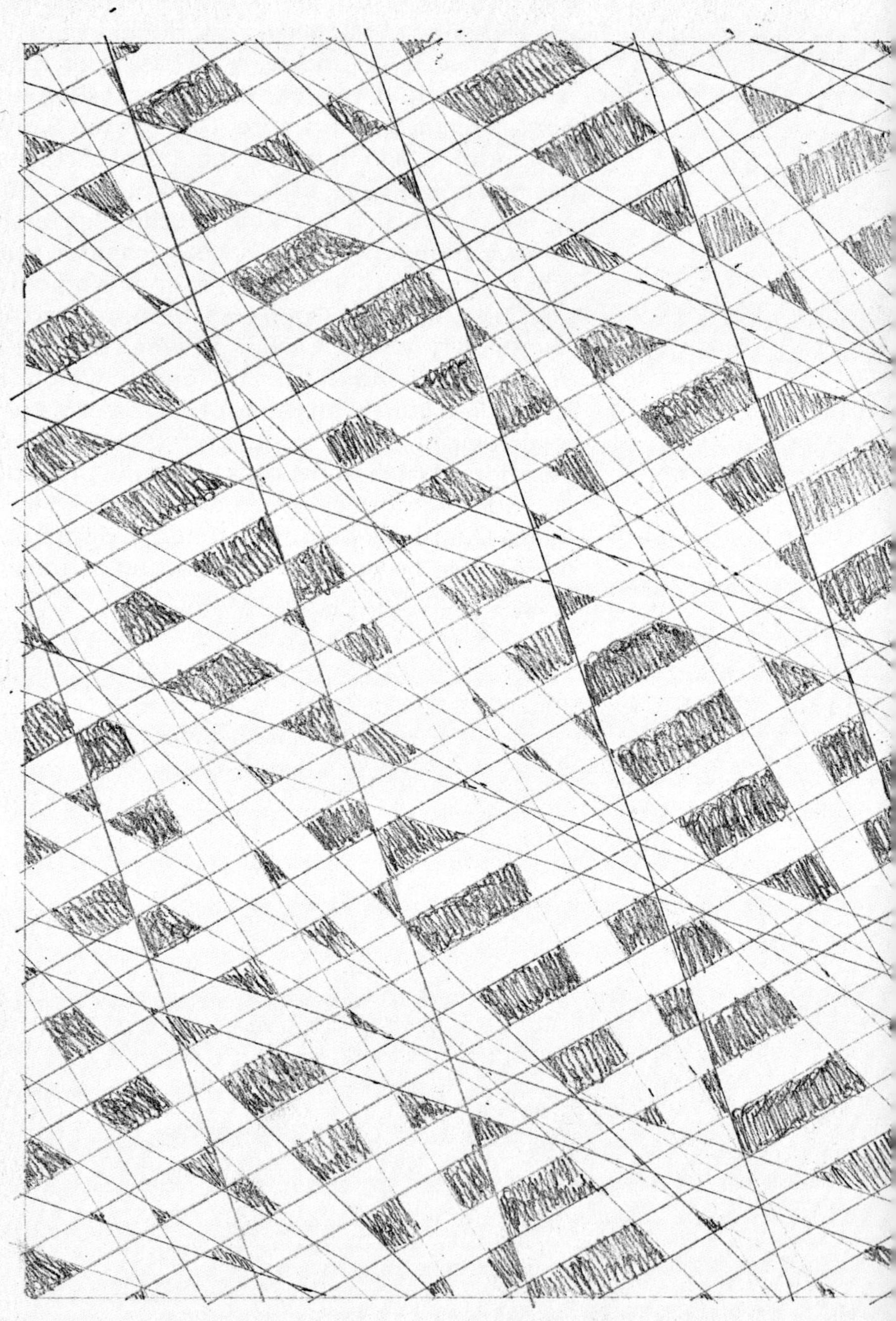

Interférence

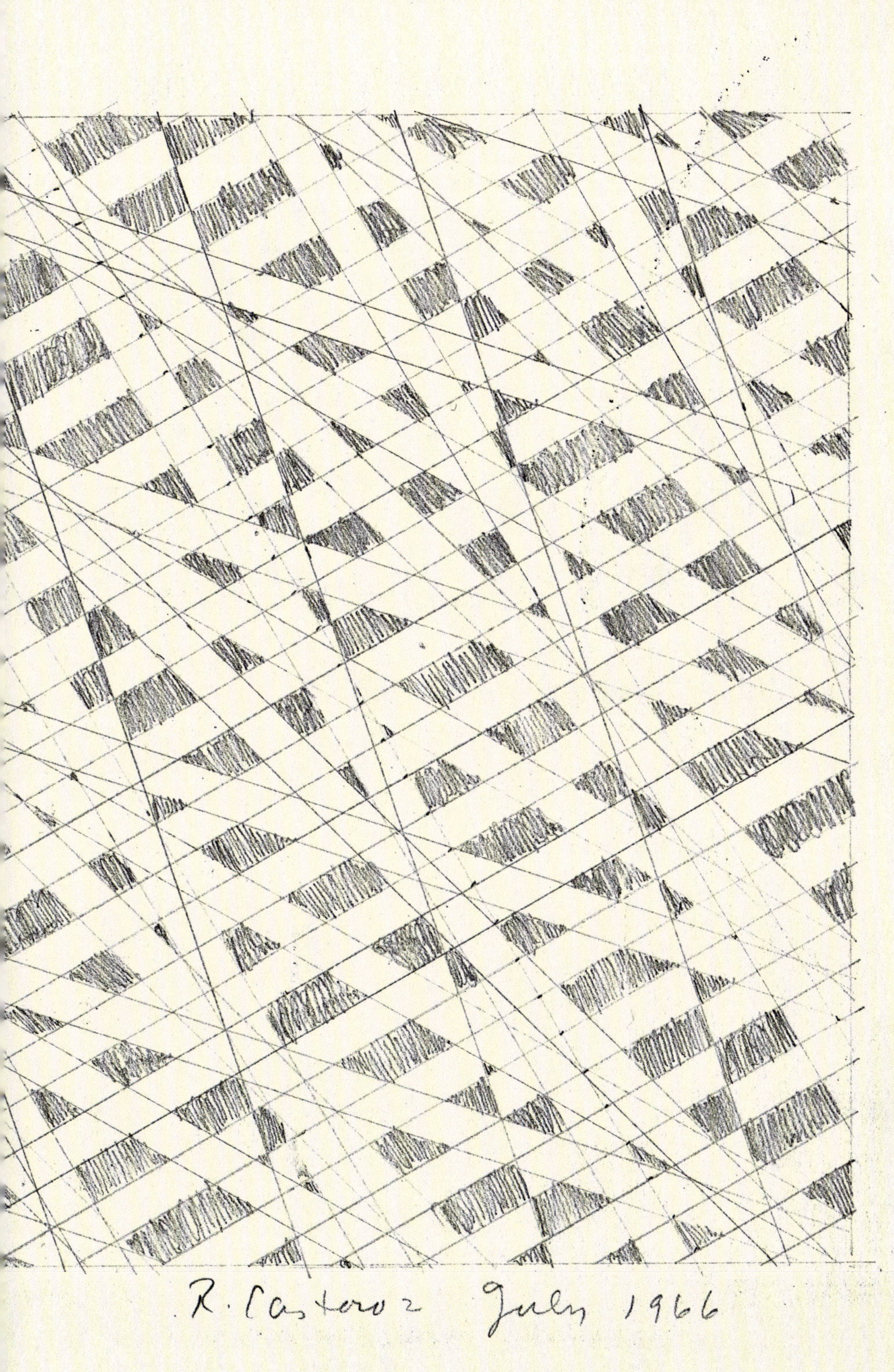

July Interference, 1966

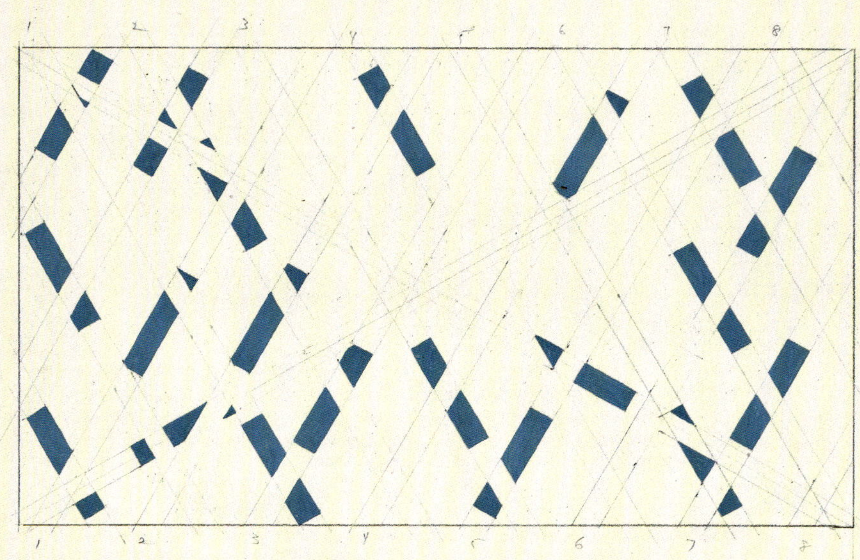

January Interference 2, 1966

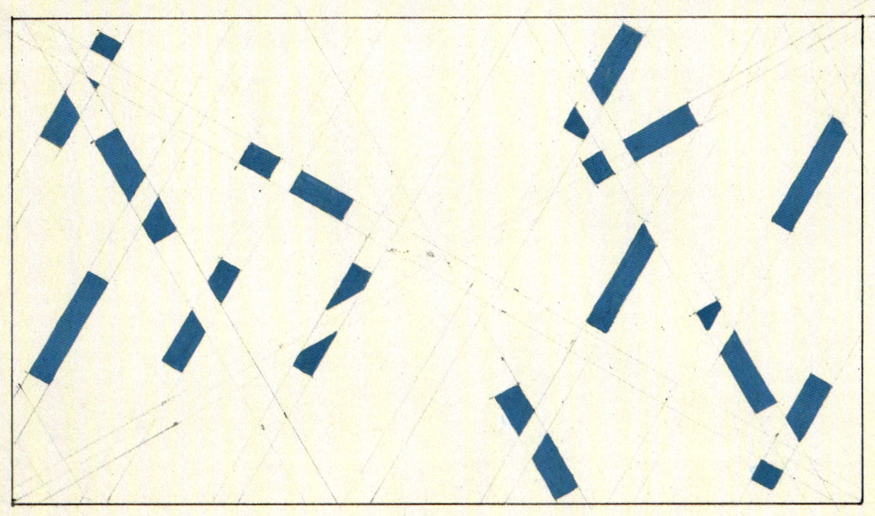

January Interference, 1966

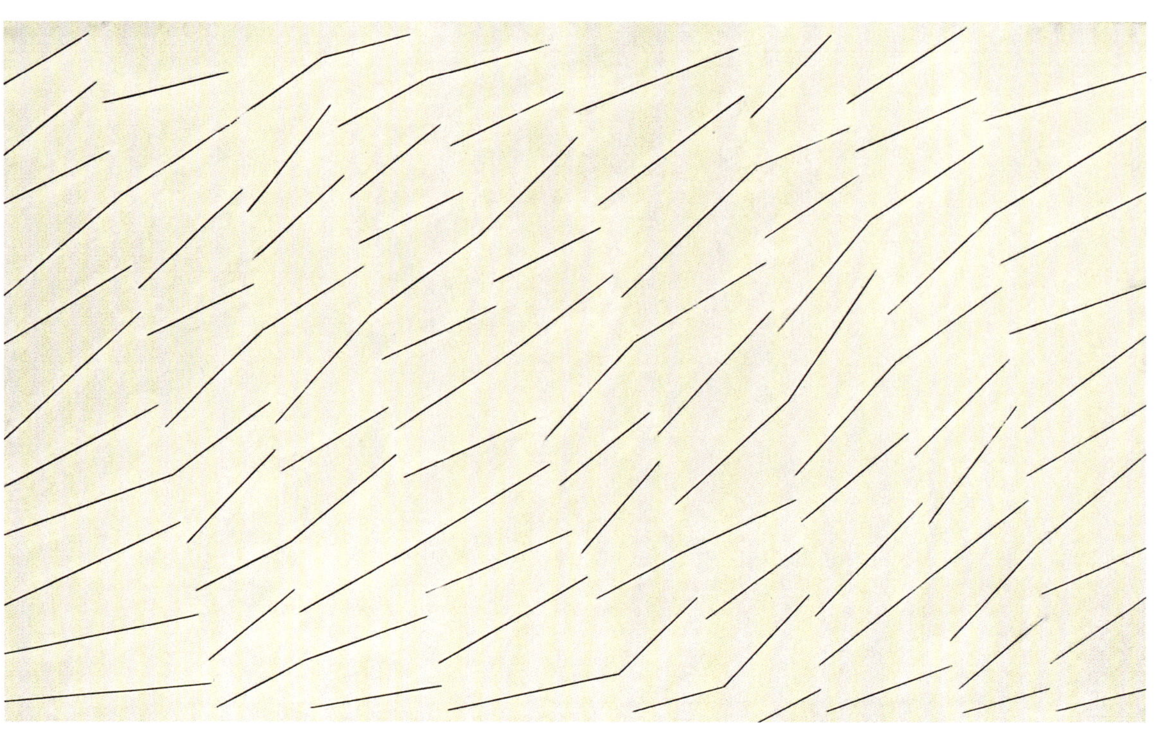

Inventory Series White and Brown, 1968

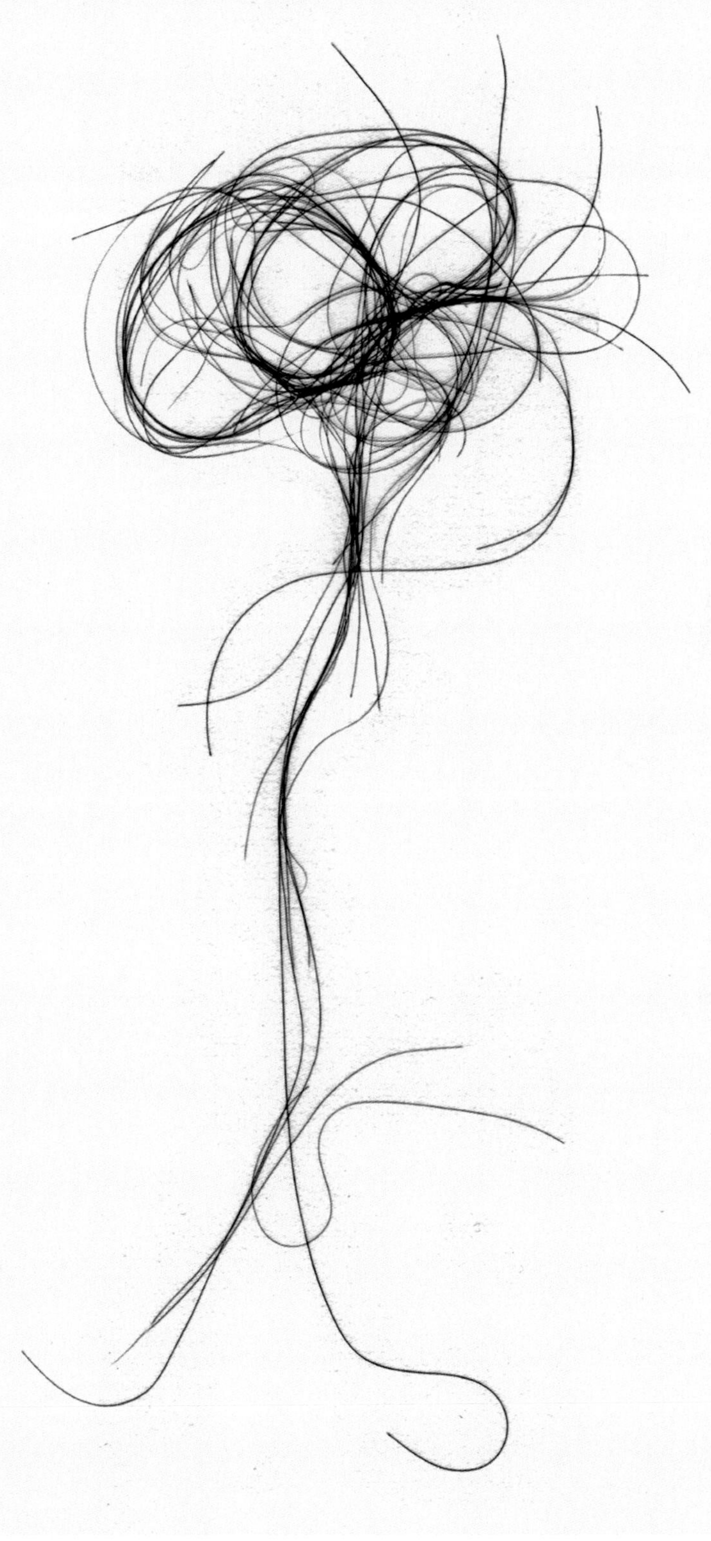

Walking Hair Brain, 2005

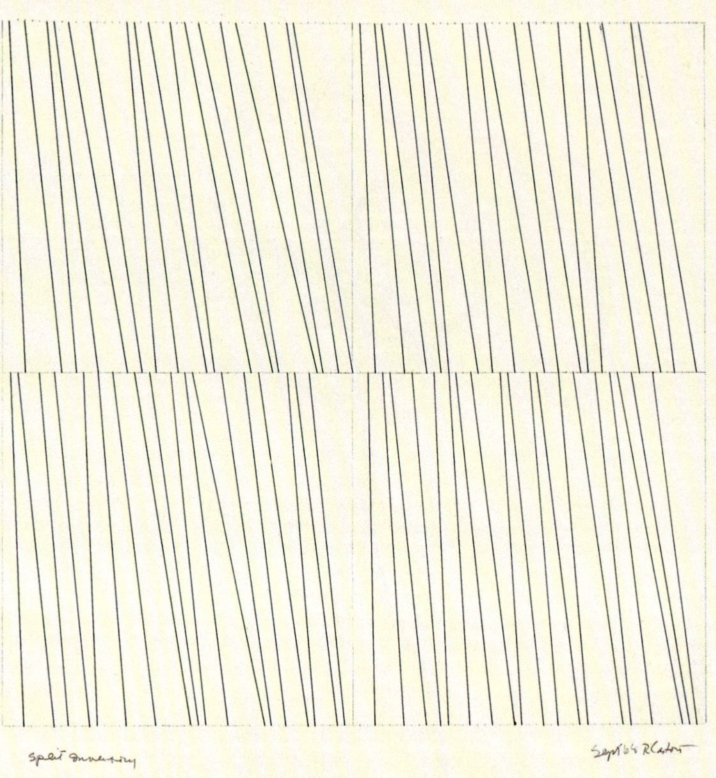

Split Inventory, 1968

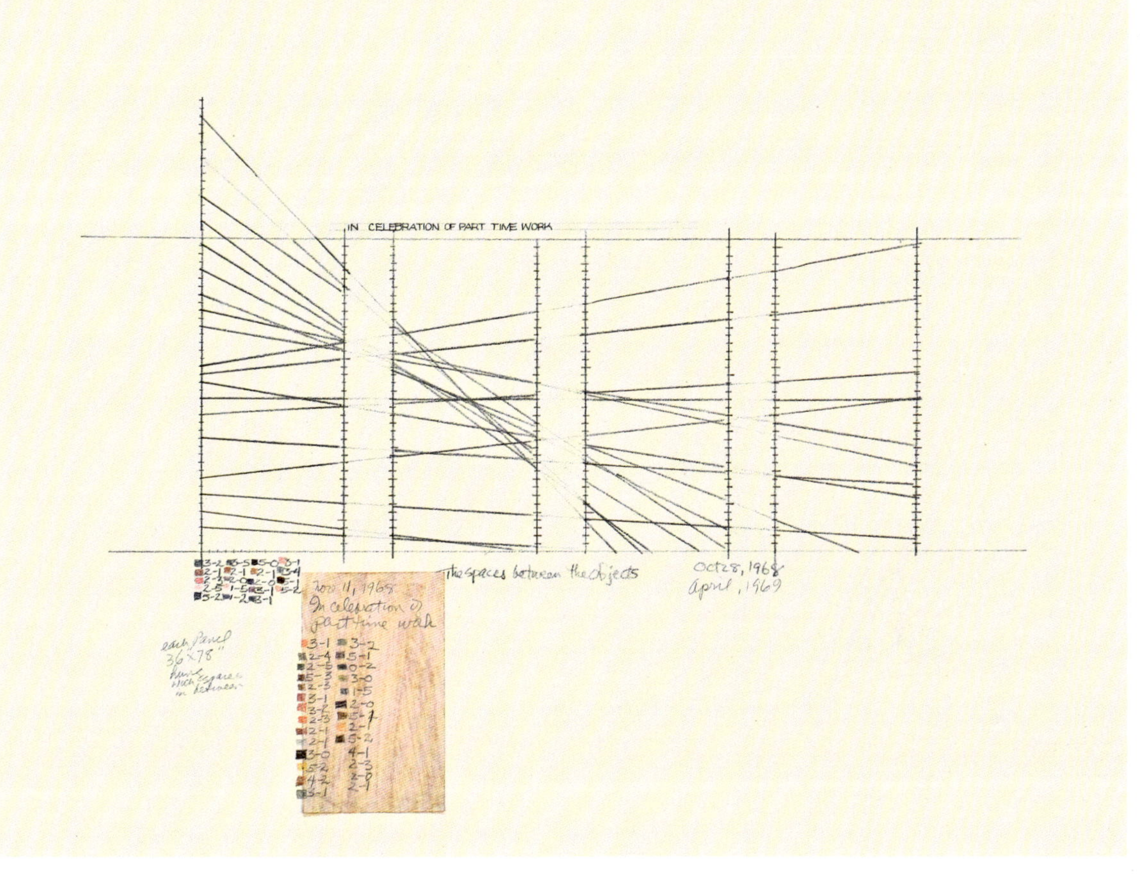

*In Celebration of Part Time Work. The Spaces Between the Objects
Oct 28, 1968; April, 1969, 1968–1969*

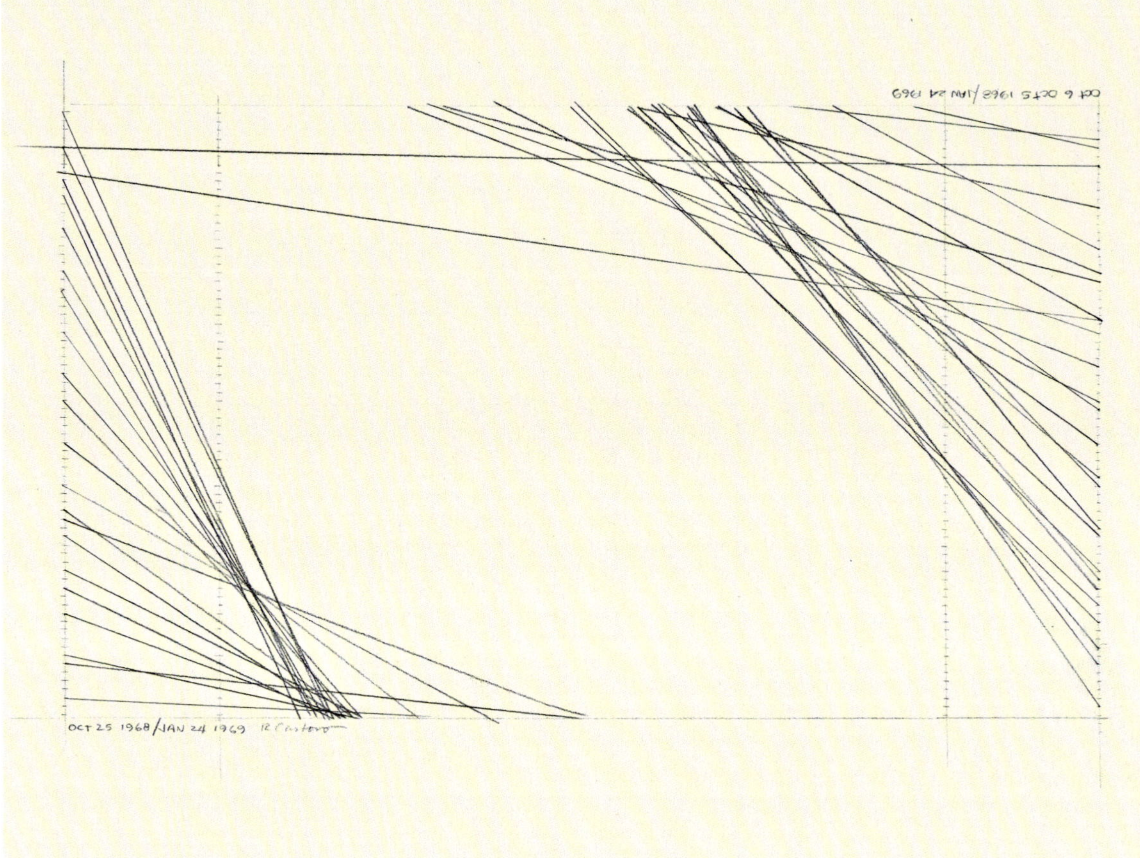

Oct 25, 1968/Jan 24, 1969, 1968-69

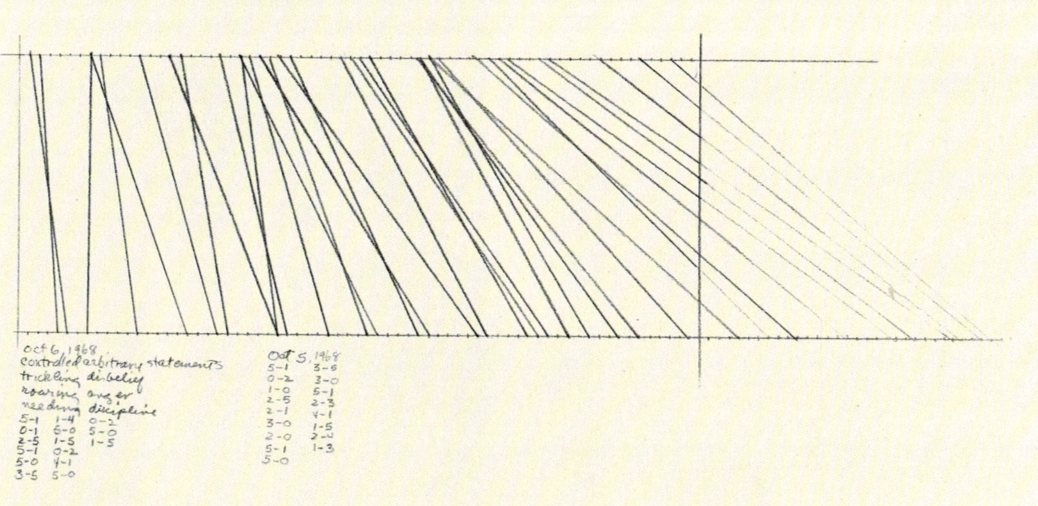

Controlled Arbitrary Statements, 1968

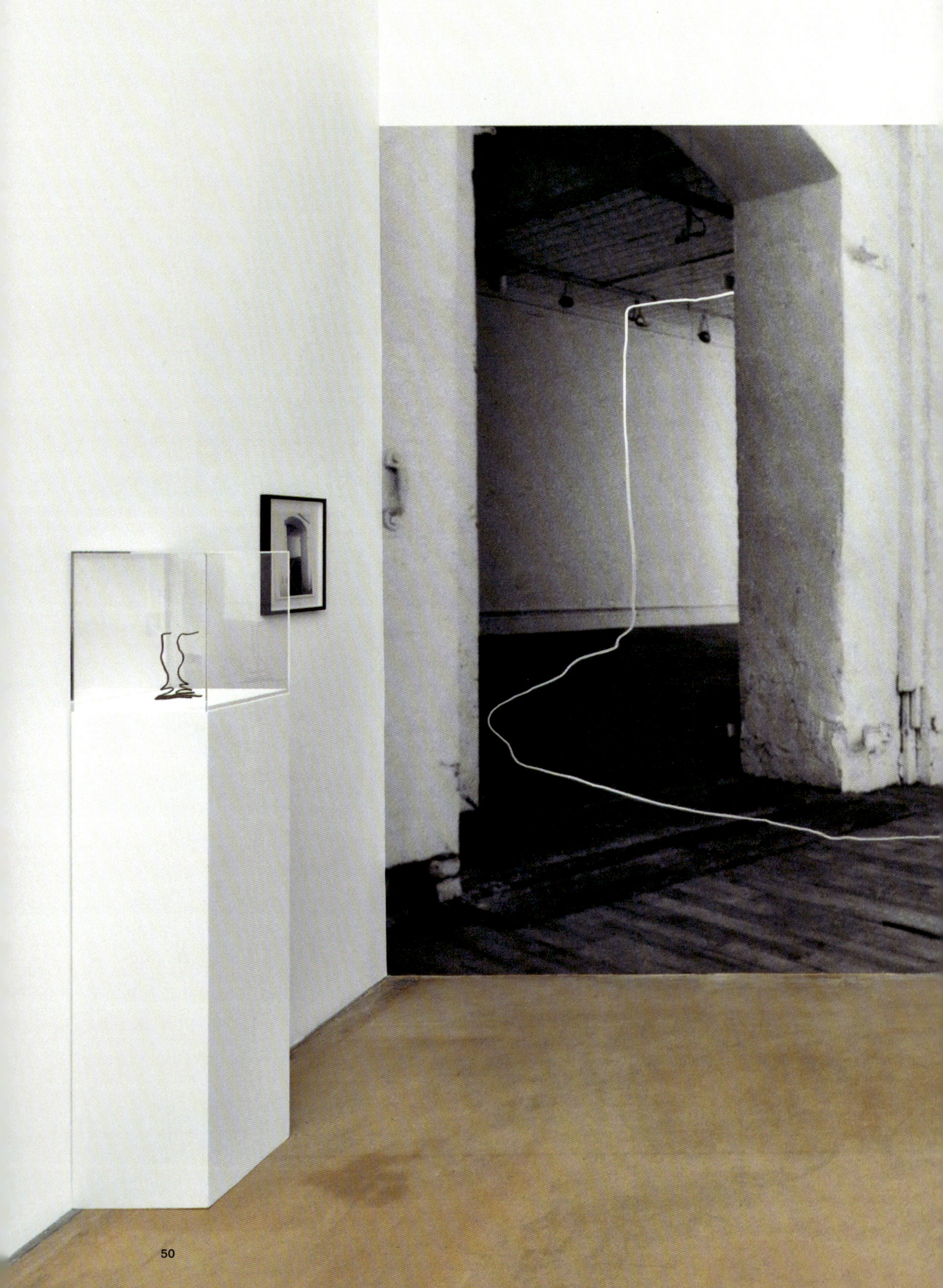

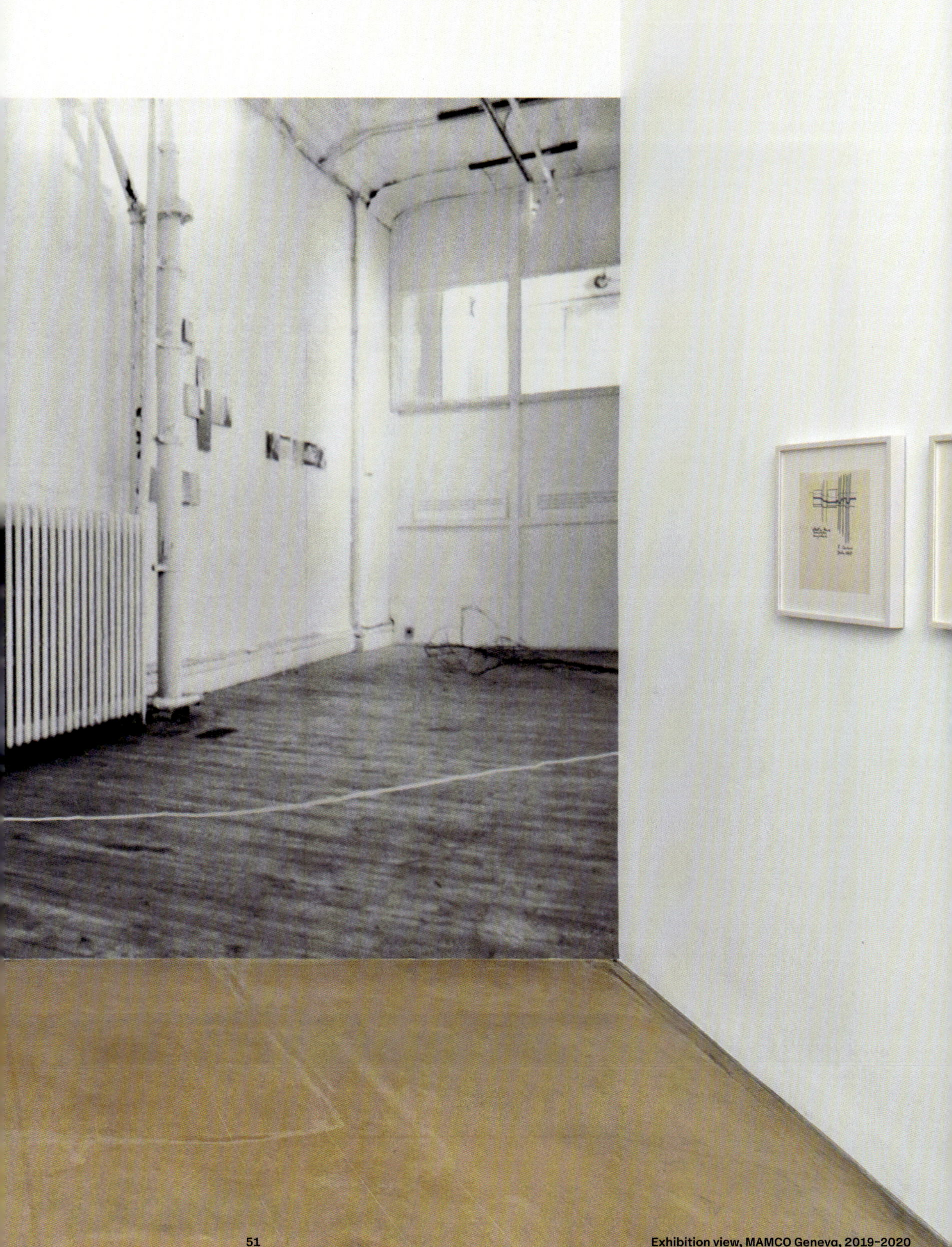

Exhibition view, MAMCO Geneva, 2019–2020

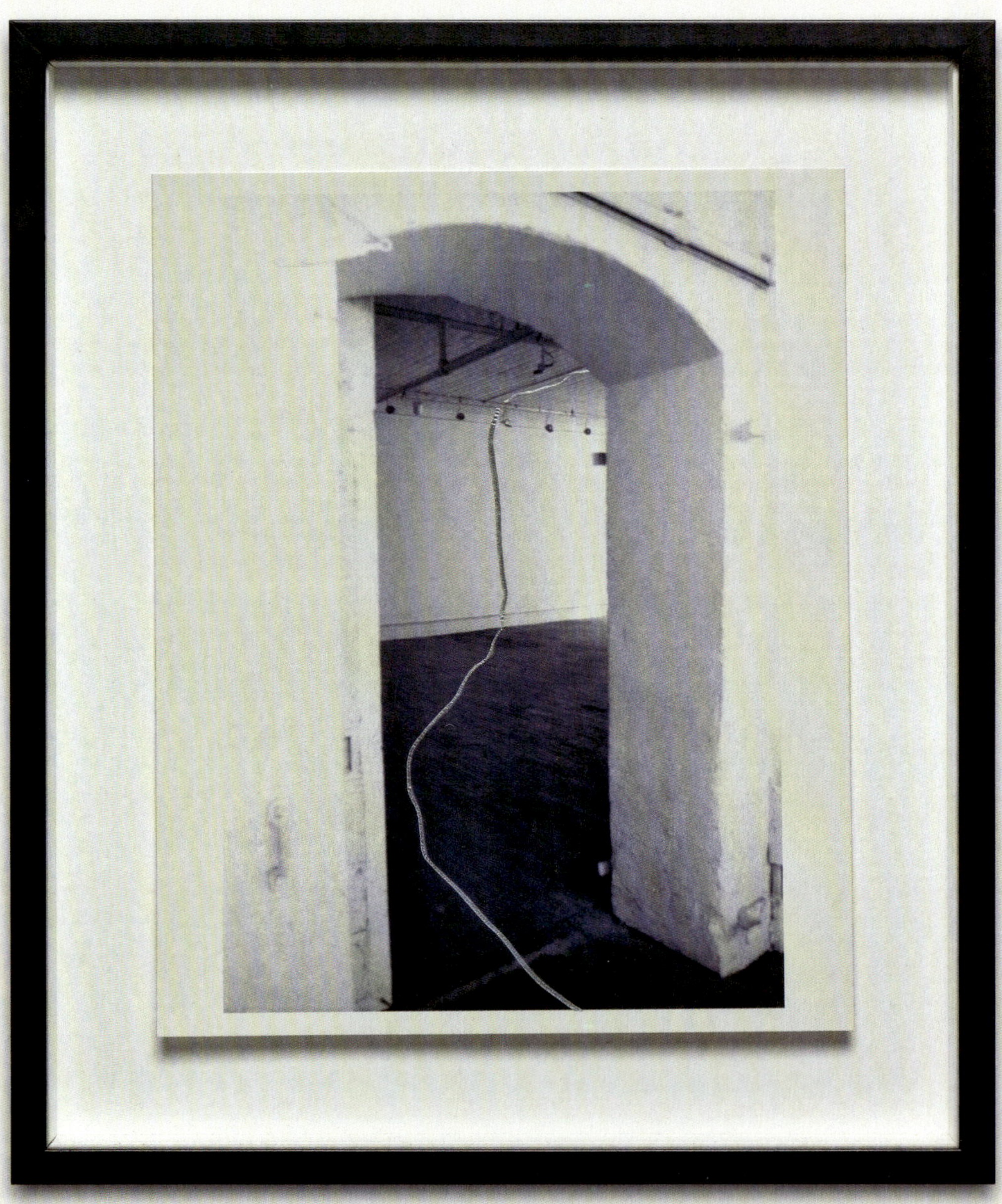

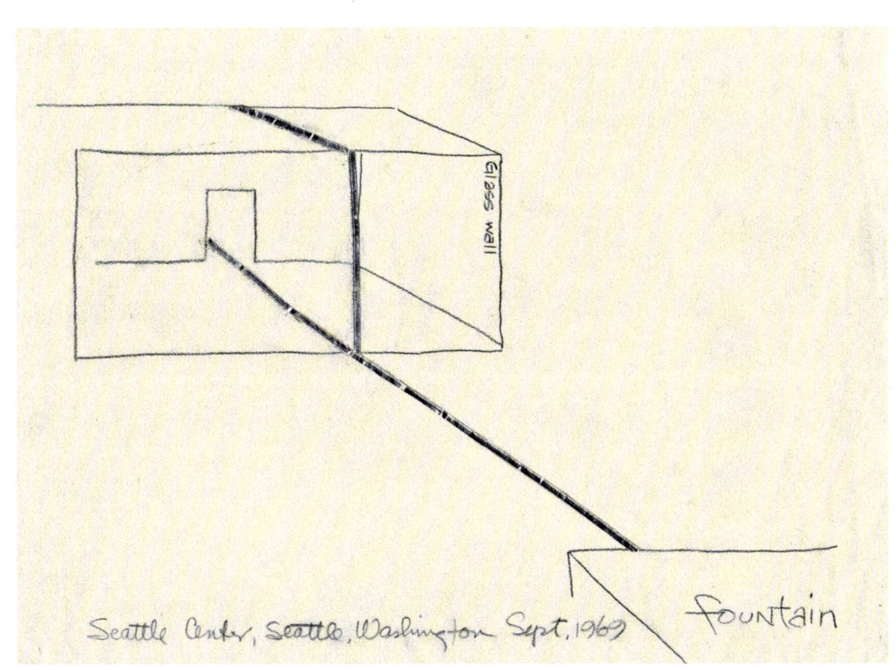

Seattle Cracking Outside, 1969

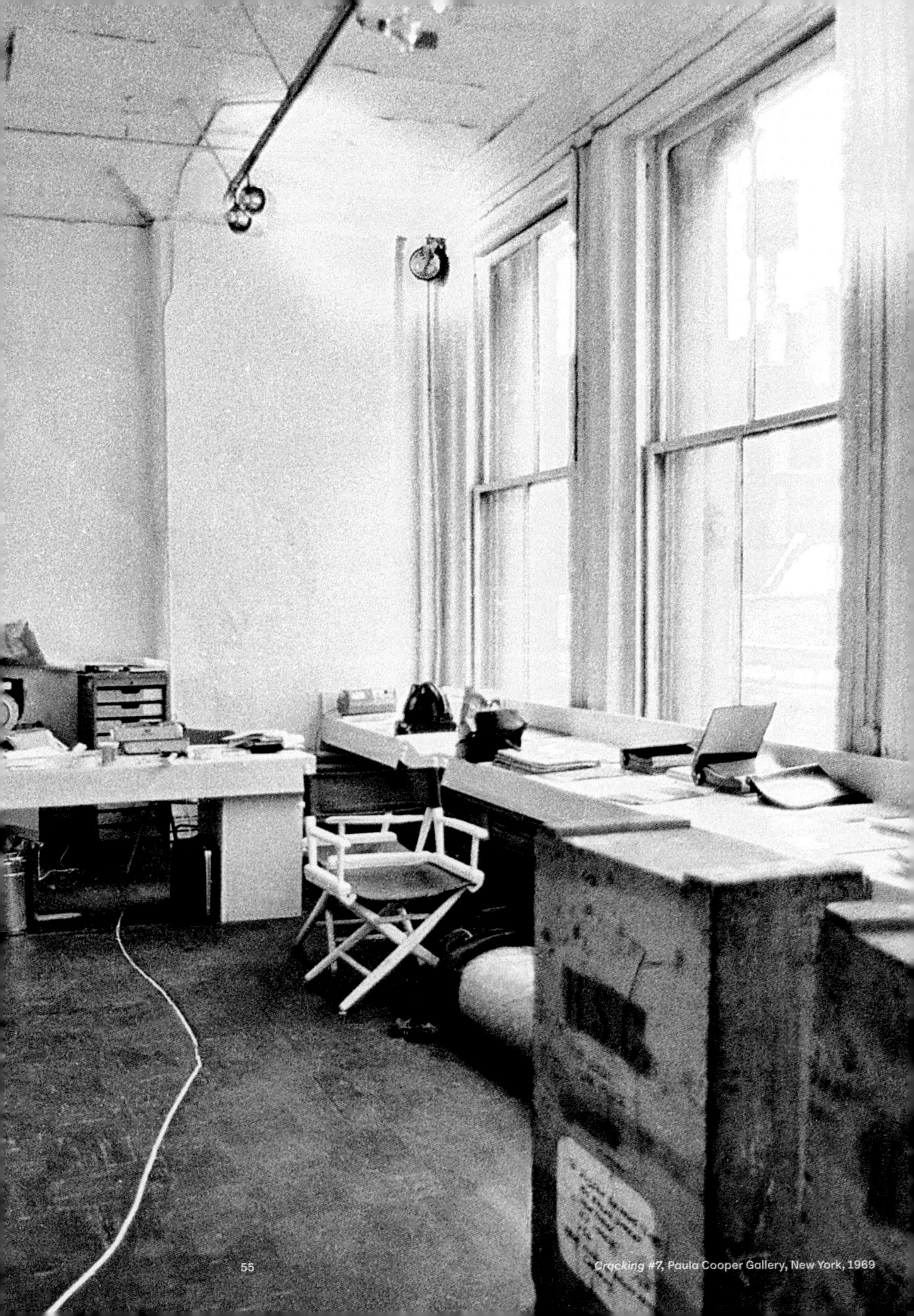

Cracking #7, Paula Cooper Gallery, New York, 1969

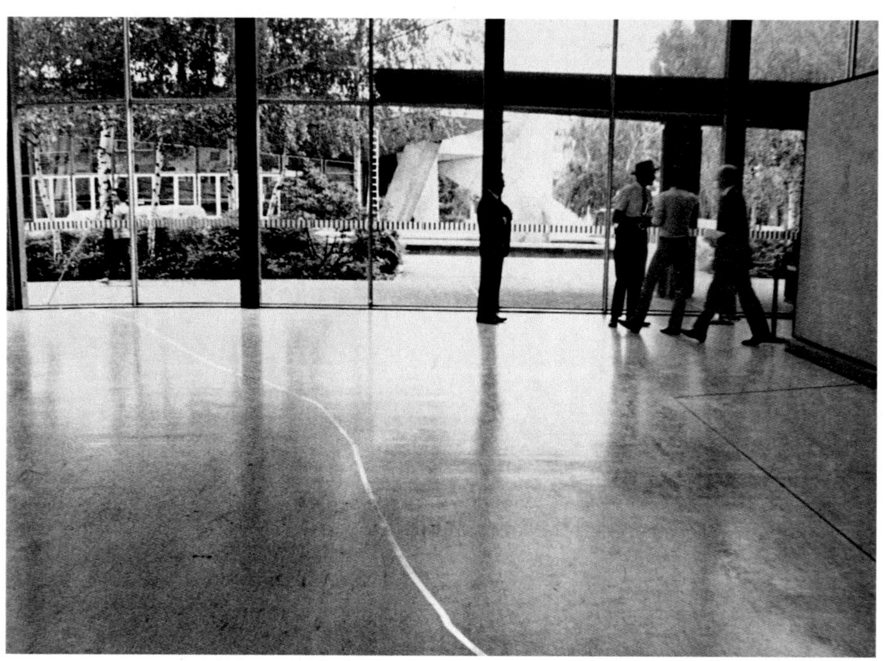

Seattle Cracking, Seattle Art Museum, Washington, 1969

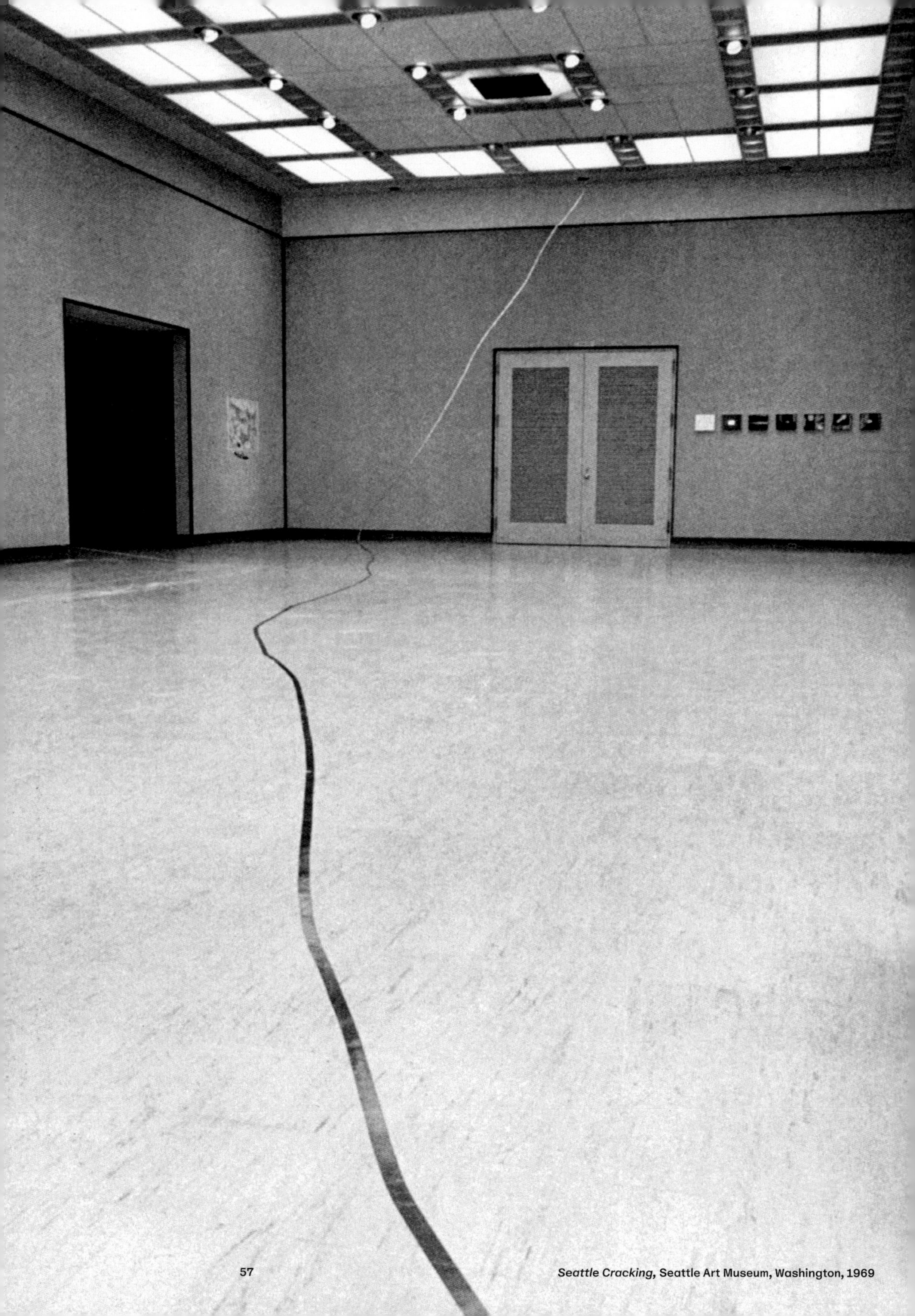

Seattle Cracking, Seattle Art Museum, Washington, 1969

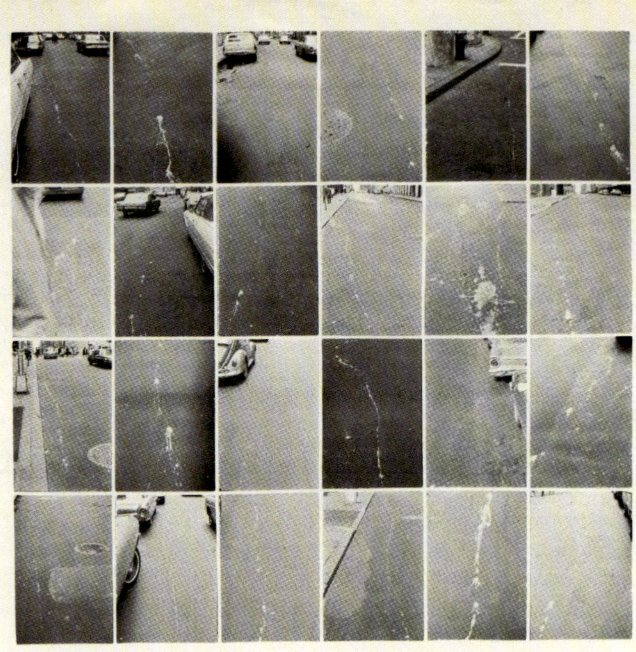

March 21, 1969

I have recently been making art out side of my studio.

On March 15, 1969, at midnight, I rode my bicycle up to 52nd Street and Fifth Avenue from my studio at Spring Street, carrying four gallons of white enamel paint.

I punched a hole in one gallon, put it on its side in the back fender basket and pedalled my bicycle up the down streets and down the up streets until the gallons were empty.

R. Castoro

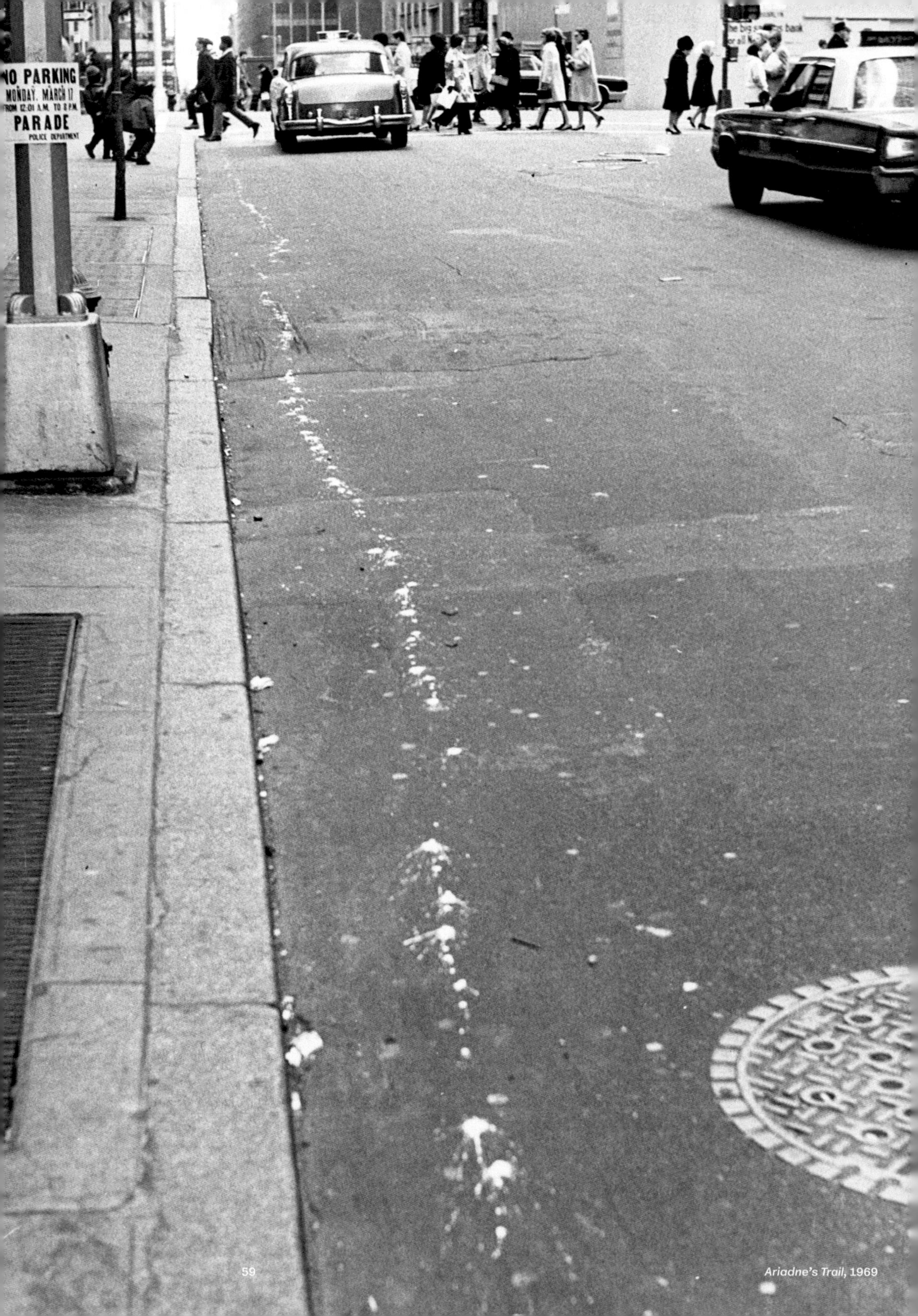

Ariadne's Trail, 1969

Ariadne's Trail, 1969

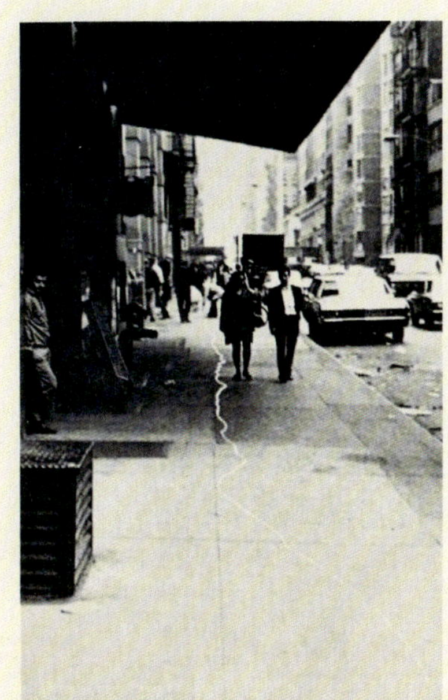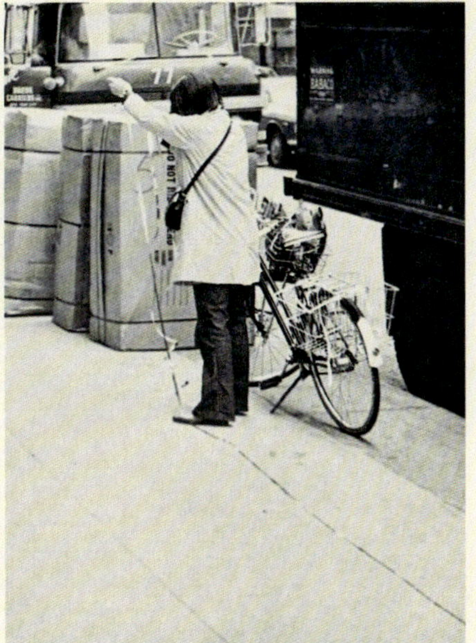

Photos: W. Dawes

April 18, 1969

How to make an atoll out of Manhattan Island:
1. Place underfoot the start of a ¼" wide aluminum tape.
2. Unroll to out-stretched arms
3. Lift knee
4. Extend foot to touch outer face of tape.
5. Fall forward keeping foot in contact with tape
6. Loosen enough of the block to allow it to fall or rise depending upon what is under street level.

R. Castoro

Atoll, 1969

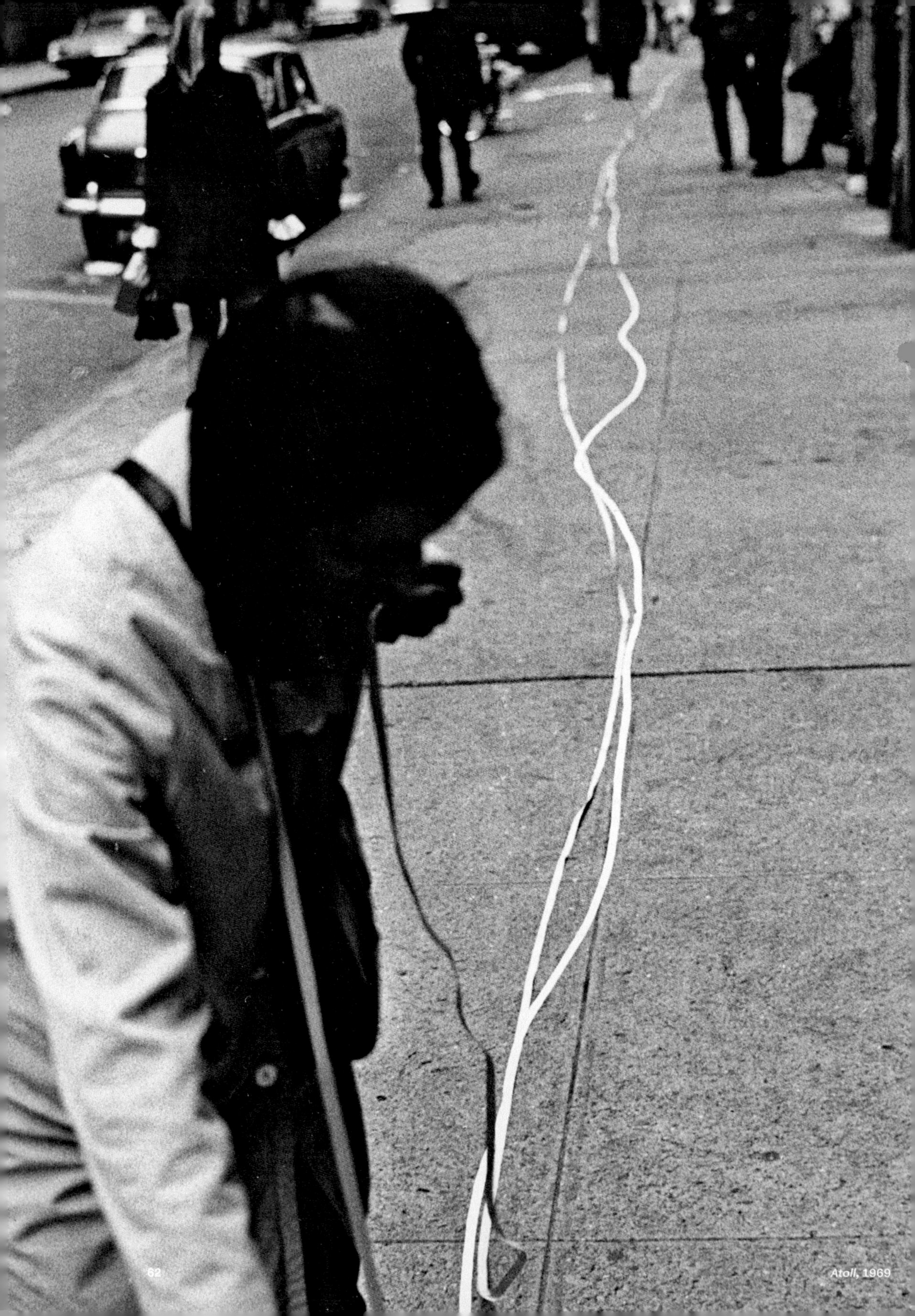

Atoll, 1969

SELF
CLOSING
DOOR
DO NOT GO THRU WHEN
RED LIGHT IS FLASHING
STOP
THIS GARAGE
PROTECTED BY
NO
PARKING
DRIVEWAY
PARK

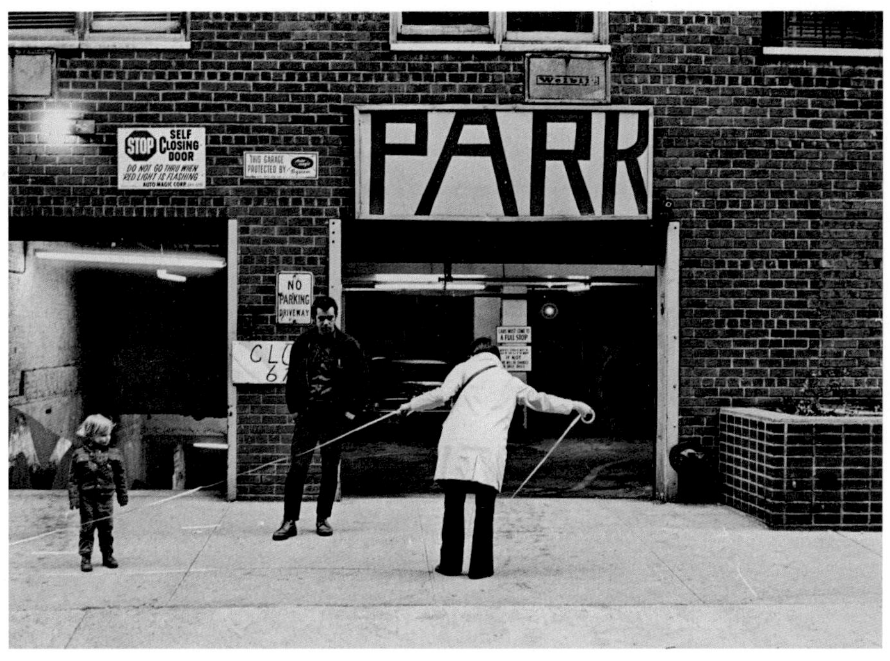

Atoll, 1969

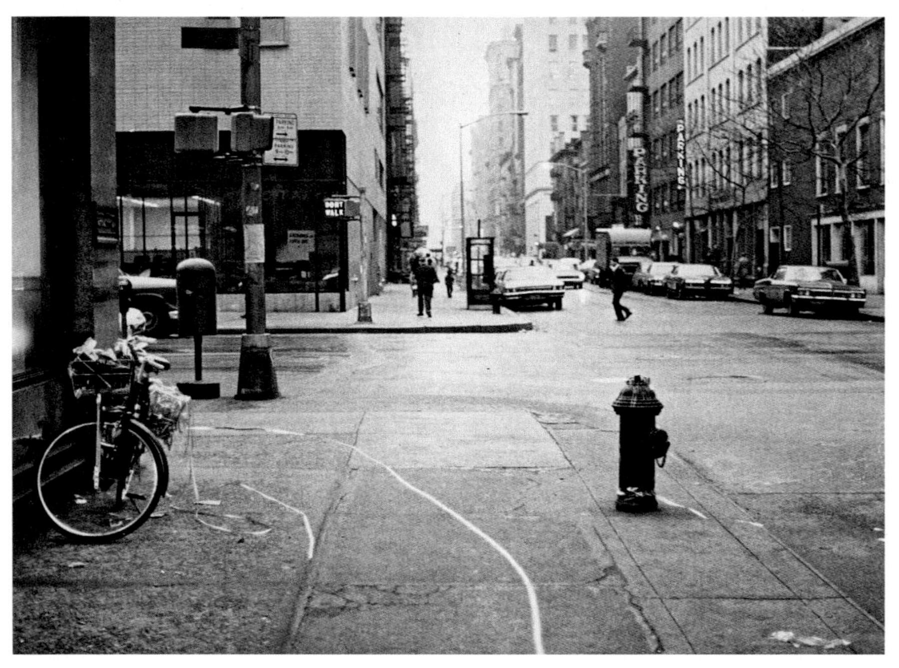

Atoll, 1969

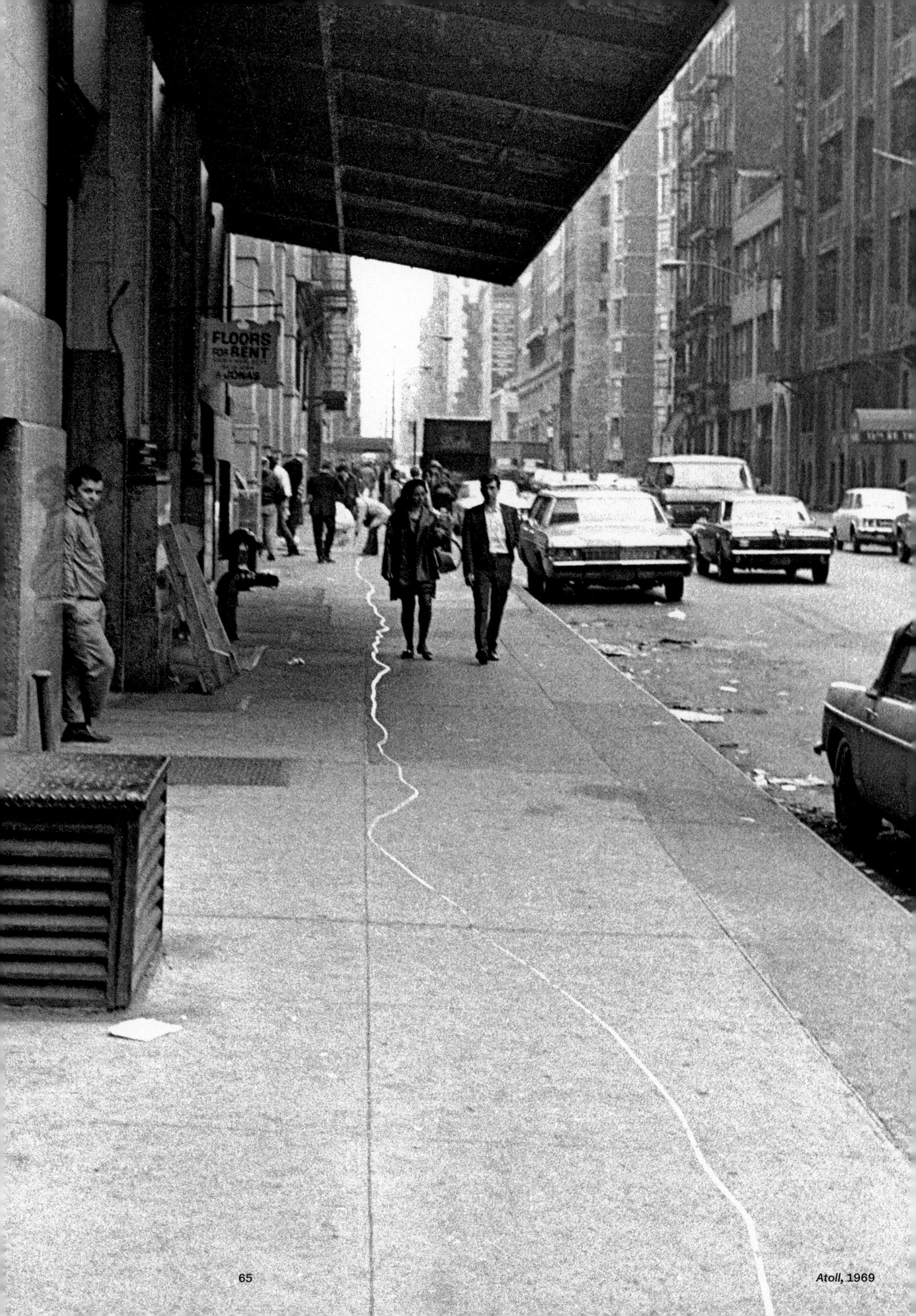

Atoll, 1969

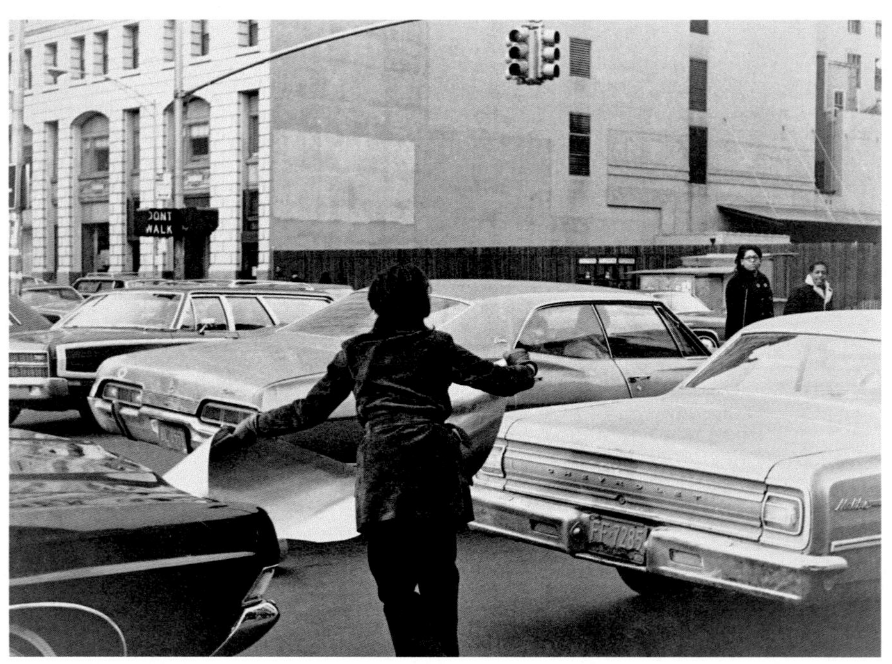

Gates of Troy, 1969

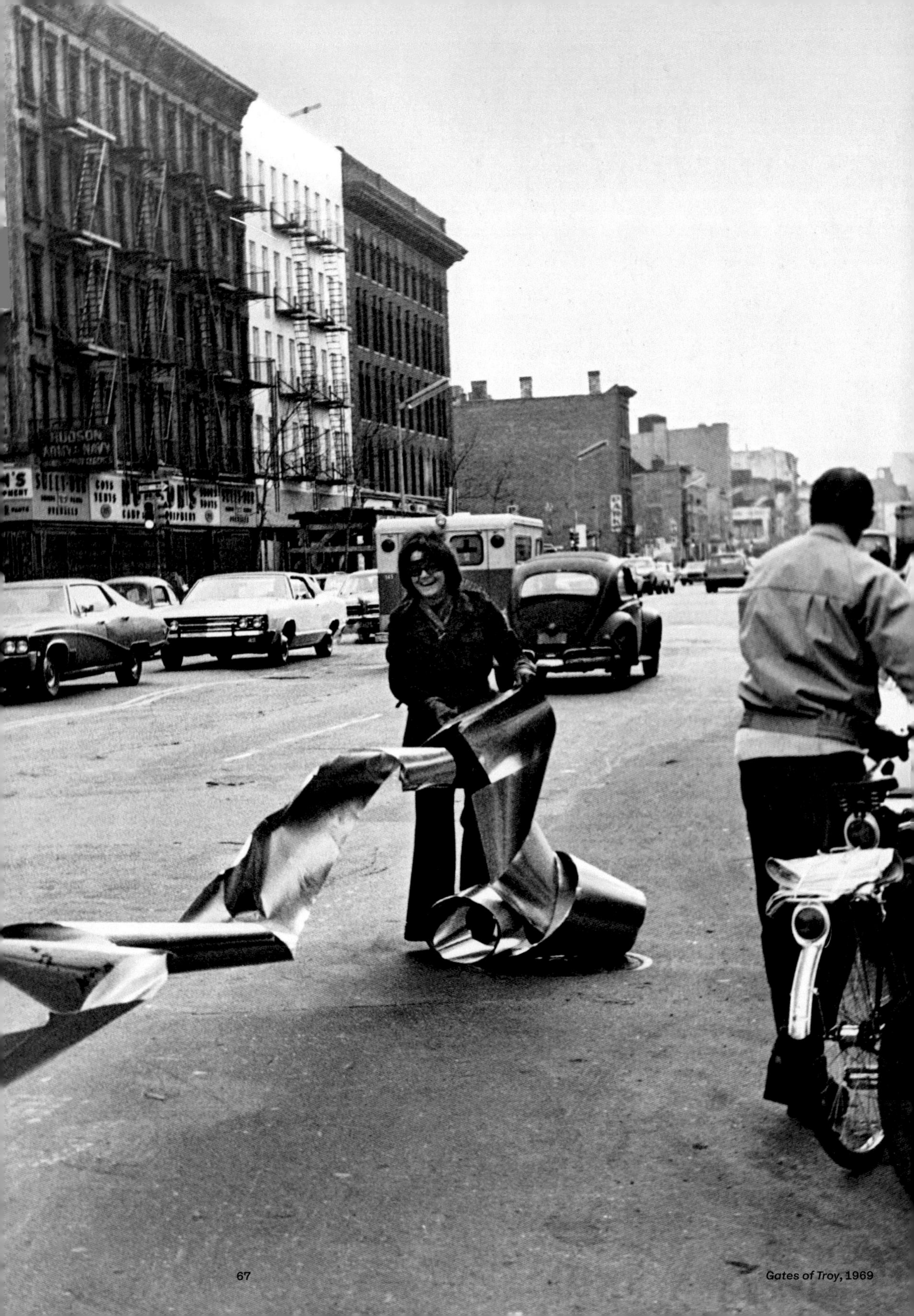

Gates of Troy, 1969

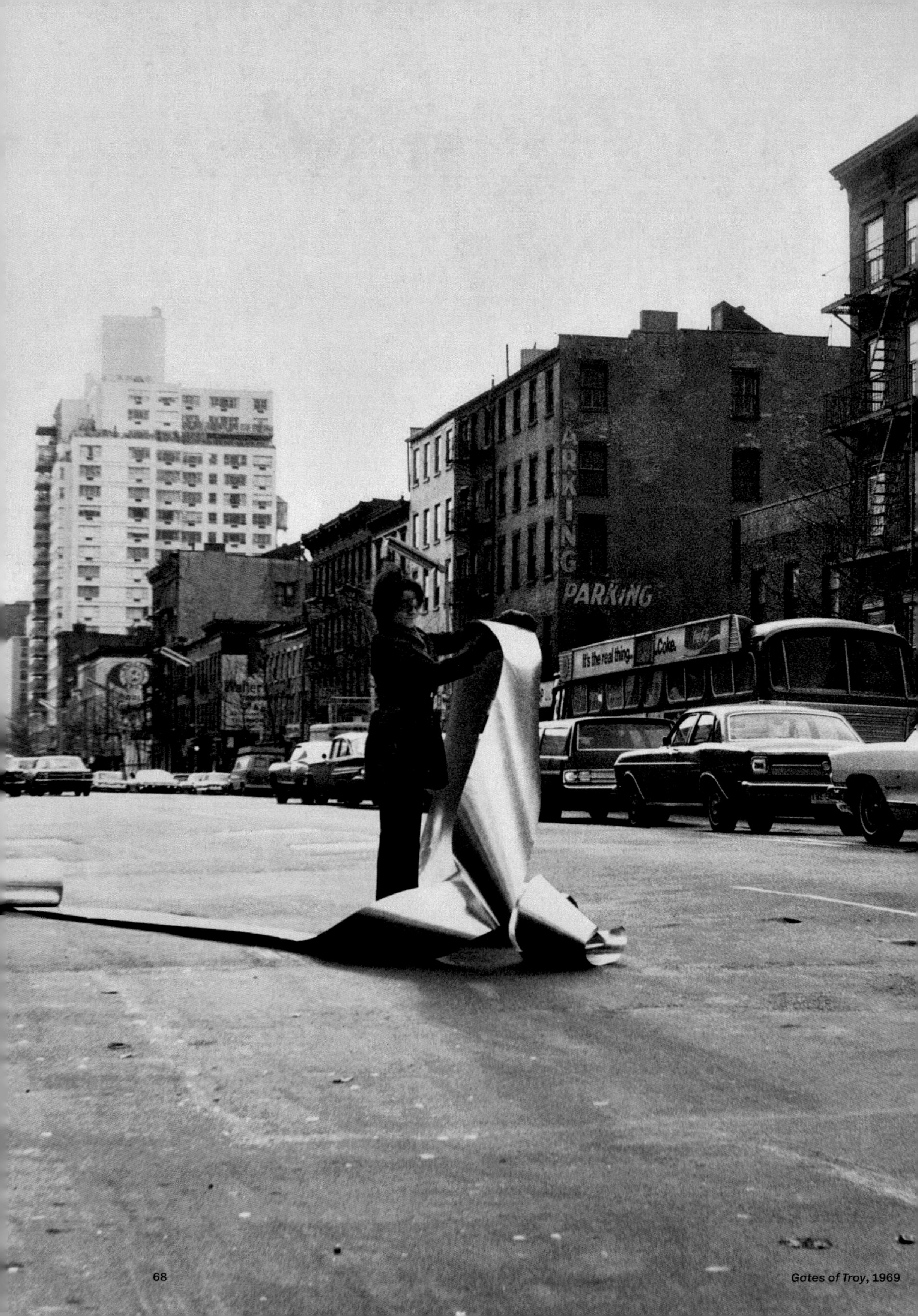

Gates of Troy, 1969

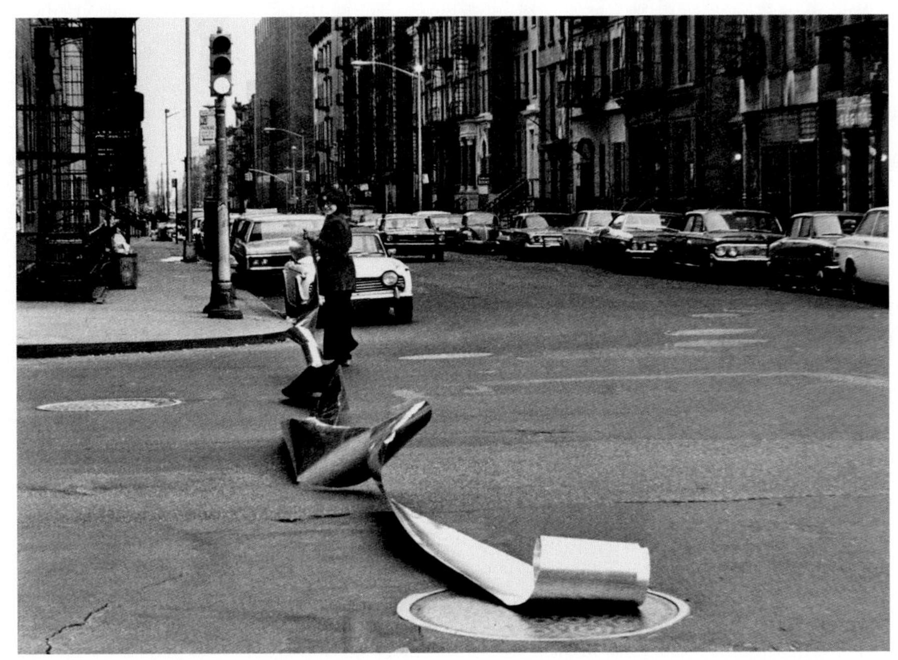

Gates of Troy, 1969

ROSEMARIE CASTORO

INVENTORY OF LINES

Laurence Schmidlin

The production of lines is among the most striking manifestations of the diversity of mediums that came to characterize the artistic practices between the 1950s and 1970s.[1] Rosemarie Castoro is unique in that her work not only participated in that trend, but became emblematic of it over a diverse range of media. As Lucy R. Lippard wrote in 1975: "Castoro's continuous activity focuses on line as a formal solution."[2] That would continue to be the case throughout Castoro's career, although the artist herself never explicitly theorized or even remarked on it. The longevity of Castoro's engagement with line also sets her apart from the rest of her generation.

Castoro explored various types of lines, pushing them into the third dimension before returning to planes, the better to free them from their support. That expansion into space, also characteristic of the period, was performed by a body—Castoro's body, her interest in choreography and dance informing her visual work and contributing to a pivotal shift in which art forms concerned with space also became concerned with time.[3] In her journal, Castoro described this shift in her own practice, bringing time to space: "At one time—time was my problem. Now, space. I want to carve space. I am carving space."[4] All of Castoro's work is intimately linked to the body, in terms of scale if nothing else. Numerous photographs show the artist in physical interaction with her works, sometimes hanging from ropes attached to the skylight of her studio, adding the lines of her body to those she drew or sculpted. In this text, I will explore the role of lines in Castoro's work over the course of her career, proceeding chronologically rather than taxonomically, as each group of pieces is the product of its predecessors. I will not consider Castoro's prolific works on paper but instead focus on her use of lines in other territories.

In Castoro's earliest paintings, produced in 1964, lines appear only unintentionally, at the boundary of geometric forms nestled together like cobblestones with the background color visible at their edges.[5] Only later would the first true lines appear in the sense of intentional marks, and not by default at the edge of a form. In her *Interference Drawings* and *Interference Paintings* (1965–1966), lines serve to construct. She traces parallel bands which intersect and break the composition into rectangles, exposing the underlying structure of each composition and documenting the process that produced it.[6] In the *Inventory Drawings* (1966–1969), Castoro again takes a construction-based approach, this time drawing lines that connect points to form an inventory of her environment, activities, and social interactions. *Inventory Plan* (1968–1969), for example, contains number-coded observations of her studio at the top and bottom of the page, connected by ruled lines. Castoro would later move even further away from the line as motif to embrace its fundamental identity as the vestige of movement. Such a departure must have been familiar—intuitive

1   See for example Carter Ratcliff's account in *Out of the Box: The Reinvention of Art, 1965–1975*, New York, Allworth Press/New York, School of Visual Arts, 2000. In particular, the chapters "From Box to Plane and Line," "Line Continued," "Line Enlarged" and "Line Erased," p. 15–58.

2   Lucy R. Lippard, "Rosemarie Castoro: Working Out," *Artforum*, Vol. 13, No. 10, summer 1975.

3   See for example Marcella Lista (ed.), *A Different Way to Move: Minimalismes, New York, 1960–1980*, Nîmes, Carré d'Art/Berlin, Hatje Cantz, 2017.

4   Personal journal of Rosemarie Castoro, June 1972 to September 1973. Rosemarie Castoro Estate.

5   Castoro, during walks through lower Manhattan, would look down at the cobbled streets and reinterpret their patterns in dynamic abstract compositions. Untitled text by Rosemarie Castoro in *MEANING*, No. 10, November 1991.

6   As Castoro explains it, she began with a mosaic of Y-shaped forms, then extended the axes of the letter until they formed a grid. Rosemarie Castoro interviewed by Claude Rutault over fax for *Le Journal des expositions*, February 10 1995. Archives of the Museum of Modern and Contemporary Art (MAMCO) Geneva, Switzerland.

even—given that the very first lines she made were likely as a dancer crossing the floor. As Wassily Kandinsky emphasized in his definition of a line as "the track made by the moving point,"[7] lines mark the convergence of space and time. The simultaneous progression of both is what sets a point in motion, most often via a tool in the artist's hand, that is, the extension of her entire body. The resulting line is a means of inscribing that track, and thus a drawing. The *Pencil Paintings* (1967–1968), with their evocative title, are composed of diagonals like the *Inventory Drawings*, but make no reference to the real. The use of large scale, such as *Arm Swing Blues* (1967), gives a physical dimension to their execution, likely around the time when Castoro stopped actively participating in dance—her pencil follows the sweep of the base layer of paint in an arc that strengthens the surface vibration.

This attention to the body and the tracking of movement led to an experimental phase in which Castoro added materiality to her lines, substituting pencil strokes with surgical tape that she wrapped around a canvas in overlapping layers in *Tape Painting* (1968). In *Aluminum Tape Painting* (1969), she employed the same technique but with aluminum foil. These new materials gave Castoro a pre-existing line and inspired her to move into real space for the *Street Works* project (editions I, II, and V) where she continued to explore the line as connector, spatial marker and tracker of movement. For *Street Works I*, she rode a bicycle loaded with a pierced 4-gallon can of white enamel paint between her studio at 151 Spring Street and the intersection of 52nd Street and 7th Avenue until the can was completely empty (*Ariadne's Trail*, March 21, 1969). For *Street Works II*, she encircled a Manhattan neighborhood with aluminum tape that she laid out by hand (*Atoll*, April 18, 1969). If we consider drawing to be the act and product of making a mark, both performances qualify. Two other works, *Aluminum Roll* (1969) and *Gates of Troy* (performance, December 21, 1969), are also based on the unrolling of a sheet of aluminum: an enlarged line whose length prevents it from becoming a surface. That same year, Castoro created the *Crackings* series in the same vein as *Atoll*, in which she divided the gallery space (with aluminum tape) or a human face (with string) in a reminder of the line's power to both separate and unite. She would return to the theme much later, in two pieces that each take the form of a pair of irregular parallel lines: in *Gallery Floating* (1996), a composition of 232 watercolors on paper installed across the walls of the Galerie Arnaud Lefebvre in Paris, and in *Fence Floating* (1999), created and set up onto the wooden rail of a collector's terrace in New York. The rest of Castoro's three-dimensional lines would be in sculpture.

In the early 1970s, Castoro's studio work began to take a more expressive turn. Working on the floor, she covered large, gessoed wooden panels with graphite in broad, energetic strokes. Her previous work in three-dimensional space, and recent developments in Minimalist sculpture, led her to give the drawn plane a

7   Wassily Kandinsky, *Point and Line to Plane*, translated by Howard Dearstyne and Hilla Rebay, New York, Guggenheim Foundation, 1947, p. 57.

physical presence and actively engage with the viewer's body. These works comprise a varying number of panels in configurations that range from a single vertical surface, dividing space like a standing screen, to self-contained volumes. Building on these works, Castoro eventually separated the action of drawing from its supporting surface, and her masses of lines became bas-reliefs representing brushstrokes. As the artist tells it, *Rotating Corners* (1971) turned so fast that a fragment of the drawing—namely a brushstroke—broke off and stuck to the wall.[8] Focusing on a single line later made it possible to move away from the wall and into three-dimensional space, as in *Small Burial* (1973), stabbing down from the ceiling. At this point, Castoro had begun to add a figurative dimension to her lines, playing on the active nature of perception. The idea for *Small Burial* was born while Castoro was lodging temporarily in an apartment in Fresno, California, that "resembled a coffin."[9] She described its genesis in vivid imagery: "I buried people on the roof and made roots growing down from the ceiling."[10] Another example of figuration can be found in her recurring use of the double-arch form (as in *Sky Tunnel*, 1973) with its intentionally sexual connotations, evoking in particular crotches.[11]

Castoro's work became still more anthropomorphic when she began to create what she called "exoskeletal auras," forms free of any abstract ambiguity: shapes modeled just enough for their symmetrical forms to suggest human silhouettes, are arranged into teeming parades and street scenes inspired by the lines outside movie theaters, where she had observed crowd dynamics.[12] The titles of these works encourage a figurative reading, sometimes through wordplay—always appreciated by the artist—as in *Street Meet* (1972), which plays on the homophones "meet" and "meat." The exoskeletal auras clearly demonstrate the sign's need for a backdrop and graphic creations' dependency on their supporting surface. Unlike Castoro's "brushstrokes"—which are themselves surfaces made from lines, the lines being so plentiful they constitute a surface—a single line does not have the same autonomy when deprived of a backdrop. In Castoro's work, the wall replaces paper as the surface upon which marks are made: the wall activates the figure it supports just as the figure activates the wall's power to act as a support. In 1973, Roberta Pancoast Smith highlighted the role of the wall in the exoskeletal auras, writing: "As before, the white wall serves as a ground for the marks which are now smaller in scale."[13] And Carter Ratcliff would conclude more explicitly, nearly 30 years later: "The wall was their page."[14] Three-dimensional lines are another matter, as the figure–form relationship does not exist per se and depends entirely on how the work is perceived in space, as the line can only be made out as such from certain points of view. Uniformization of the exhibition space thus becomes important to the wall's ability to serve as an imaginary surface.[15] When *Beaver's Trap* was shown at the Hal Bromm Gallery in 1978,

8   Barbara Rose, "1972. Living the Loft Life," *Vogue*, August 1, 1972.

9   Castoro 1991, *op. cit.*

10   Rosemarie Castoro quoted in John Perrault, Review of gallery-shows, *Village Voice*, December 12, 1973.

11   Francis Naumann, "Rosemarie Castoro," *Artforum*, Vol. 12, No. 6, February 1974.

12   Lisa Lilienthal, "Teaching SU art students stimulates new visiting artist," *The Daily Orange*, September 23, 1975.

13   Roberta Pancoast Smith, "Rosemarie Castoro: Tibor de Nagy Gallery," *Artforum*, Vol. 11, No. 9, May 1973.

14   Ratcliff, *op. cit.*, p. 39.

15   For example, in 1973, Dorothea Rockburne explicitly requested the Bykert Gallery in New York to paint the rooms white (including the floors) so as to create a continuous space for her exhibition of *Carbon Paper Installations* and *Drawings Which Make Themselves*.

Tiffany Bell noted that "the whiteness of the room, which makes it more difficult to distinguish the angle where the walls and floor meet, tends to emphasize the suggestion of an arrested movement —the instant before the balance is destroyed—in that it complicates one's sense of the flatness of the floor. One's understanding of the space is concentrated on one's perception of the stakes."[16] One minute, the square formed by the installation of 42 wooden stakes is discernible, the next minute they flatten into a single plane. Castoro had painted the walls and floor of her studio white, which contributed to this flattening effect. In photographs taken there, the linear sculptures appear as if drawn on a sheet of paper, like in reproductions of land artworks. The all-white backdrop was also used in exhibitions of Castoro's work, in line with the ideal of the white cube, precisely in order to render uncertain the distinction between plane and volume.

Castoro not only created lines (using various techniques) but also used pre-existing lines inherent to materials, both industrial (ropes, cables, string, etc.) and organic (hair, branches, etc.). Such materials are not in and of themselves drawings—which presuppose the intent to signify—but rather arise from what I have called "graphic capacity."[17] In a series of small sculptures produced in 1976 (including *Book's Underconsciousness*), pieces of steel wire extrude from white outer forms, revealing the energy within and rendering visible the sculptures' internal supporting structures.[18] The accumulation and irregularity of the wires evoke pencil hatching—particularly when one compares the completed works to Castoro's preparatory drawings, which they faithfully translate—and, from a distance, produce a shadow-like effect. She would later free the lines from the plaster and sculpt them into the shape of an angle (as in *Inside Corner*) which forms its own base. Inspired by the sticks she would throw for her dog while playing in the woods,[19] Castoro also created installations entirely from branches that she cleaned, cleared of any excess growth, and lightly trimmed and polished. The ambiguity as to whether or not a line can be considered a drawing is resolved when that line seeks to represent a form: Castoro's *Georgia Branch Dance* (July 16, 1974) is thus indeed, as she herself called it, a "sculptural drawing."[20] The ephemeral performance work was created with students at Berry College in Mount Berry, Georgia, and was composed of long branches that were collected and implanted into the earth, first in a line, then an angle, then a circle. Castoro also made use of human hair in her practice: first evoking it in the titles of her brushstroke pieces (such as in *Armpit Hair Coming from the Corner of a Room*, 1972), later collecting her own hair from the bathtub drain and using it in small compositions on paper (1993–2010) or arranging it to represent a human figure (*Walking Hair Brain*, 2005).

While Castoro essentially employed and created two types of lines as categorized by the anthropologist Tim Ingold— traces (a mark left following an action) and threads (use of a

16   Tiffany Bell, "Rosemarie Castoro," *Arts Magazine*, Vol. 52, No. 9, May 1978.

17   See Laurence Schmidlin, *La spatialisation du dessin dans l'art américain des années 1960 et 1970*, Dijon, Les presses du réel, 2019: in particular p. 25–26, 42–43, 109, 114–121. On the differences between "drawn" and "sculptural" lines, see also Laurence Schmidlin, "'One might say drawn': Three-dimensional Drawing, Linear Sculpture, and the Concept of Graphic Capacity," *Master Drawings*, Vol. 59, No. 2, 2021, p. 243–258.

18   Castoro/Rutault, *op. cit.*

19   Gail Ernsberger, "Going to the Max," *Manhattan Plaza News*, September 1987.

20   Personal journal of Rosemarie Castoro, February–August 1974. Rosemarie Castoro Estate.

21   Tim Ingold, *Lines: A Brief History*, London/New York, Routledge, 2007.

22   Ernsberger, op. cit.

23   Georgette Gouveia, "Artists take fleeting moments and make them permanent," *Westchester Newspaper*, May 27, 1990.

24   The term "drawing in space" comes from Julio González (1932), and was employed by modernist critics such as Clement Greenberg in the 1940s to describe the work of artists like Anthony Caro and David Smith. See Schmidlin 2019, op. cit., p. 110–115.

25   Peter Schjeldahl, "Now and Then It's Nice Just to Look at Things," *Sunday New York Times*, August 20, 1972.

26   Anonymous critic quoted by Gordon McConnell in "Rosemarie Castoro: The Magic of Her Art. Making the Horizontal Vertical," *Colorado Daily*, February 4, 1977.

27   Lawrence Campbell, Review of gallery-shows, *ARTnews*, Vol. 72, No. 3, March 1973.

28   Castoro/Rutault, op. cit.

29   *Ibid.*

pre-existing resource)[21]—her visual vocabulary in fact included yet more linear modes, such as in the *Flashers* series (1978–1981), enveloping forms that evoke raincoats. These sculptures, constructed from sheets of steel and aluminum, were inspired by the shape of a crumpled $20 bill folded so as to stand upright.[22] In addition to the lines formed by folds along the metal surface, there are the outside edges of each *Flasher*, which the human eye perceives as lines due to the form's division of space. Castoro would also use folds as indicators and break down their volumes into planes (as in *Crystal People*, 1981). She appears to have been dissatisfied with this technique, however, as she quickly returned to creating facets on a mass, all while accentuating their borders and folds (in *Kings*, *Queens*, and other series inspired by chess pieces, starting in 1984). In 1985, she began drawing at the opera and at contemporary dance performances, where she sought to "take that fleeting moment and make it permanent."[23] These line drawings served as the basis for planar sculptures, after which the surface disappeared once again, leaving lines to create self-sufficient forms. In 1994, Castoro began to create wall-mounted linear portraits made of welded steel that cut through space (including the *Sarcophagi* and *Ice Breakers* from 1994 to 1996, and the moving bodies of *Dancers and Lures*, 1995–1997). Still others were placed into a space (*Head Floatation*, 1999). These volumeless sculptures dissolve into abstract lines when deprived of a backdrop, or if the viewer is not standing in the right place; for that reason, they could be qualified as anamorphic. By extending the physical reach of drawing through her multimedia practice, Castoro revived, in a sense, the tradition of "drawing in space"— a metaphorical descriptor for a type of slender sculpture composed through a process like drawing.[24]

Contemporary critics struggled to categorize Castoro's work in terms of medium. The materiality and spatialization of her lines would make them seem to be sculpture, but sculpture that has lost its mass and expresses a graphic capacity. In the critical rhetoric of the times, her brushstroke pieces thus "may be 'drawing,'"[25] or her works produced a "double movement, making a sculptural element pictorial and a pictorial element sculptural."[26] Some critics, unwilling or unable to decide one way or the other, considered Castoro to have worked at a media crossroads. Lawrence Campbell, for example, wrote that she "continue[d] to explore new paths for her combinations of drawing, painting and sculpture."[27] While Castoro "consider[ed] [her]self a sculptor" despite "probably think[ing] like a painter, with three-dimensional responsibilities,"[28] she also explained that "to make the transitory nature of drawing to become solid and permanent as painting and sculpture, the boundaries of the three disciplines were transgressed."[29] It was through line that she accomplished that transgression, situating herself a step back to the mediums.

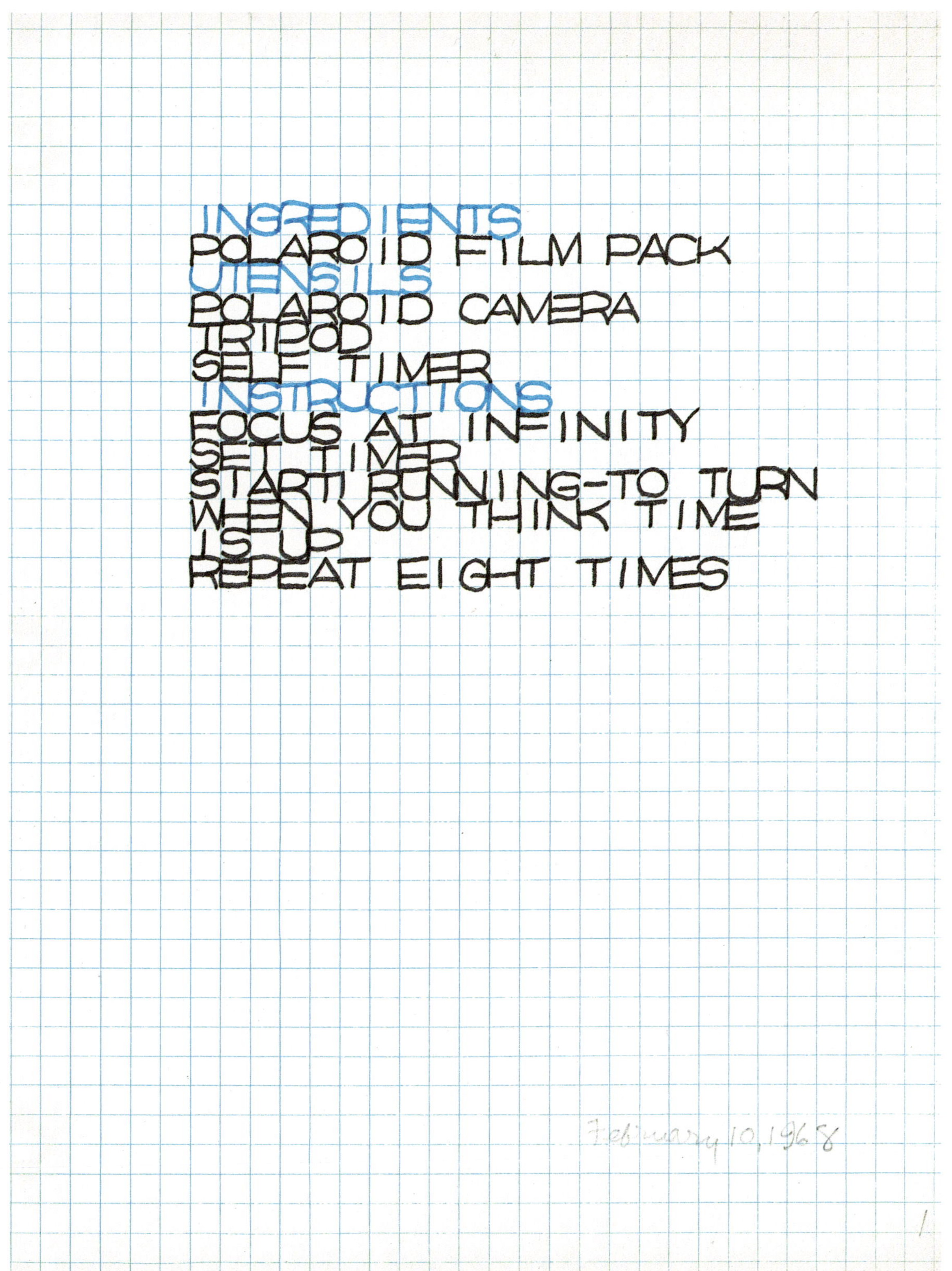

INGREDIENTS
POLAROID FILM PACK
UTENSILS
POLAROID CAMERA
TRIPOD
SELF-TIMER
INSTRUCTIONS
FOCUS AT INFINITY
SET TIMER
START RUNNING—TO TURN
WHEN YOU THINK TIME
IS UP
REPEAT EIGHT TIMES
February 10, 1968

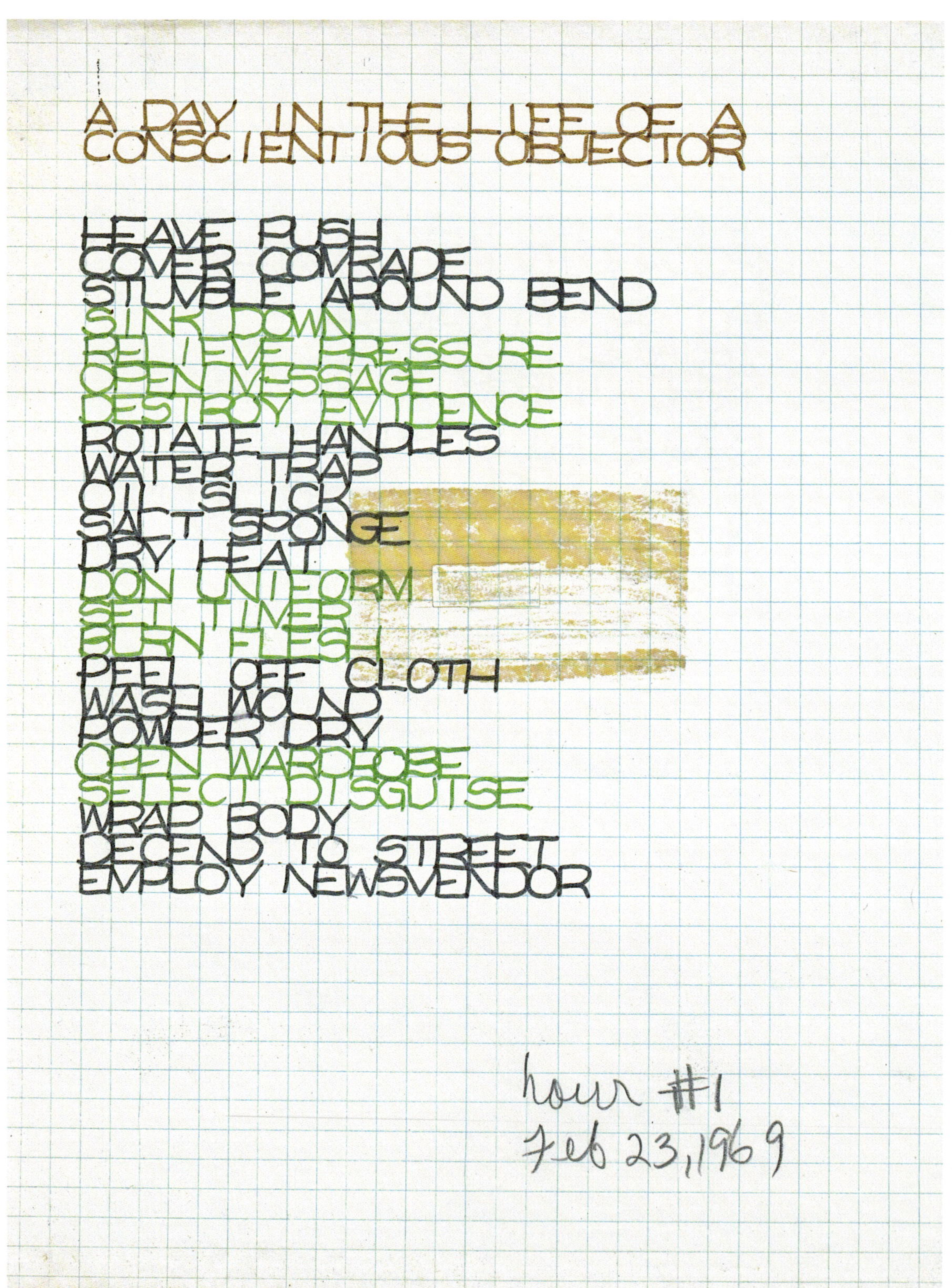

A Day in the Life of a Conscientious Objector, February 23, 1969, Hour #1, 1969

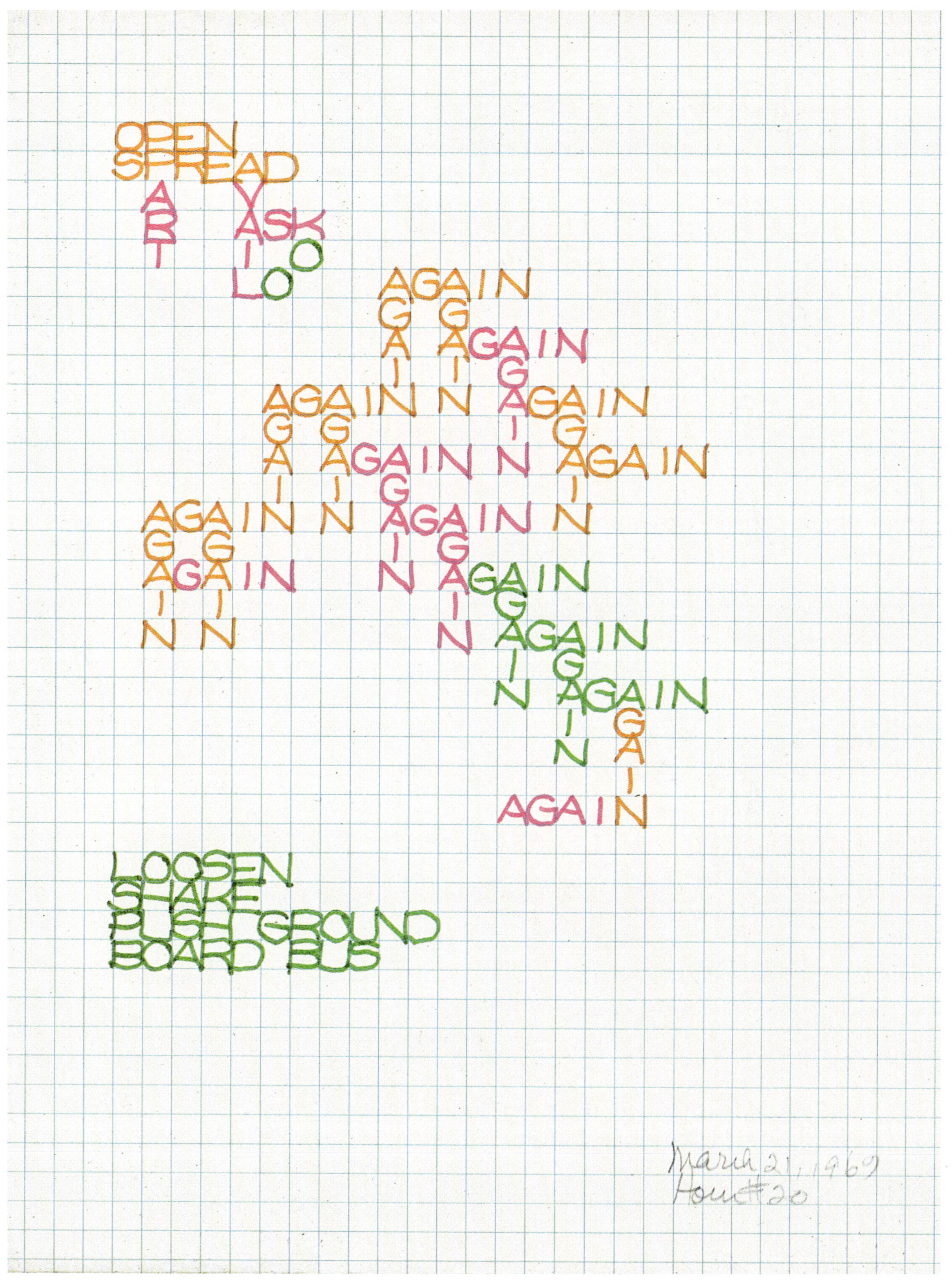

A Day in the Life of a Conscientious Objector, March 21, 1969, Hour #20, 1969

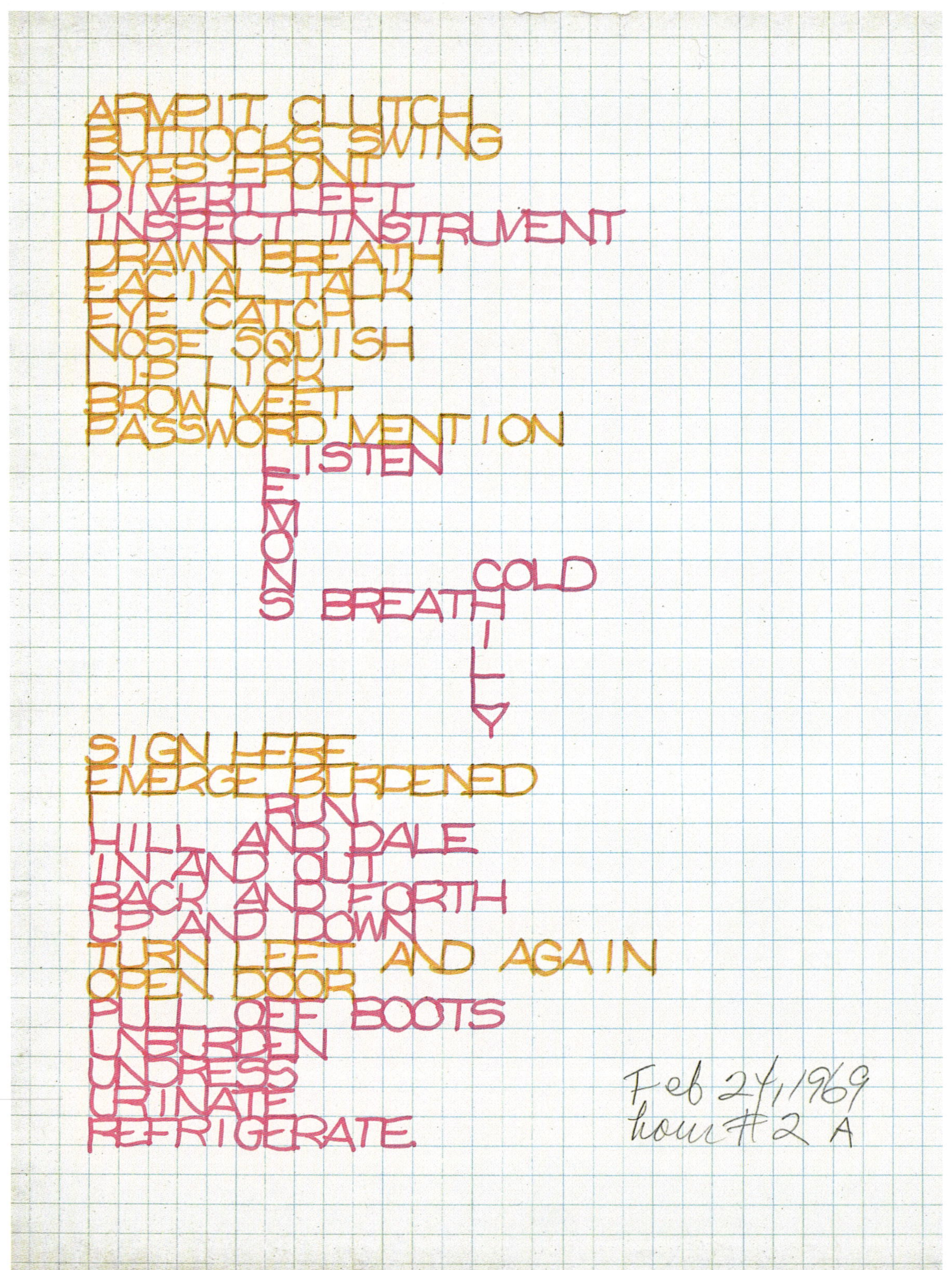

A Day in the Life of a Conscientious Objector, February 24, 1969, Hour #2A, 1969

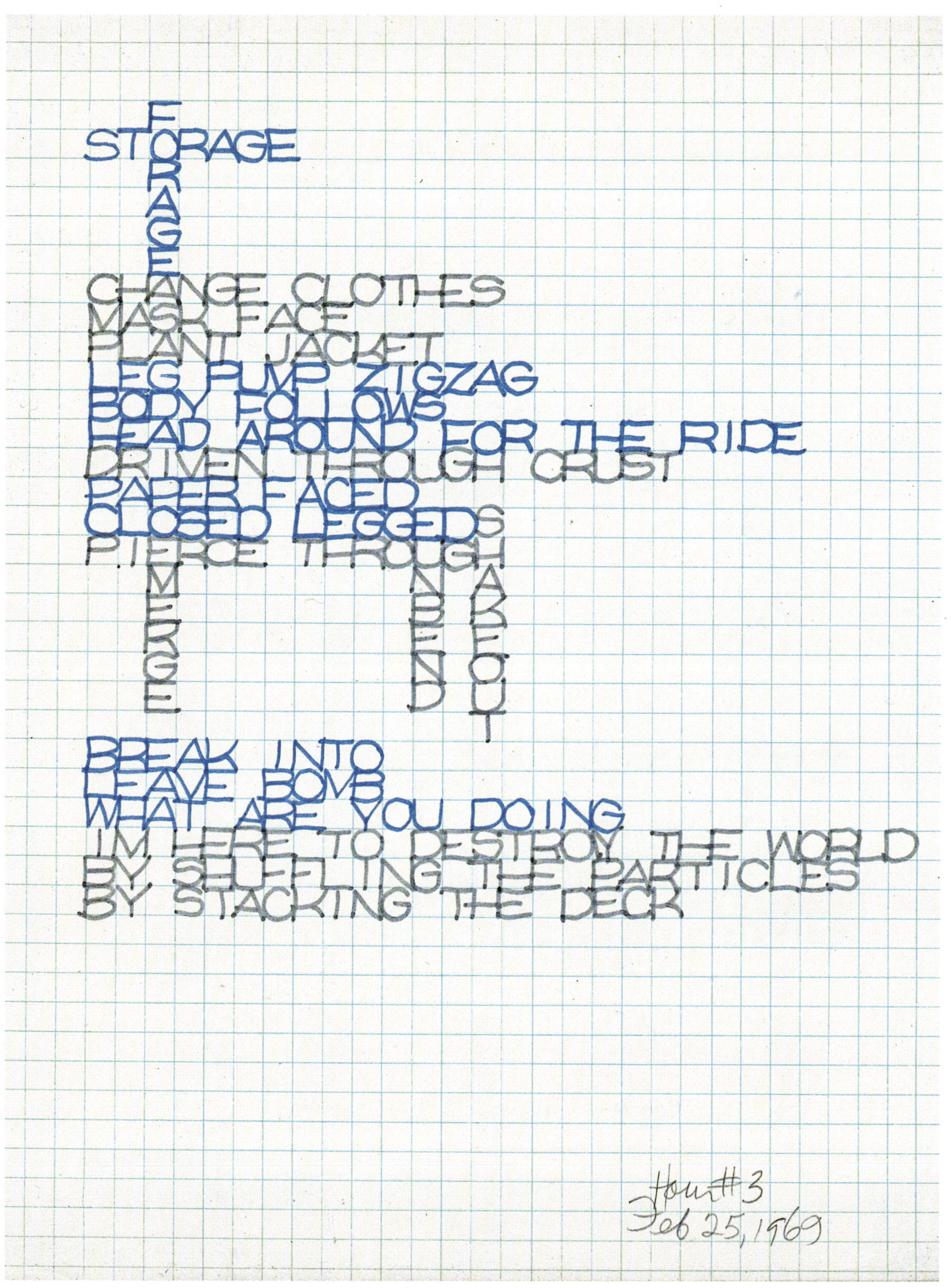

A Day in the Life of a Conscientious Objector, February 25, 1969, Hour #3, 1969

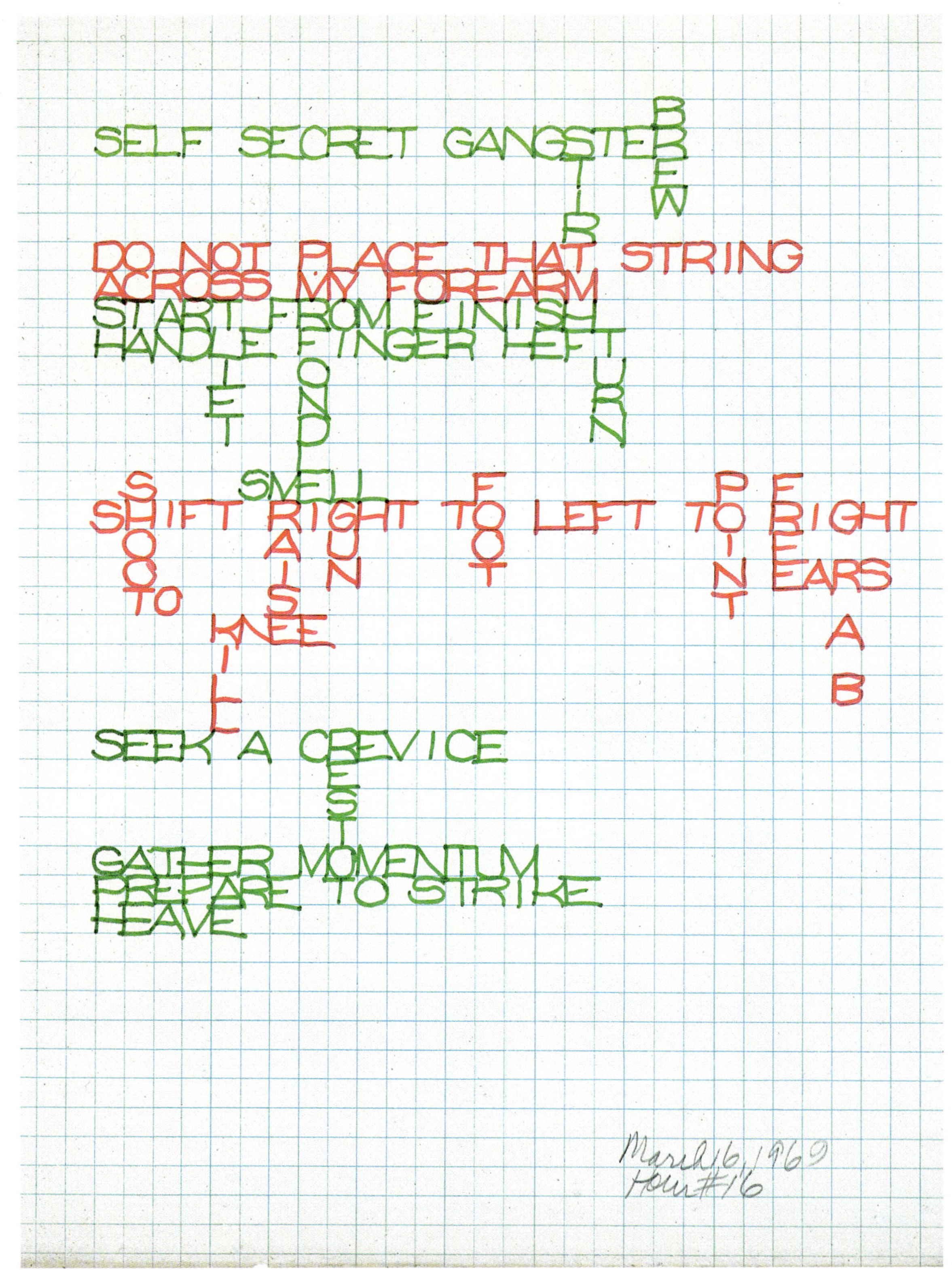

A Day in the Life of a Conscientious Objector, March 16, 1969, Hour #16, 1969

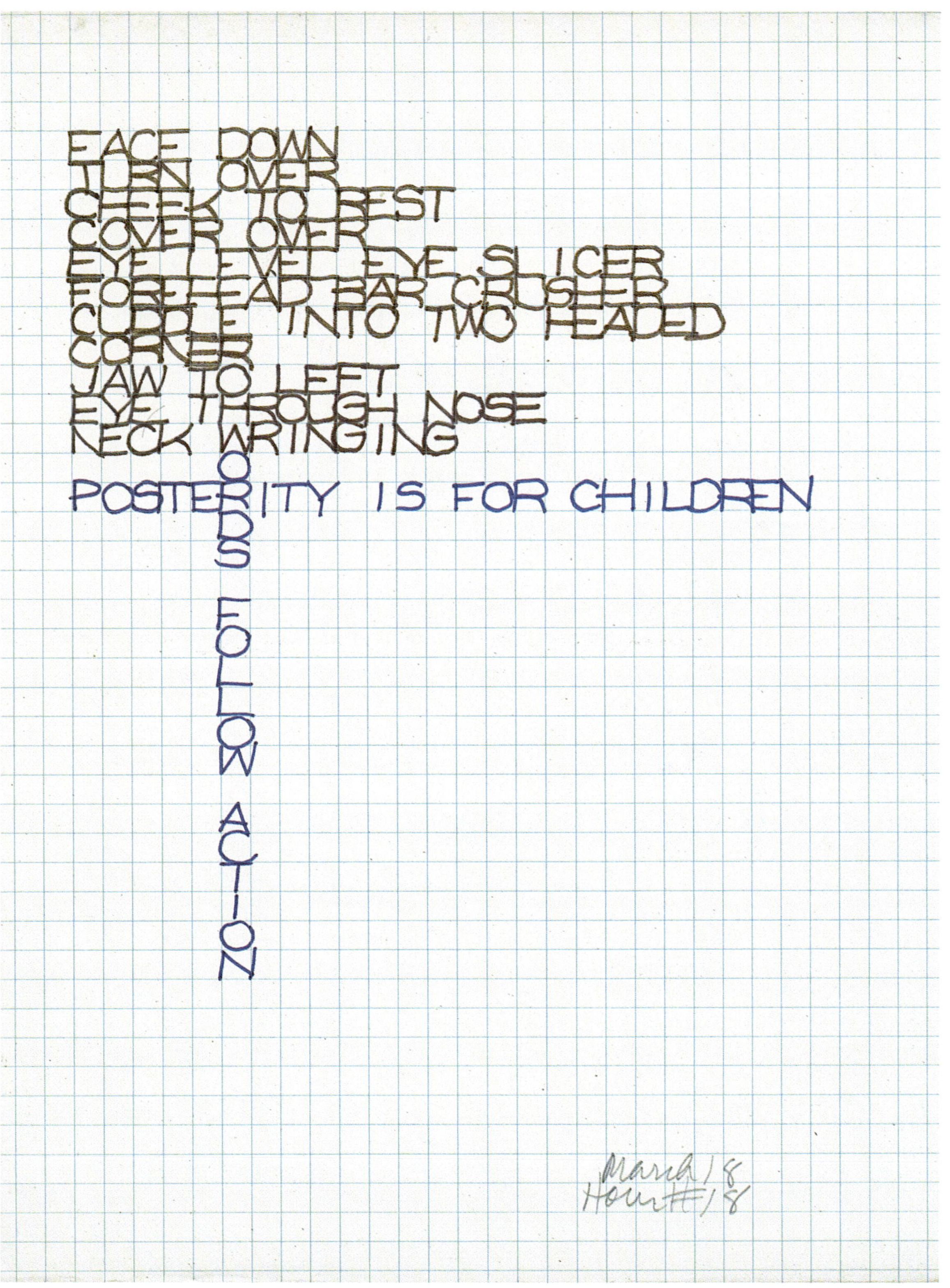

A Day in the Life of a Conscientious Objector, March 18, 1969, Hour #18, 1969

LOVE'S TIME
FEBRUARY 26, 1970
6:15 P. M. -
MARCH 1, 1970
3:30 P.M.

Minutes	Activity
0-7/43	From the start of push button push through rock music relaxation to work daily on writing and reading
0-17	From resolution through waiting for guest to unbathroom to March 21, 1970, springtime
0-15/55	From train leaving Spring Street to arriving at Whitney
0-33/55	From leaving Whitney to leaving Whitney
0-20/50	From going downtown to dinner to inventory for party
0-36/15	From arrival of dinner guests to finishing dinner
0-25/11	From check getting to funny and brilliant
0-600/9	From a left hand to Italian Bouilabaisse for dinner
0-18/57	From some kind of beginning again through list making and phone calling to drawing with a hard stick on gessoed masonite is a call for help
0-8/1	From putting it out there on the walls of the studio to notes are things that have to be crumpled and thrown away
0-26/30	From note taking to not wanting to eat until wordly dinnertime
0-8/15	From standing in line waiting to check out groceries to thinking about providing myself with food to last through the weekend
0-6/17	From still waiting on line to is this yours honey?
0-12/43	From bagging groceries to what do I need other people to bring me?

Minutes	Activity
0-11/1	From storing food to I would prefer it if you did not come to my birthday party on Sunday. I will pick up my final papers this afternoon
0-29/7	From going out to reaching Liberty Street by walking for it
0-1/16	From the top of a cavern to the ground level
0-2/24	From not waiting to coffee sipping
0-13/15	From dish clatter water spraying sugar bowl sliding bacon frying, utterances, whispers, chair dragging paper snapping bottle rattling counter banging money changing utensil dropping syrup squirting soda goggling cup piling telephone ringing wirebrush cleaning hot water sizzling chair scraping utensil gathering plastic cup popping whip cream squirting newspaper rattling spoon dumping whip cream pushing paper bag snapping lid slamming soda water wishing egg scrambling to where shall I go for three weeks?
0-55	From where I am to where I am
0-32	From where I am to wherever I happen to be
0-7/12	From right here to package getting
0-1/17	From elevator descending to street leveling
0-21/51	From Liberty leaving to water watching
0-43/42	From lobster rattling next to paper enveloping to return home walking
0-66/17	From I am working to ending dinner
0-21/4	From the beginning of the end of dinner to dinner guest leaving
0-27/42	From leaving to Atlantis' invasion of Egypt

Minutes	Activity
0-22/7	From history thinking to over compensation
0-42/14	From leaving stoned out of my mind to look for someone to buy me a whip
0-13	From the search for a whip to the finding of a friend
0-34/24½	From an unorganized sense of order to putting something there
0-20/7	From breathtaking to slandering and cursing
0-135/15	From starting to make time at St. Adrian's to arousing into the day and somehow being carried
0-31/23	From an uplift to the start of work
0-165/53	From vacuuming to splitting
0-12/50	From entering and exiting to the arrival of the IRT local
0-54/5	From leaving in taxi after seeing likenesses of drawings of mine in hair of movie
0-27/23	From onward to no answer
0-9½/57	From needing to go away to still being here
0-63/20	From leaving through frippery of musical comedy war movie to sitting in St. Adrian's
0-5/26	From ordering white wine to reading over "Love's Time" and improving the legibility of my quick handwriting
0-55	From clarity and legibility to what kind of poetry do you write

Minutes	Activity
0-16/20	From music playing of time filling to table right of me in words leading to poetry
0-11/36	From my own word through being here seated to more than one other to me is public
0-2/16	From tomorrow is my birthday to others sitting around me
0-1/13	From four at my table with one empty wine glass to I'll have some too
0-2/45	From a ten year study not so long please to how to deal with psychological time
0-8/9	From saving the world through reserving the self in doing to going to dine
0-6/3	From coq au vin no appetizer through easy music hamburger loving you too long cash register lettuce leaf in my time the eve before my party through take it or leave it if you have the choice
0-2/55	From lettuce salad eating to two guests seated
0-1/53	From continuing dinner to departure of guests
0-30/46	From departure of guests to finish of main course
0-3/40	From plate full of chicken bones to how can you stand being away from me
0-35/25	From sipping coffee to paying check after dinner
0-27	From start of leaving through midnight of going to arriving at Spring Street
0-24/14	From a toast to my friend the performancer on my birthday through coffee sipping to finishing triptych and starting sextriptych

Love's Time, February 26, 1970 6:15 P.M.–March 1, 1970 3:30 P.M., 1970

Minutes	Activity
0-7/17	From looking for numbers to calling a birthday guest and exchanging images, slices of reality, pieces in places
0-24/14	From boiling water to drawing is what I am doing
0-12/29	From old fashioned traditional solid grounded to full blown inspired young give it all away
0-14	From concentration of attention through waiting to calling
0-10/22	From reading vacation time to finish amending and deleting
0-8/26	From editing to AnnaLee's call before leaving from home
0-	From on their way here to it's not snowing for the first time in a few years but maybe three times in 31 years and I have been stingy but at 9:45 PM tonight I will start another piece to a stop watch stopped by time

Rosemarie Castoro

RUNNING

1. Returned from 30 paces waving my four year old
   hooded sweatshirt

2. Returned from 27 paces ignoring one curiosity car

3. Returned from 54 paces draping my four year old
   hooded sweatshirt around my shoulders while passing
   a two toned sedan

4. Returned from 45 paces strutting and smiling
   broadly

5. Returned from 43 paces not yet turned around

6. Returned from 56 paces although the self-timer
   went off earlier than expected

7. Returned from I forgot to write down the count
   after littering the street with a wad of yellow
   paper

8. Returned from 57 paces wearing my four year old
   hooded sweatshirt

9. Returned from 84 paces after having to force entry
   into one of the deserted buildings on your right
   to open the back of the camera to clean the steel
   rollers and wasting three hitherto unexposed pieces
   of film

Rosemarie Castoro
March 21, 1970
through noon
Washington Street
New York City

ROSEMARIE'S WRITING TIME

Sarah Lehrer-Graiwer

1   Lee Lozano, *Private Notebook 4*, p. 16 (1969).

2   Bruce Hainley, *Under the Sign of [sic]: Sturtevant's Volte-Face*, Los Angeles, Semiotext(e), 2013, p. 219.

3   Around this time, she exhibited text-drawings in *Language III* at Dwan Gallery (1969) and published statements in *Artforum* (1970) and *ARTnews* (1971).

4   Werner Pichler's email to author, June 26, 2022.

At the end of the eighteenth hour, she concluded, "Posterity is for children/Words follow action." Hour #18 in Rosemarie Castoro's *A Day in the Life of a Conscientious Objector*, 1969, describes a series of tortured head movements and "neck wringing" before reaching its declarative conclusion: the way it's written, the two lines crossing perpendicularly, it could also be read in reverse, "Words follow action/Posterity is for children." Either way, the pejorative implication is that posterity has a lot to do with words (and vice versa) and that she was not especially fond of children. Words may seem residual and secondary while action—in the studio, in life—is primary. Her friend Lee Lozano arrived at a similar if more extreme position just a few blocks away, writing that any matter, text included, is merely "a precipitation, a sediment, the ash from an idea."[1] By putting things down on paper, writing is always in some relation to a historical record, a "longlastingness" that's easily mixed up with ego, validation, and the fear of death. Elaine Sturtevant would also agree when she stated, defiantly: "I am not interested in being a 'Great Artist'/That's real medieval thinking."[2] An emergent feminism coincided with the development of an interior space in which art addresses direct experience and holds up a mirror to lived psychological processes, activating a feedback loop. The point is, in her art and life Castoro would use writing to observe and understand herself more than display, communicate, or perform an agenda. She began keeping a journal in 1969 and, after 1970,[3] her ongoing writing and habitual play with words remained mostly private. Language was there, parent at her birth as an artist and persistent to the end, if concealed within like an engine. Writing was a core strategy for Castoro, a way to generate ideas that elevated her objects and powered her art's next moves. Because writing is action too—thought in action.

Born and bred in Brooklyn as the oldest of four daughters, Rosemarie cared for her younger sisters as a self-described "child-mother."[4] Coming of age as an artist in the early 1960s, she studied graphic arts, printing, and painting at Pratt Institute, earning her BFA there in 1963 at age twenty-four. That same year she married Carl Andre and in 1965 they moved into the SoHo loft at 151 Spring St that would remain her studio, home, and sky-lit sanctuary to the end. She was in the thick of it. Her circle was large and heady, an epicenter of a generation of artists redefining the field as they experimented radically with new ways of thinking about perception, producing form, and turning art into action. She dialogued with artist and writer friends like Sol LeWitt, Lawrence Weiner, Hollis Frampton, Larry Zox, Neil Williams, Barbara Rose, Frank Stella, Richard Long, Lucy Lippard, Robert Smithson, Jan Dibbets, Agnes Martin, and Lozano among so many others. She was there at the bars with the rest of them—Cedar Bar, Dillon's, Max's Kansas City—often showing up after work to drag home Carl who might otherwise stay out past dawn.

As a student, she pursued dance and choreography alongside her visual studies, becoming president of Pratt's dance workshop and plugged in (like many of her peers) to the wildly influential laboratory of new and everyday movement that was fomenting at Judson Dance Theater. She performed in Yvonne Rainer's *Carriage Discreteness* in 1966, alongside her husband and twelve other performers of pedestrian traffic. Dance remained foundational though she basically stopped performing in public after school: she "decided to center her creativity on her performance in the studio rather than performing on the stage."[5] A slew of private, self-timed Polaroids of herself (clothed and naked) suspended by ropes in front of and posing with her work in the studio attest to the persistence and centrality of dance as a vital modality she aligned with sculpture, carving space. The way her body feels doing *this* next to *that* is a major part of the work's concern and interest—and led to her anthropomorphic, anatomized, narrativized take on formal abstraction. After Pratt, she explained, "[t]here were no more dancers that I could use and I didn't want to wait and develop a dance company. I wanted to make art every single day."[6] From the start, she prioritized a disciplined dailiness —day in, day out, hour to hour—that she framed as a kind of compulsion, later calling herself a *Maximust*, instead of a Minimalist. At the same time and while attending Pratt, she worked a day job:

> I studied graphic arts because, when I wanted to go to art school, I had to pay for it myself, so I went to school at night and worked during the day. And since I was an artist, I learned how to do paste ups and worked for an insurance company doing those and mechanicals, which was fun because it was just making lines and putting type in. … So, with that, I learned more, I was more proficient in triangles and T-squares and I've used them in my work. I think that whatever you do to make money, or do besides your profession, can work itself into your profession. So nothing's wasted.[7]

"Nothing's wasted" is an ethos to live by: everything gets folded into artmaking, consciously or not, because it is conditioned by candidly lived experience. Not only is nothing wasted, but real, practical, brass-tacks, day-to-day economic necessities become integral and subtextual to structure, material, and content. That the personal is indeed political was a burgeoning awareness. Since she earned her living doing paste-ups and tweaking details of text, it was natural that the skillset and experience had a major impact on what developed in her studio.

She applied a systematic, technical approach in combination with an extremely graphic and vivid aesthetic. Castoro's plastic play with the body of letters fueled meticulously penned Concrete poems and text-drawings on graph paper in a stylized and

5   Rosemarie Castoro, *ROSEMARIE CASTORO, short version_5feb08.doc*, unpublished.

6   "In Conversation: Rosemarie Castoro with Alex Bacon, *The Brooklyn Rail*, October 5, 2015, https://brooklynrail.org/2015/10/art/rosemarie-castoro-with-alex-bacon.

7   Ibid.

standardized font that conveys care, deliberation, and regimentation, as well as an unadorned elegance and roundness that reads feminine. She went further by homing in on a single letter while intensifying the possibilities of its formal presence, in her highly optical "Y" paintings which were the first she exhibited after school, showing them in group shows at Tibor de Nagy and Stable Gallery in 1966:

> [Painting] told me to look at the edges, of how the edges intersected space, and so I was able to then take that Y form and deal with the tips of the Y, with the edges of the Y. I also came out of the graphic arts, which means that I dealt with calligraphy, I dealt with typesetting, I dealt with letters, I dealt with linocuts, and I dealt with the hard edge of something ...[8]

The hard edge of something, as an image, suggests a great many things, emotional as well as physical in nature. Her objects often address edge limits, corners, ceilings, perimeters, and parameters in a way that comes out of dealing with type and text. The "Y" works from 1964–65 reflected her employment, schooling, technical expertise, the way she spent much of her time, and what her imagination did with all those things. It was also a bit of subtle wordplay as she mulled her chosen medium: "'Y' painting: question with its own answer."[9] She thought about language, especially titles, through metaphor, association, punning, homophones, alliteration, and often slippage across languages. Over the five decades she made art, wordplay (frequently with bodily or sexual innuendo) was the transformational logic by which Castoro framed work, from sculptural installations like *Tree Point Perspective* in 1977 and *Beaver's Trap* (Castoro meaning beaver in Italian, beaver being gendered slang in English) in 1977–78 to her standing metal *Flashers* from 1979 and small hair collages titled things like *Hair Piece* (2004) and *Meine Heir* (1993).[10] Some works had unofficial secondary titles: *Side by Side* (1972) was also called *Race to Become a Hook*, while *Bangs* (1972) was also *Chest Hair of a Giant*. She made small pen drawings tracking the phonetic and spelling relations of words, the kind of adjacencies that emerge from a chain of mishearings or misreadings, like a game of telephone: one from 1975, begins with "BE A MAN I SAY THAT IS TO SAY" which becomes "AYE MANICOTTI TIS TO STAY" and "TERRA COTTA TEATRO STATION" and thirteen further turns of the screw to arrive at "TEA TITTLE LED DELI" and, finally, simply, "THE TITLE." Words—and titles—would help articulate the fast flow of her thinking.

Years into growing nationwide protests against the Vietnam War, Castoro's ambitious 24-part text-drawing from 1969, *A Day in the Life of a Conscientious Objector*, reads as part Concrete poem, part linguistic abstraction, part short story, part confession, and part political protest. By the end of that same year, a draft lottery for conscription was instituted for the first

8   Ibid.

9   Rosemarie Castoro, *2010resume2*, unpublished.

10   Castoro prefaced the set with the description: "DNA self-portraits lifted from a bathtub strainer in recognition of the difference between architecture and sculpture, which is, plumbing."

time since World War II. Comprising 24 pages of text drawn with colored felt-tip pens on graph paper, it would be her largest text-based work. Every page is an hour in the day of the work's title, so that the first page is hour #1 (dated Feb 23, 1969) while the last is hour #24 (dated March 26, 1969). With few exceptions, she tackled an hour (a page), in order, per day. Writing in all caps with two, three, or even four colors on a page, she often used a chromatic shift to both break up blocks of text and indicate shifts in register or content, like between declarative actions and dia-logue. Tight kerning crams letters against one another and stacks rows of text close on top of each other in the grid, making the reading experience slow and labored. Visually, if not also otherwise, it is a dense read, at points challenging legibility, requiring re-readings and deciphering—and conveying all the weight and uncertainty of a long, most trying day.

  A Day in the Life is obliquely narrative, registering fleeting glimpses of story in terse, unpunctuated fragments in the vein of her Concrete poems, such as "COVER COMRADE," "RELIEVE PRESSURE," "DESTROY EVIDENCE," and "SELECT DISGUISE," all from hour #1. Or, "BREAK INTO/LEAVE BOMB/WHAT ARE YOU DOING/IM HERE TO DESTROY THE WORLD/BY SHUFFLING THE PARTICLES/BY STACKING THE DECK" in hour #3. There are indica-tions of both violence and sensuality. There are mundane moments. She writes in short staccato lines, single words or phrases only a couple long. The choppiness is basic and guttural, a broken and hurried expression of storytelling that teeters on collapse and desperation. She includes passages of sound effects, clickety clacks and crackles. Mostly she lists commands, tasks, verbs, and physical actions, reminiscent at times of Lozano's drawing of verbs she used for painting titles (1964–67) and Richard Serra's *Verb List* (1967–68). Still, Castoro seems far more invested in developing drama and character in a culturally specific way than the poems or conceptual experiments in text typically undertaken by her (mostly male) peers. *A Day in the Life* exists not only as a series of text-drawings on paper but has also been performed as a kind of script read aloud and projected as a slideshow.

  Utilizing the graph paper, each letter fully fills a square in the grid which makes the reader more aware of the binary vertical and horizontal components structuring most letters and how much of writing can be described by a small palette of lines —a proto-digital, even robotic kind of hand-scripted font. Many drawings in the set intersperse vertically-oriented words inter-secting with standard horizontal lines of text, forming crossword-puzzle or Scrabble-board layouts which multiply the order and ways lines can be read in sequence, adding a non-hierarchical array of parallel possible reads. The gameboard grid of graph paper echoes, too, an urban map or strategic game like chess, of which Castoro was a long-time player, continuing to play regularly with Andre at a neighborhood restaurant after their

11   "The Materialist,"
The New Yorker, November 27, 2011,
https://www.newyorker.com/maga-zine/2011/12/05/the-materialist.

12   In her journals, Castoro
frequently calls both herself and
her art "containers": from "The
artist is a container," to "my panels
are my containers," (Sept 1, 1970)
to "a sheaf of paper/a blank
canvass/some kind of container"
(October 10, 1969). See *Rosemarie
Castoro: Focus at Infinity*, Barcelona,
MACBA, 2017.

13   Castoro,
2008NarrativeResumeED.doc,
unpublished.

14   Rosemarie Castoro journal,
November 21, 1970.

divorce.[11] Yes, it is the sense of modularity and accumulation of units so central to the then contemporary Minimalist aesthetic that also infused her use of language. But, this grid-based emphasis on individual letters as building blocks connects not only to the Concrete poetry and sculpture of her husband and others like LeWitt, Smithson, and Morris. It is also the expression of a fundamental understanding of structure, analyzing a thing, one step at a time, according to its constituent parts. The affinities extend as far back as childhood when her mother, Camille, worked as an embroidery beader for haute couture fashion like Oscar de la Renta and her father, Michael, was a milkman, both occupied in their different ways with the perpetual filling and repetition of similar units within a grid.

The Concrete way words are positioned on a perpendicular axis also suggests an echo of her (contemporaneous) freestanding panels covered with graphite (retaining associations with writing) that take on qualities of folding screens or crisscrossing partitions, room dividers that she called "containers" for herself, as she did other sculptures to come.[12] An explicit bridge between language positioned along intersecting axes and architectural containers holding space for the artist is found in a small work, also from 1969, called *Non-Correspondence Letter* that can be manipulated at hinged joints so that its three congruent rectangular panels fold like a document being fit inside an envelope. Castoro's work, across media, is embodied and visceral, concerning physical movement. There is the suggestion to walk around them, as though understanding words on a page as objects or obstacles in space. The quasi-architectural panel configurations led to wall sculptures of large brushstrokes, sawed out of Masonite: "In my second show, *Rotating Corners* turned in my mind, I released the brushstroke. Out came Pitman shorthand, the basis for drawing symbols of people's names, words, and body parts."[13] Pitman shorthand script is a phonetic shorthand she riffed on in fanciful approximations of friends' names—*Guinness Martin*, for example, being a play on Agnes Martin—that privileged fluidity and speed in writing, different indeed from the precise print of her Concrete poems.

In the late 60s and into the early 70s, Castoro employed writing and text as a vehicle for self-analysis through selective record—and timekeeping. She developed projects tracking data and logging information that documented her activities and their duration as well as things like the spatial arrangement of objects and people around her. Mostly, she tracked time and duration. She was methodical. She used a stopwatch to clock the time between events, from doing one thing to doing another. And that activity of timing things makes both time and the activities timed more real, more concrete, more contained: "What is time but the measure of activity. What is activity but the manifestation of thought."[14] The stopwatch could get a handle on time, both breaking it up into manageable units and making it solid, giving it form with measurable shape. Her attention to rigorously recording daily life in terms of durational increments amounted to an ethical demand. In an undated note, she wrote, "Art is fast life. It is the cramming into a corner a lifetime of one moment." While on the other hand, complementarily, she wrote in a public statement, "Information is not art. To experience art one has to have time for an arrested moment."[15] Art had to do with the kind of speed that could cram a lot into a moment and the arresting of that moment, both at the same time. Time, too, was a container.

February and March of 1970 were especially productive, yielding several significant text-based works structured around timekeeping: *Vacation Time: February 16, 1970 through February 20, 1970*; *Love's Time: Feb 26, 1970–March 1, 1970*; *Eclipse: 6:43 AM March 7, 1970*; and *Running* (March 21, 1970). A year after composing *A Day in the Life*, she pushed her ongoing interconnected interests in daily experience, narrative, duration, and language into more personal territory. As opposed to the handwritten text of that earlier effort, these more data-driven text pieces are typed in list form, all but *Running* arranged so that a column on the left under the heading "Minutes" records times, while a column on the right under the heading "Activity" describes corresponding actions. Resetting the stopwatch with each new entry, Castoro formats each duration as zero to some number of minutes and seconds, like 0–32 or 0–18/16. Reading the log, one feels the repeated jolts of the clock's constant resetting. The logic of one thing after another echoes an affectless worldview in sync with the modular construction of Minimalist sculpture and anti-expressive, colloquial approach to choreography practiced at Judson. In fact, the stopwatch formulates a technical and athletic relation to time, like a dancer's—do this for this many minutes then that for that many minutes, according to a choreographic score or stage directions.

While the activities she measured are often straightforward and mundane studio or domestic tasks (i. e., "From stirring gesso to cutting new discs for sander"), her descriptions frequently spin off into poetic digressions (ie, "From old fashioned traditional solid grounded to full blown inspired young give it all away"). She includes notes on hygiene, diet, work, business, relationships, exercise, daily routine, outings, and the very making of the piece she is composing. There is a sense that all time, at that time, was also a matter of waiting and anticipation, some kind of preparation. How was the durational aspect of the everyday felt on her 31st birthday when *Love's Time* was made? Was it a seamless drifting flow or was it a stuttering series of starts and stops, abrupt changes and obligations pulling her in different directions? How could language capture time at the time that she was separating from her husband with whom she had lived for nearly a decade and whose intellectual companionship was major and enduring? Her

15   Rosemarie Castoro's statement for Art Workers Coalition April 10, 1969.

16   Lucy Lippard, "Rosemarie Castoro: Working Out," *Artforum*, Summer 1975, https://www.artforum.com/print/197506/rosemarie-castoro-working-out-37660. Lippard responded, "These constitute the best 'fiction' I have read about the life of an artist."

17   Ibid.

texts describe a personal, lived, corporeal form of Conceptualism, foregrounding her subject position and voice while her most prominent peers (again, mostly male) seemed to deny any with clinical distance. She said, "I sometimes watch myself in time by recording my activities with a stopwatch."[16] Similarly, painting was "where you watch yourself"[17]—indeed all artmaking was an analytic drug, a voyeuristic and exploratory out-of-body experience. For Castoro, language facilitates observation, keeping track of herself, taking stock and staying on track. She watches herself and we read her—we read her watching herself. She clocks in and she clocks out. Soon after these stopwatch works, she quit her day job, instead opting to live off her savings, grants, awards, and occasional sales. Taking time into her own hands.

And so, the overwhelming majority of writing Castoro did has remained private, either unpublished and not displayed or, on rare occasions self-published in the smallest of runs. Her husband since 1985, Werner Pichler, remembers the small (4×6 inch) white cards and black felt-tipped pens, like sharpies, she kept on hand for drawing and making notes. She made drawings rearranging the letters of her name and Werner's. She wrote one-liners, puns, and aphorisms on scraps of paper and in word documents on her computer: i. e., "The early word gets the bone" (1980) and "Do fetus wear shoes?" (December 3, 1982). She wrote quite a few versions of professional narrative resumes, one of which recounts her beginnings in the scrambled guise of a woman named Eiramesor Orotsac. She wrote a series of poems about smoke, ash, debris, wind direction, and the state of her city after September 11, 2001. And, looking herself hard in the eye in 2006, she did eye chart drawings to approximate the badly compromised vision she'd had since childhood, when she was teased for wearing glasses as thick as coke bottle bottoms.[18] Without contact lenses, Werner says, she was practically blind. The drawings show her left and right eye vision as a field of buzzing static, blurred light and dark where rows of bold letters should be—no hard edges here. As much as dealing with the hard edge of something visually, she was also listening to letters and language to feel their edges in the air and in her body—her mouth, her breath, her ear. Cutting and recutting, splicing and shuffling, running together and recombining fluidly. The chart she based the drawings on reads like a free associative run-on poem, letters diminishing in size:

18   Pichler email to author, June 26, 2022.

ECDROMNEWTONSAPPLEPLATOSCAVECASTOROSMO
UNTAINRANGEHIHOSILVER

Including herself in the litany, posterity, some 37 years later, looks rather different: a reductive shorthand for sure, and still for children, but collectively adding up to a teeming and varied cultural landscape that she's committed to contributing to—and a mountain range, no less.

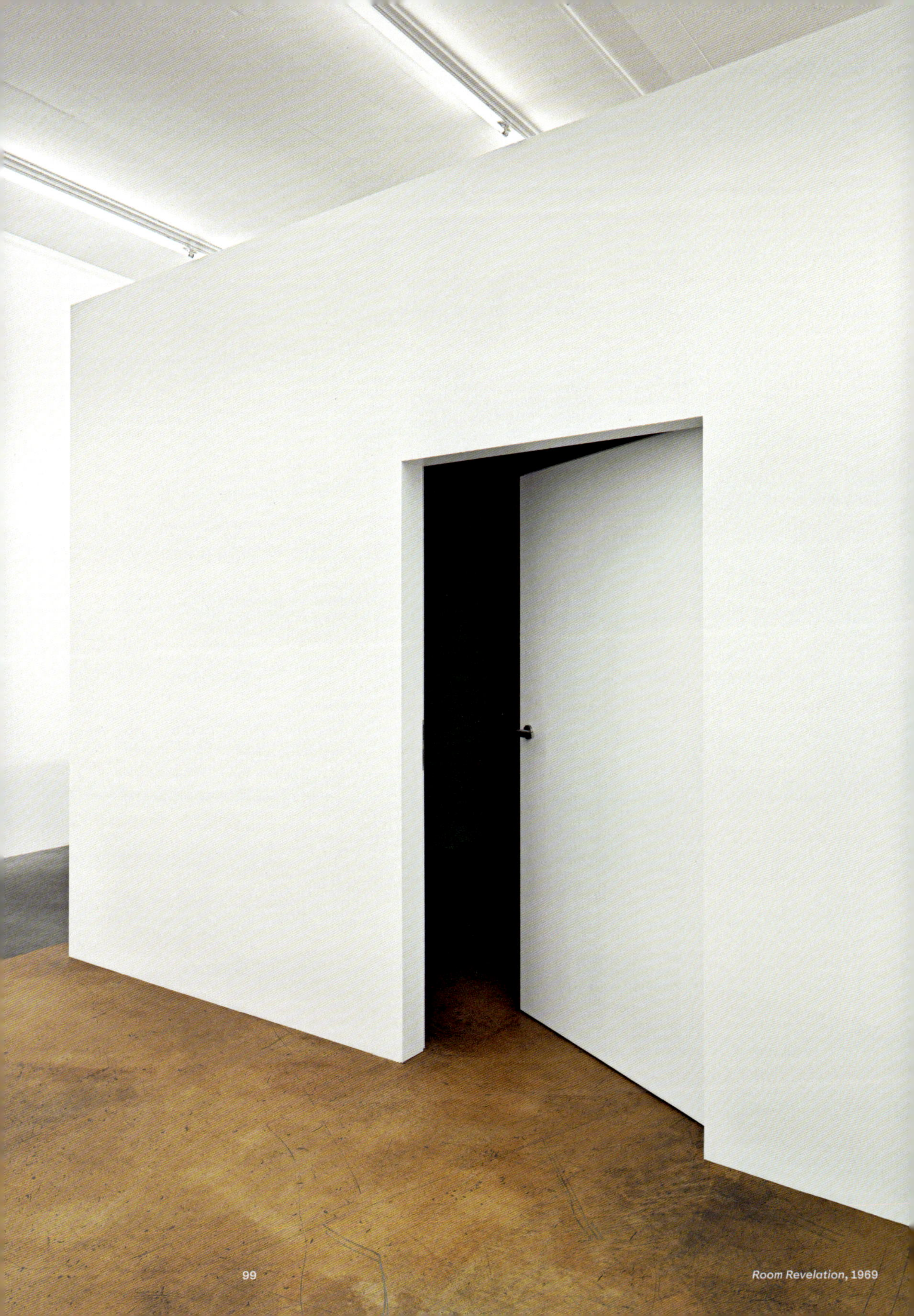

Room Revelation, 1969

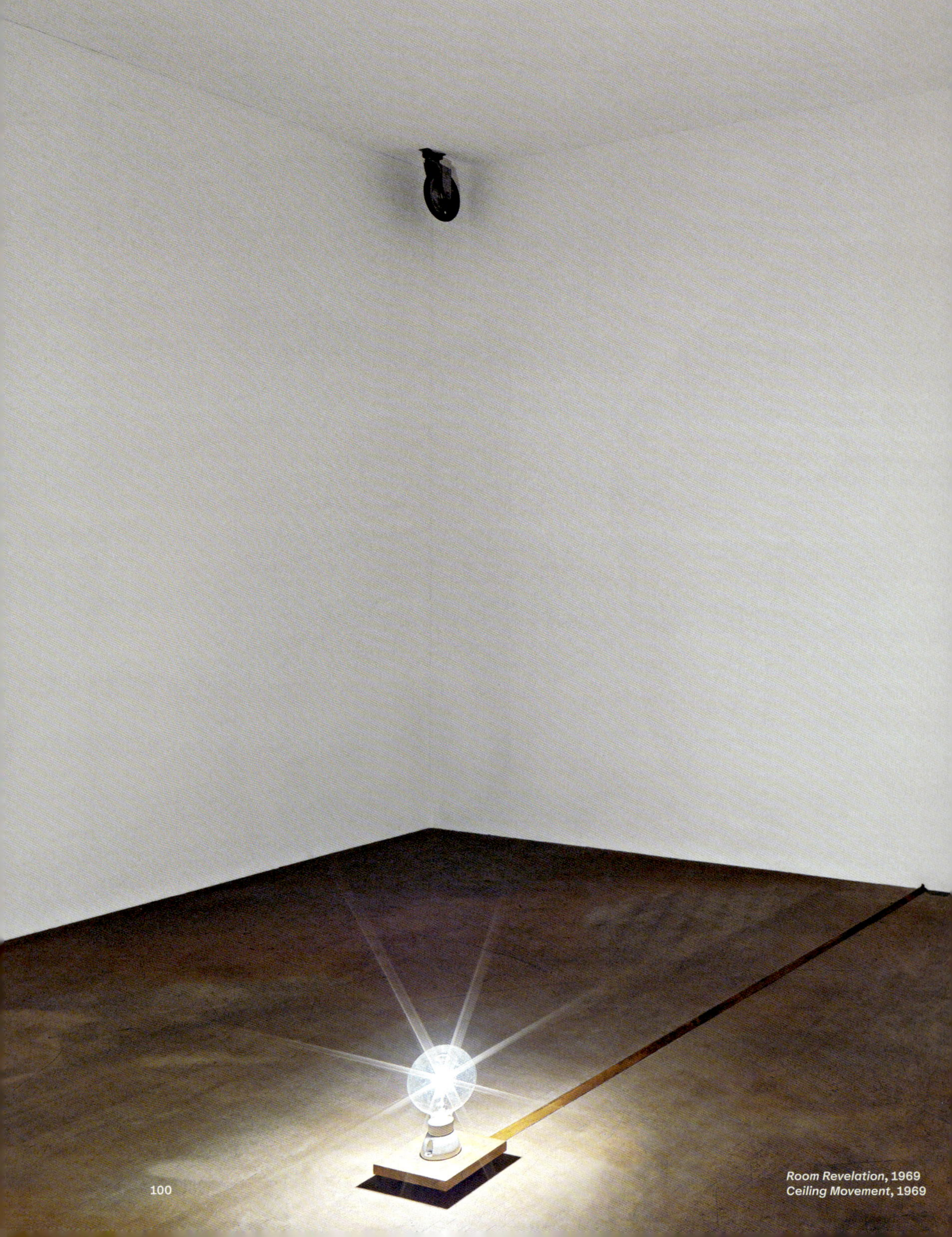

Room Revelation, 1969
Ceiling Movement, 1969

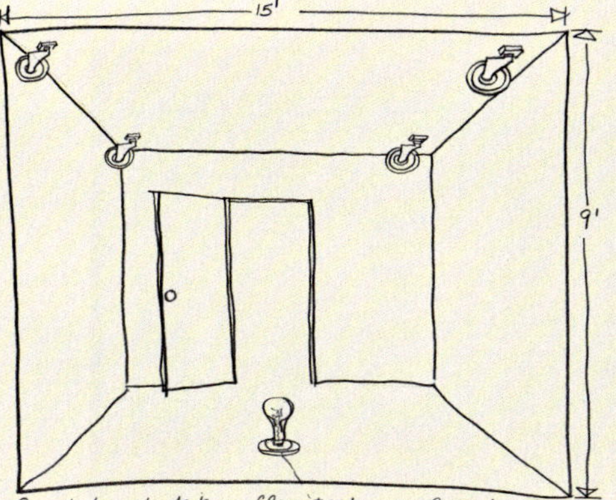

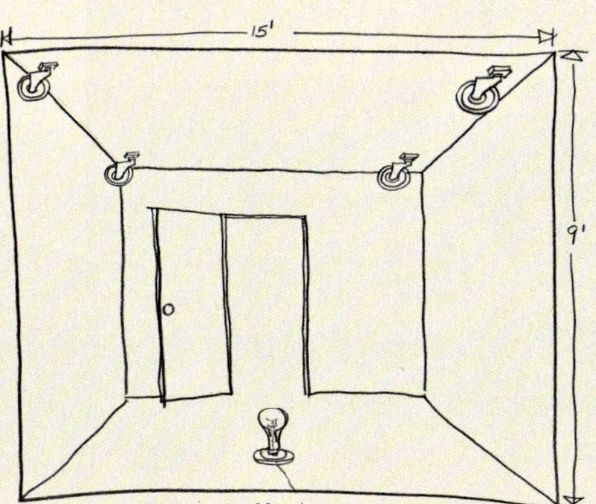

Room Revelation, 1970

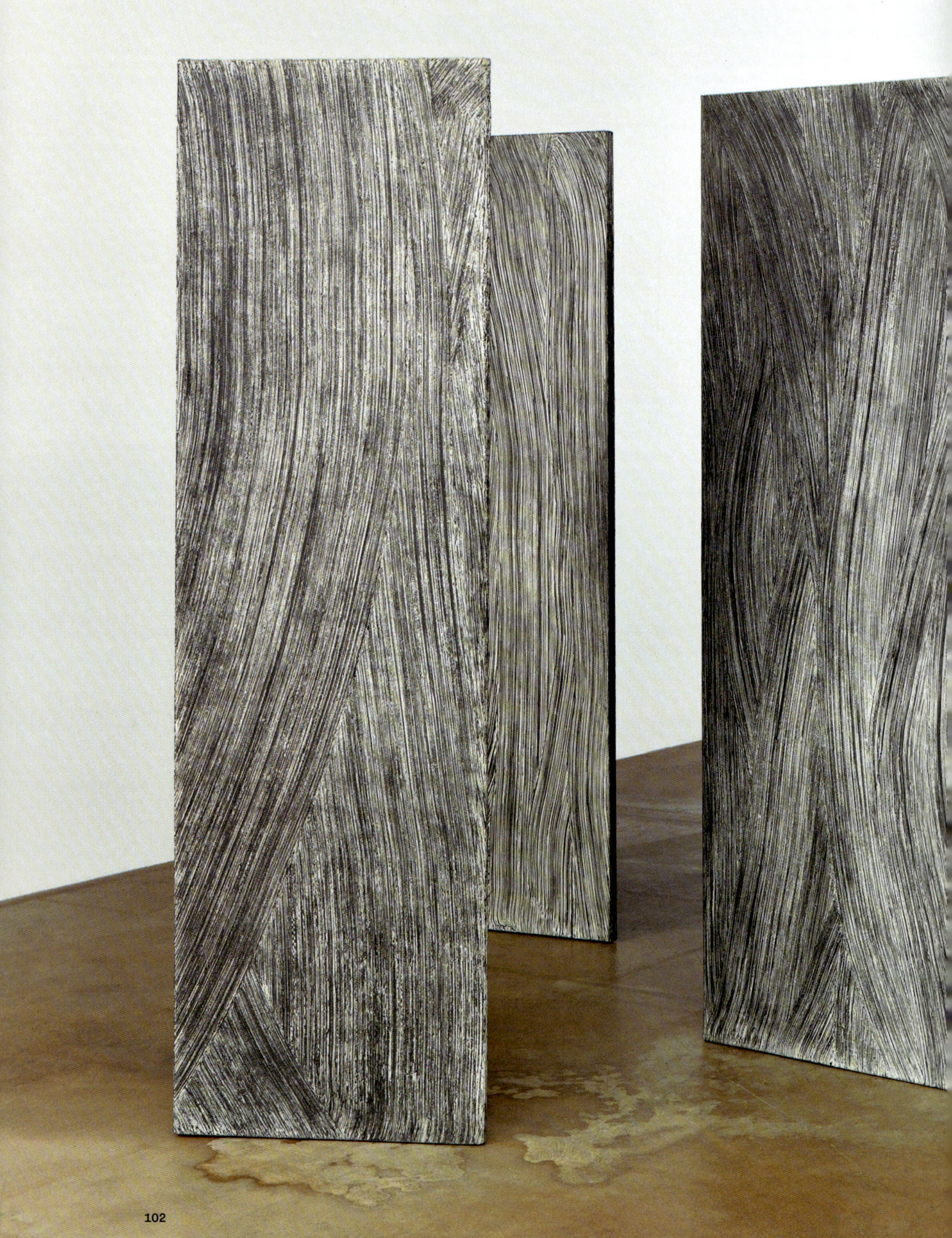

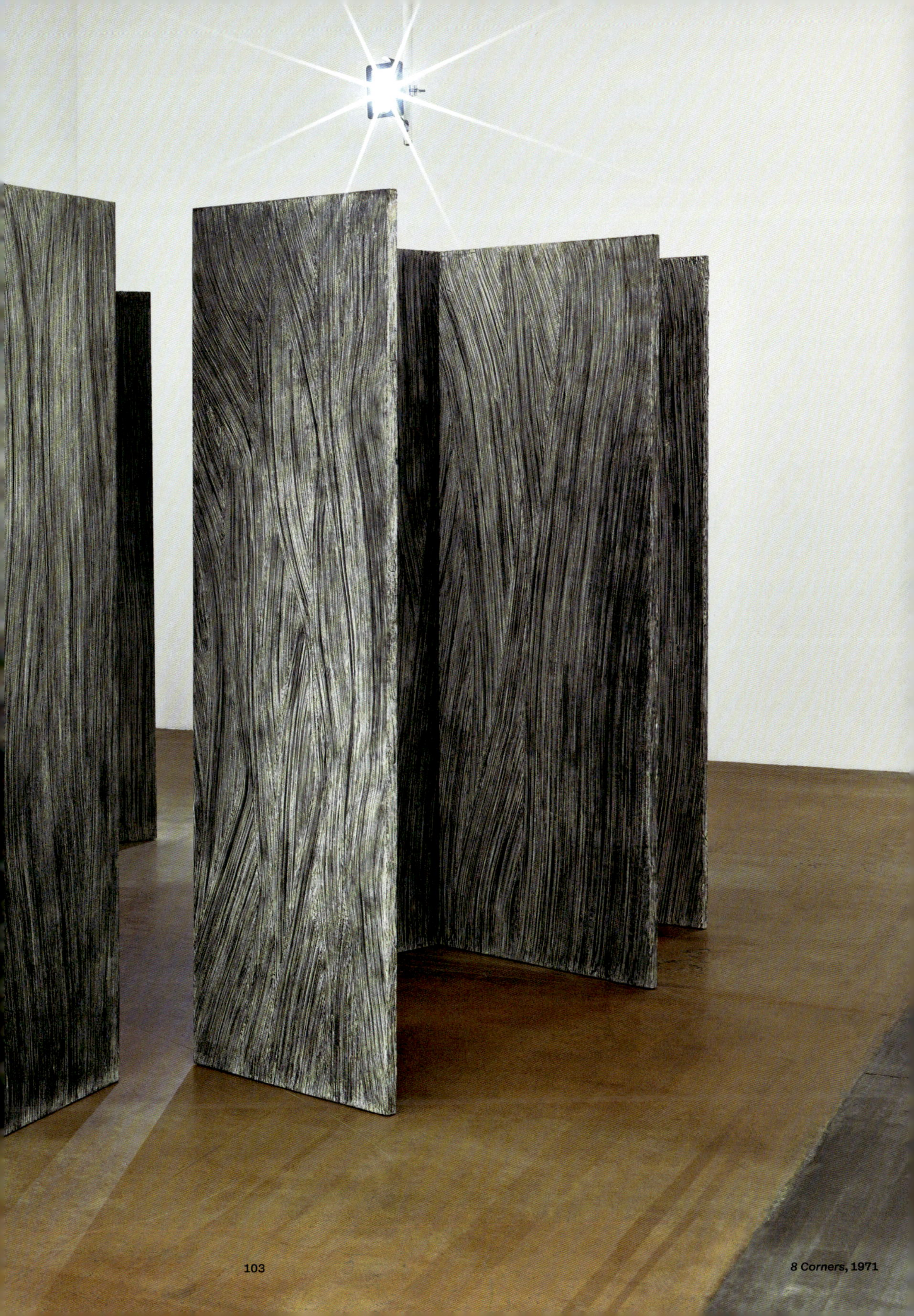

8 Corners, 1971

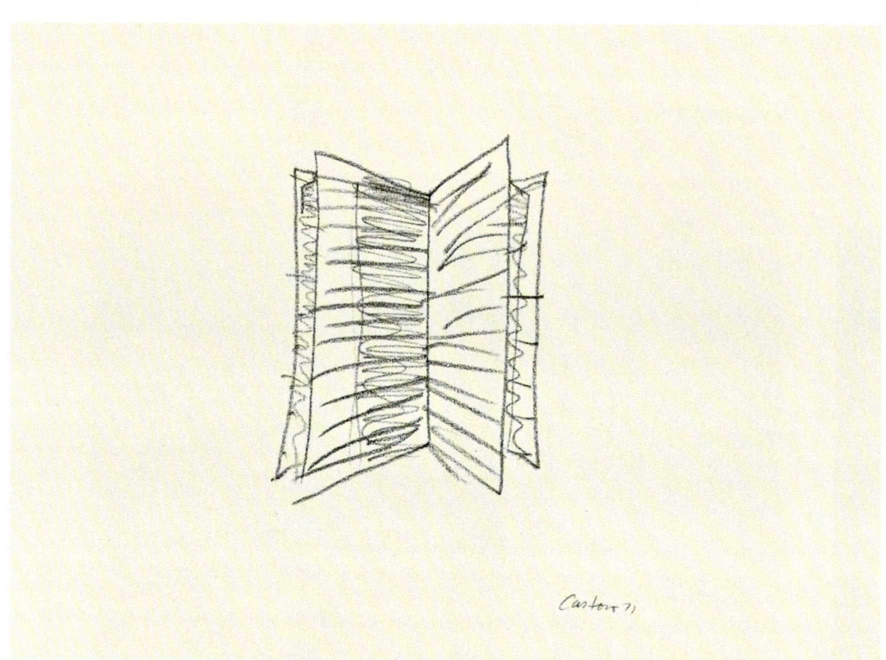

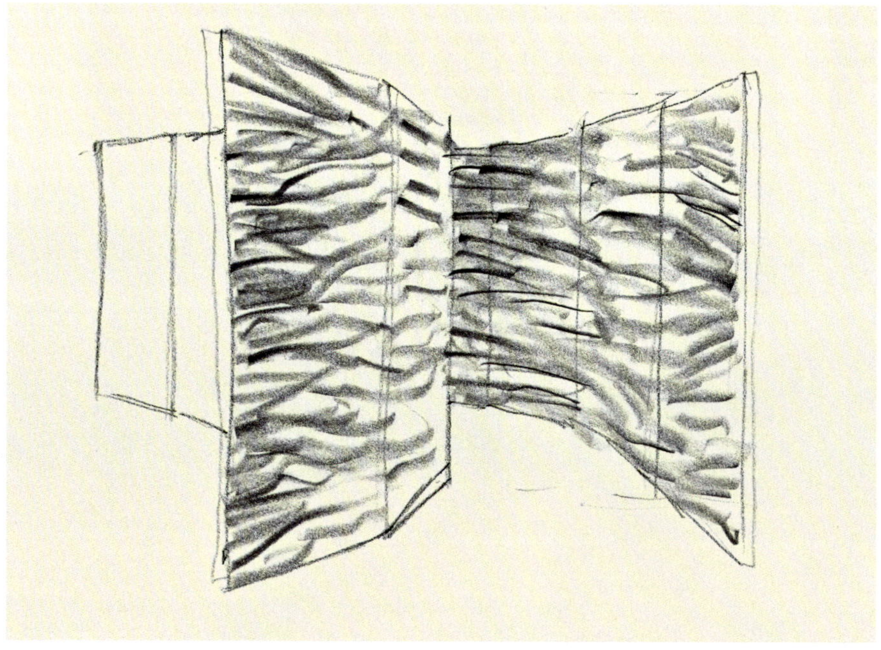

Rotating Corners, 1971
Cold Sake, 1971

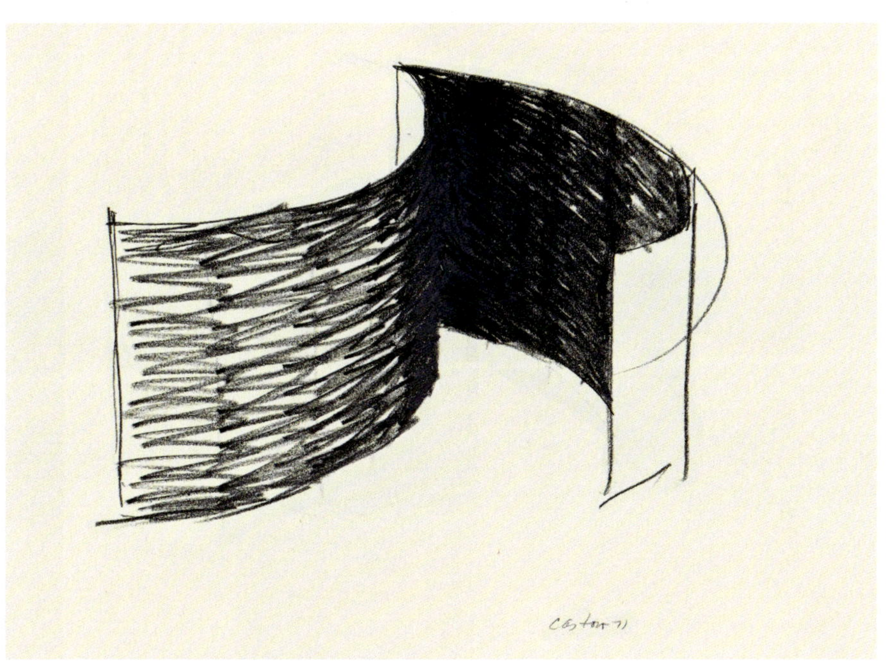

Cold Sake Deep Reflection, 1971

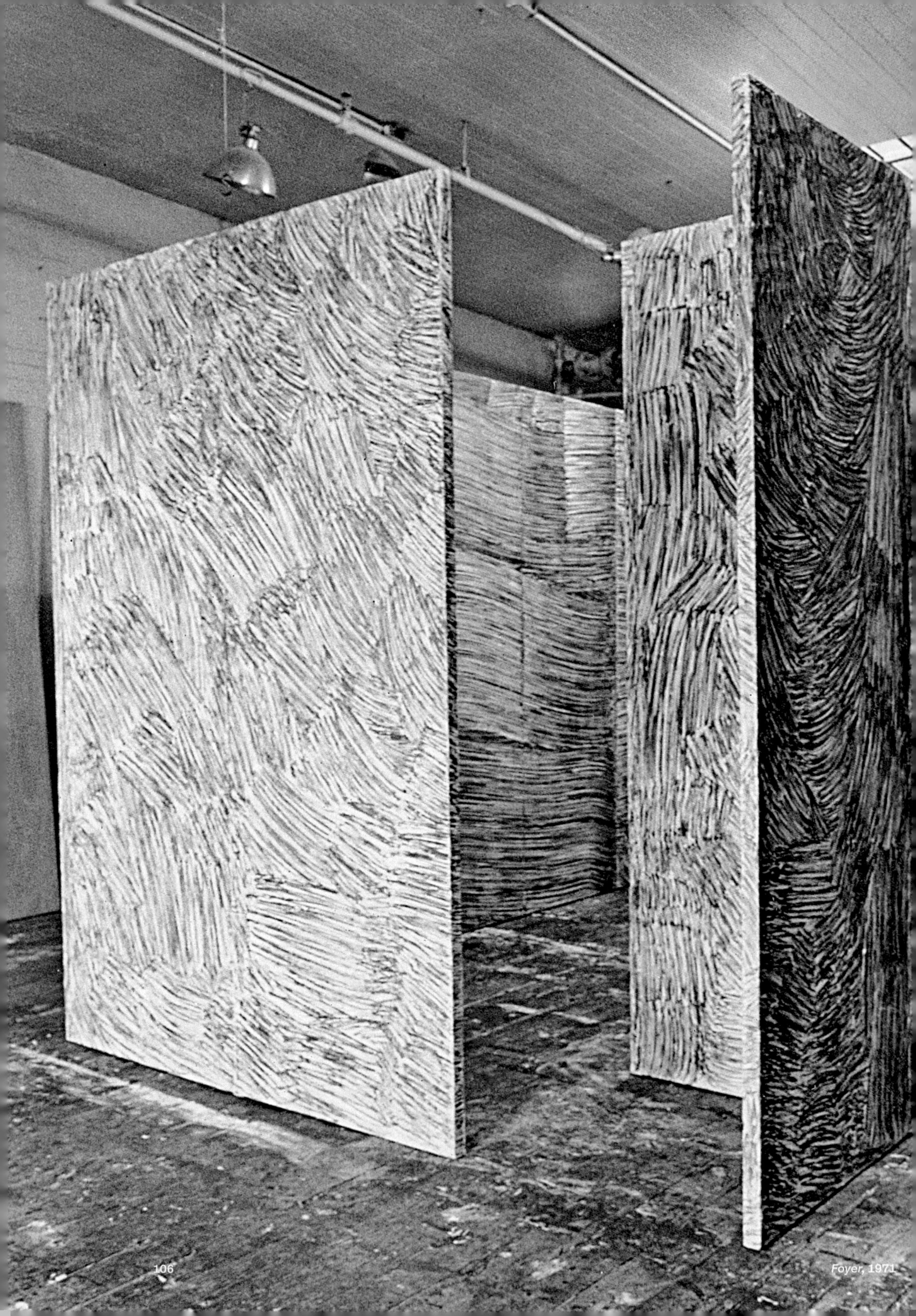

Foyer, 1971

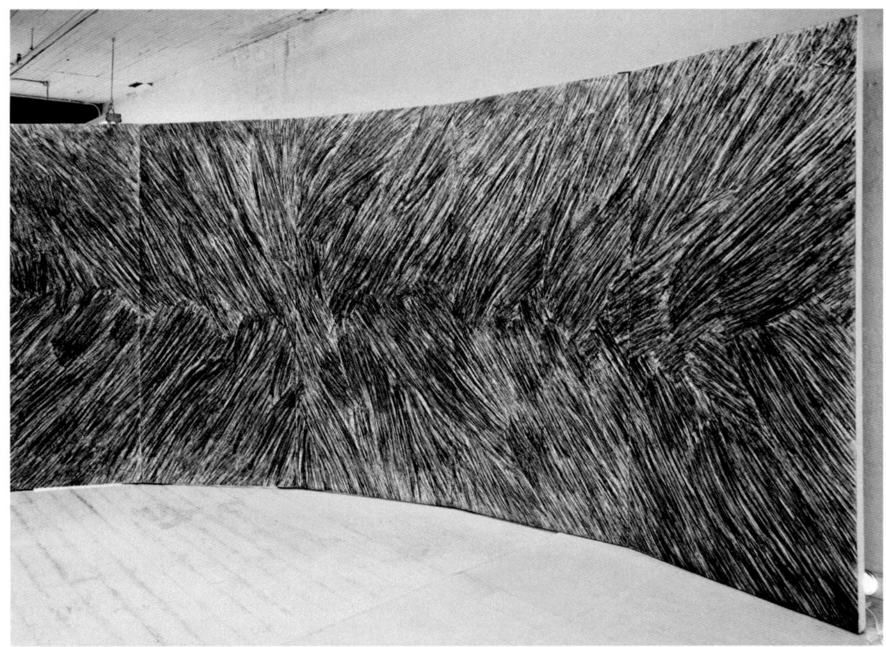

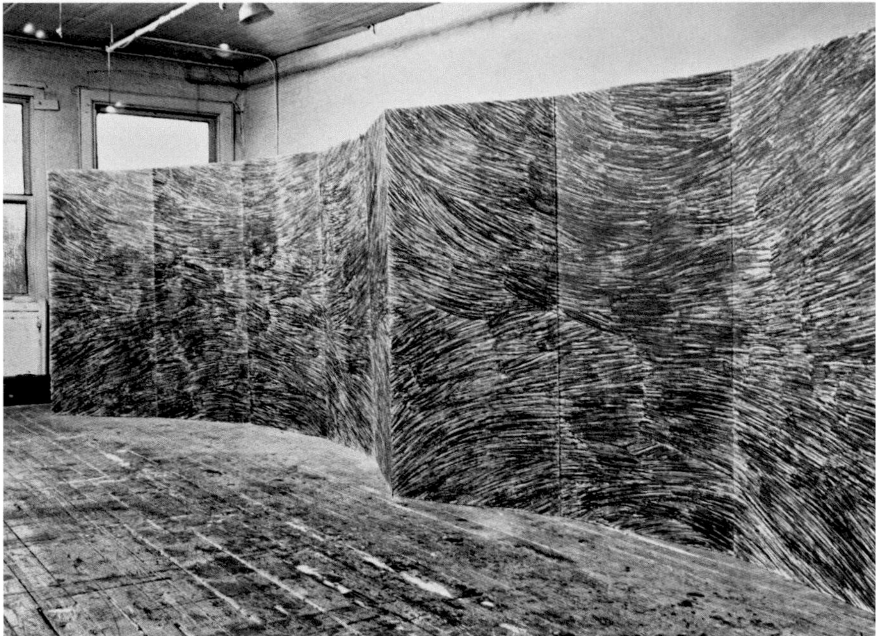

Spine on its Side, 1970
Two Curves, 1970

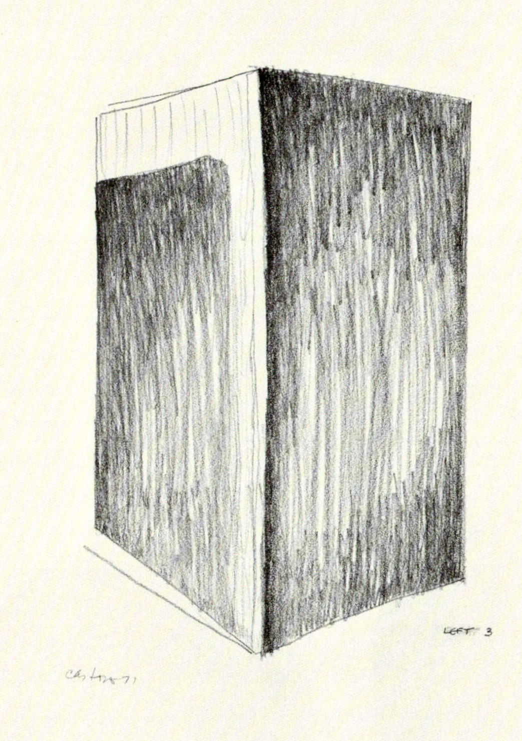

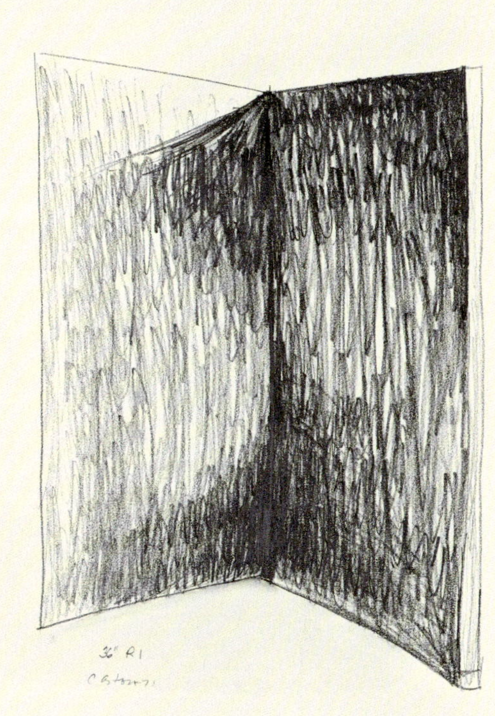

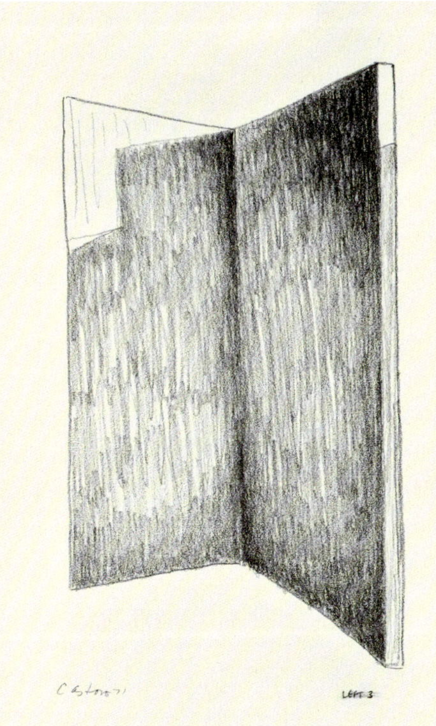

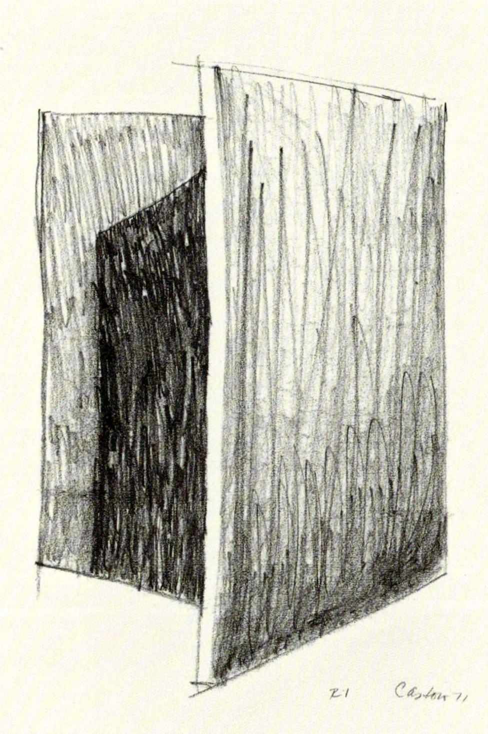

Corners, 1971

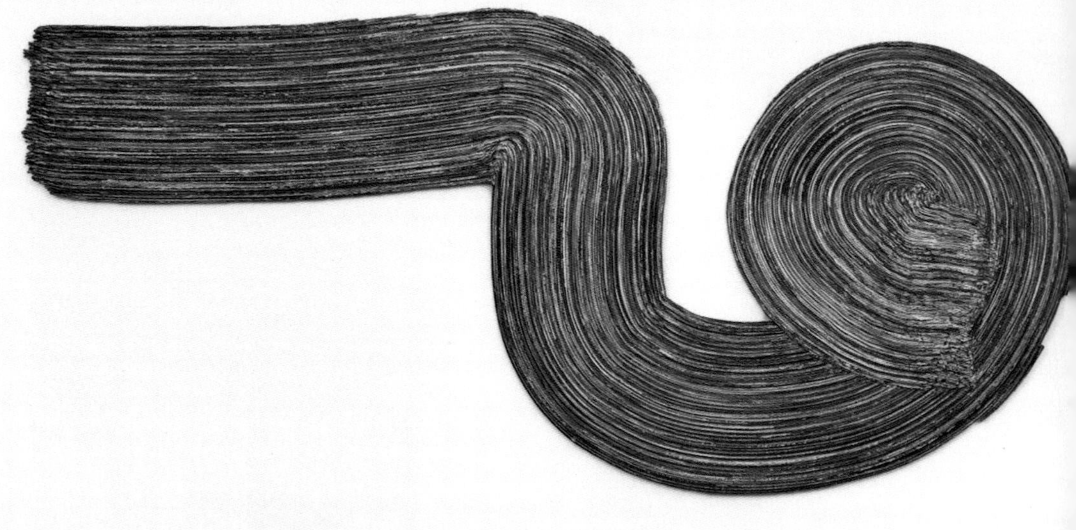

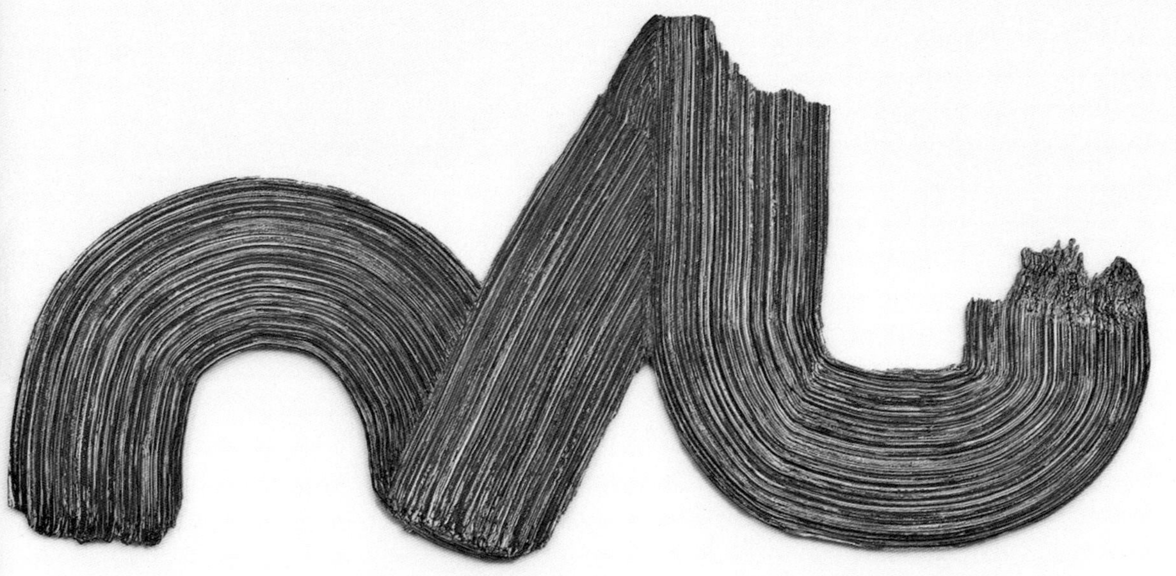

Guinness Martin, 1972

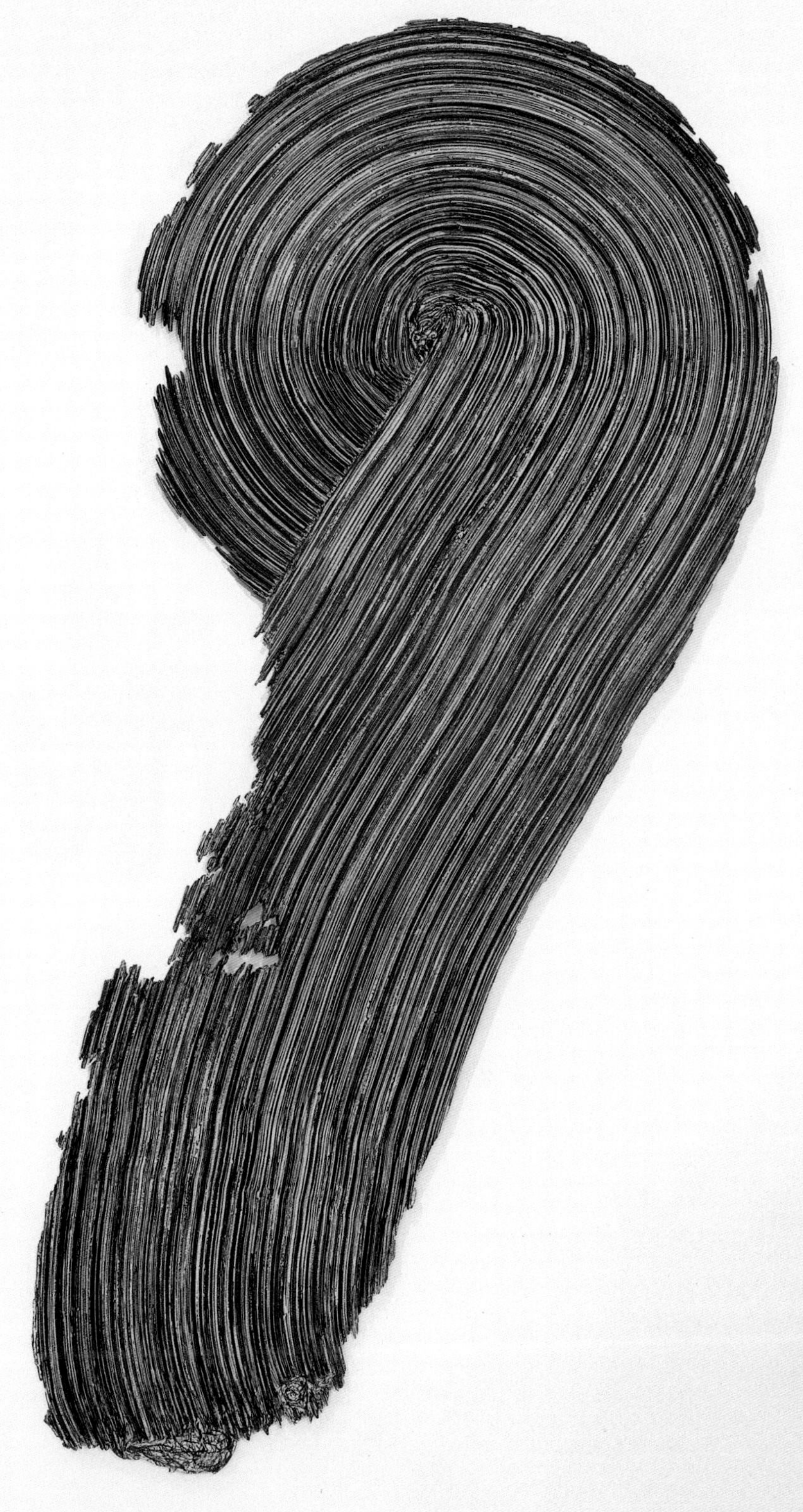

St., 1972

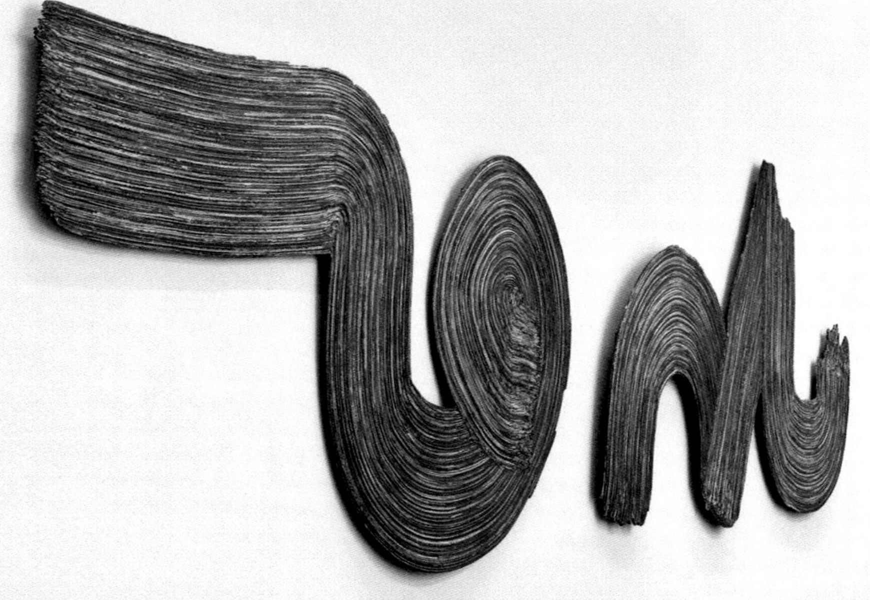

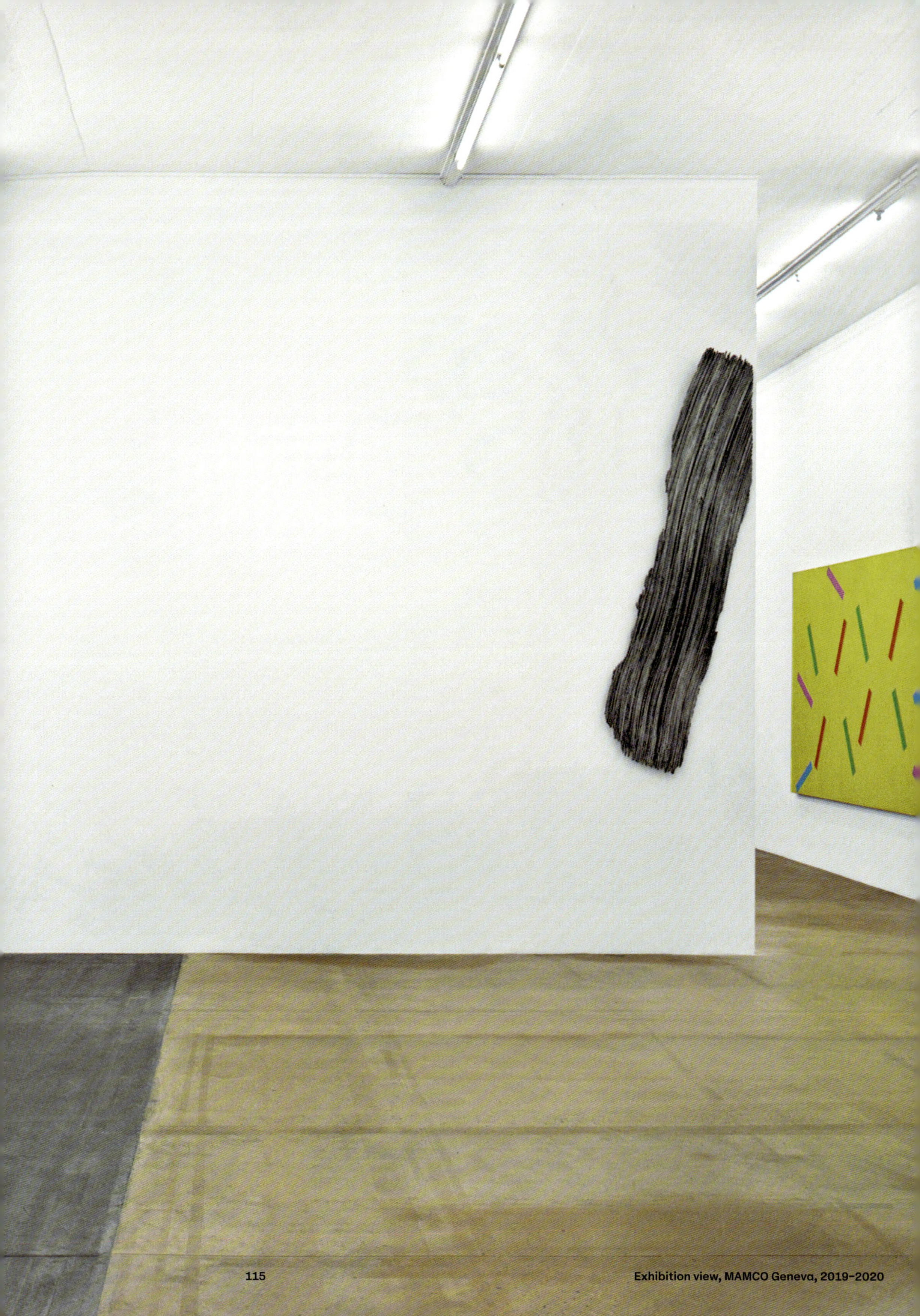

Exhibition view, MAMCO Geneva, 2019-2020

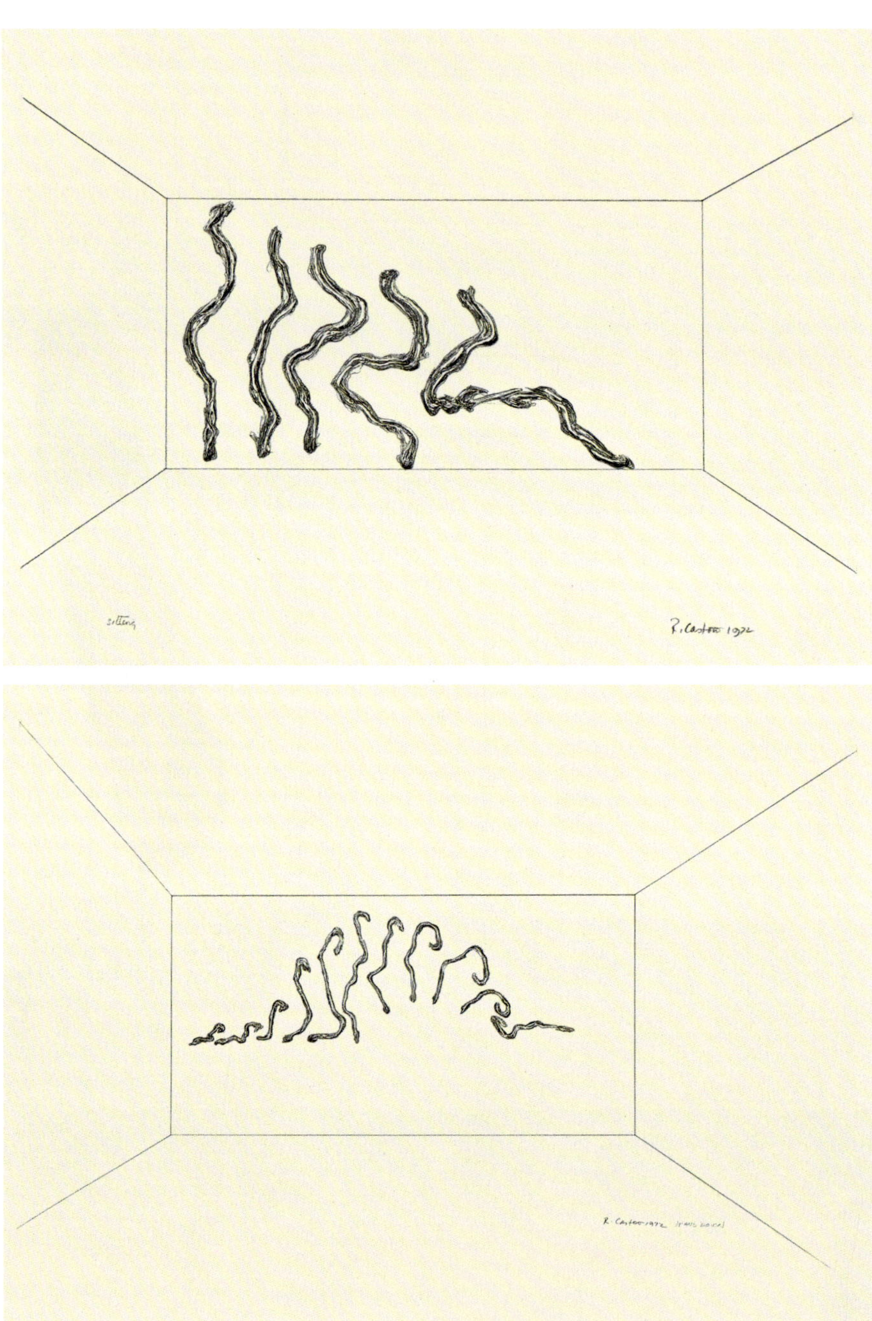

Sitting, 1972
Up and Down, 1972

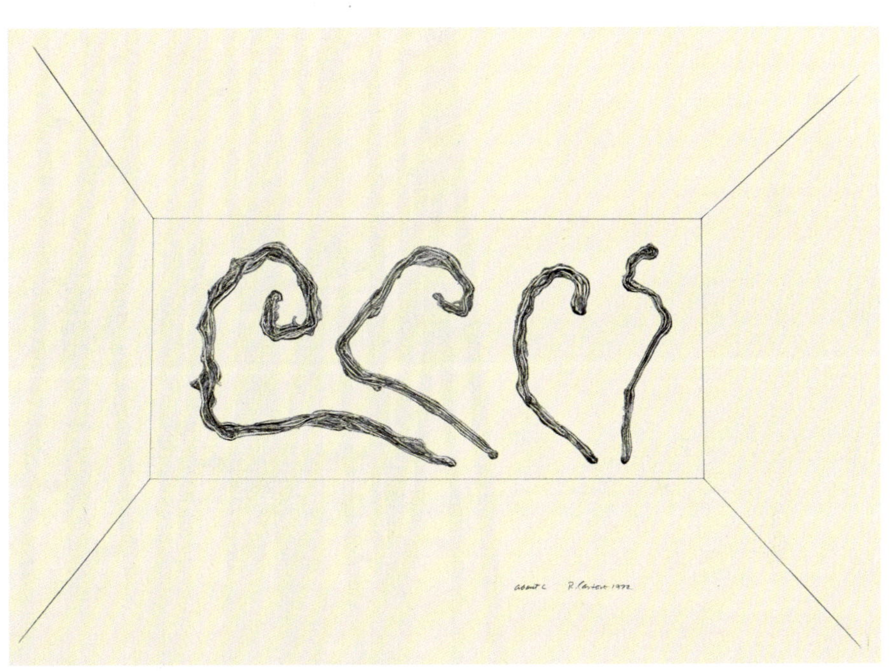

About C, 1972

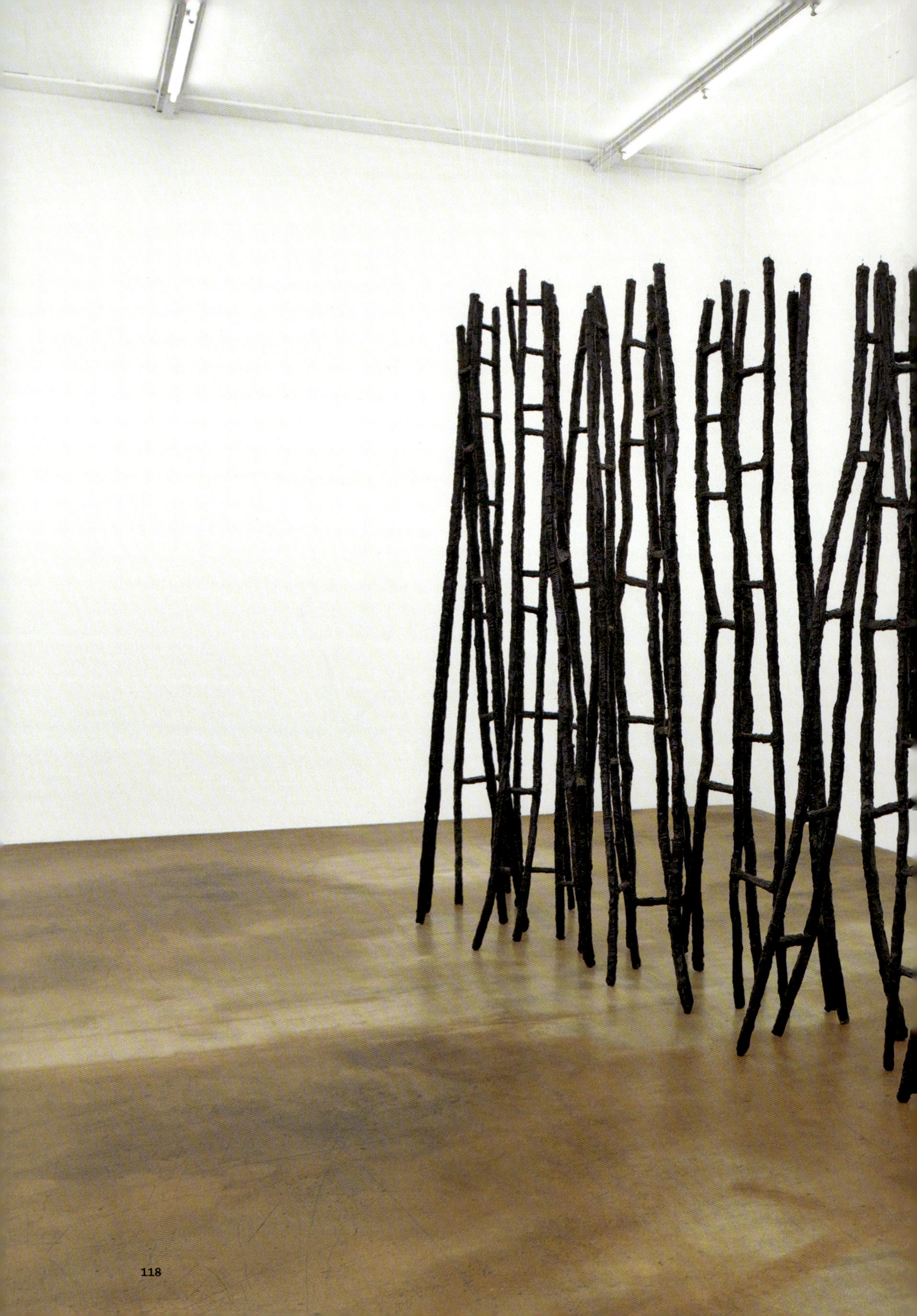

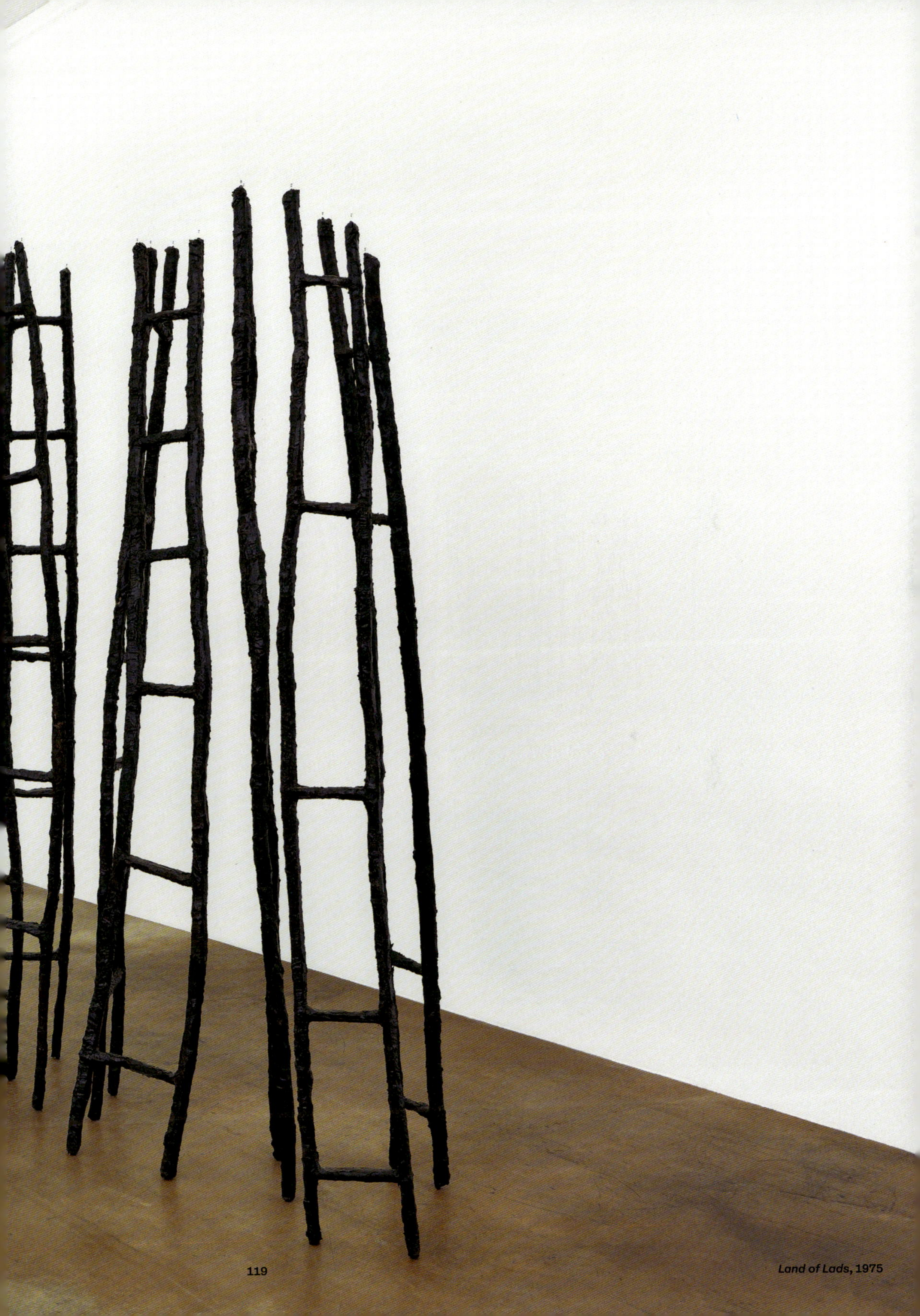

Land of Lads, 1975

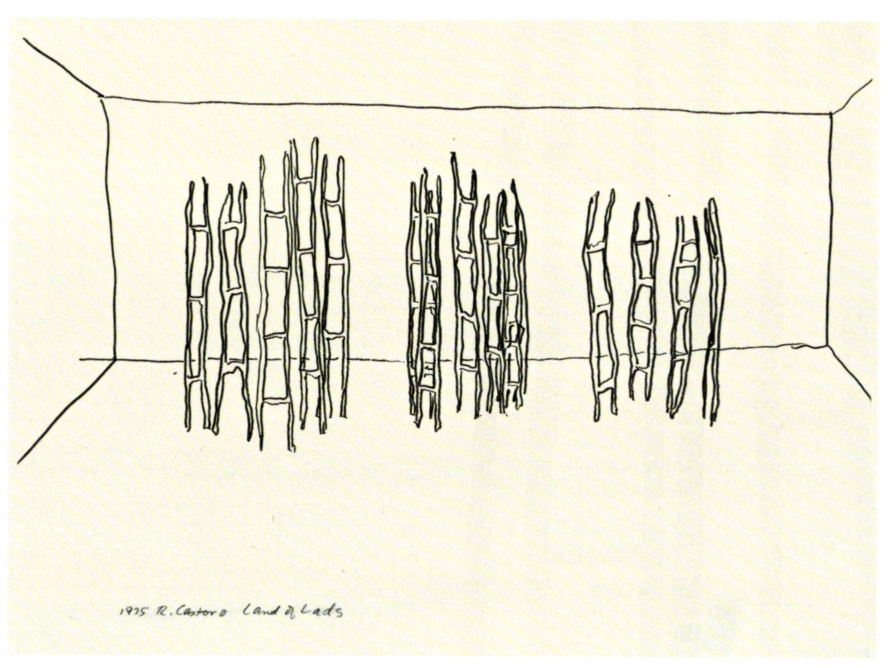

Land of Lads, 1975

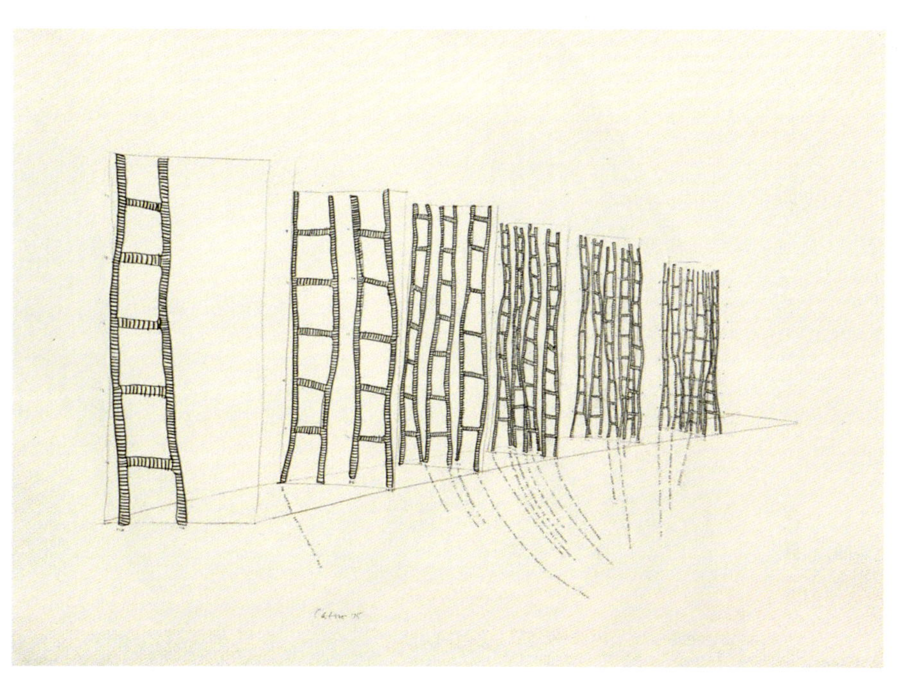

Untitled, 1975

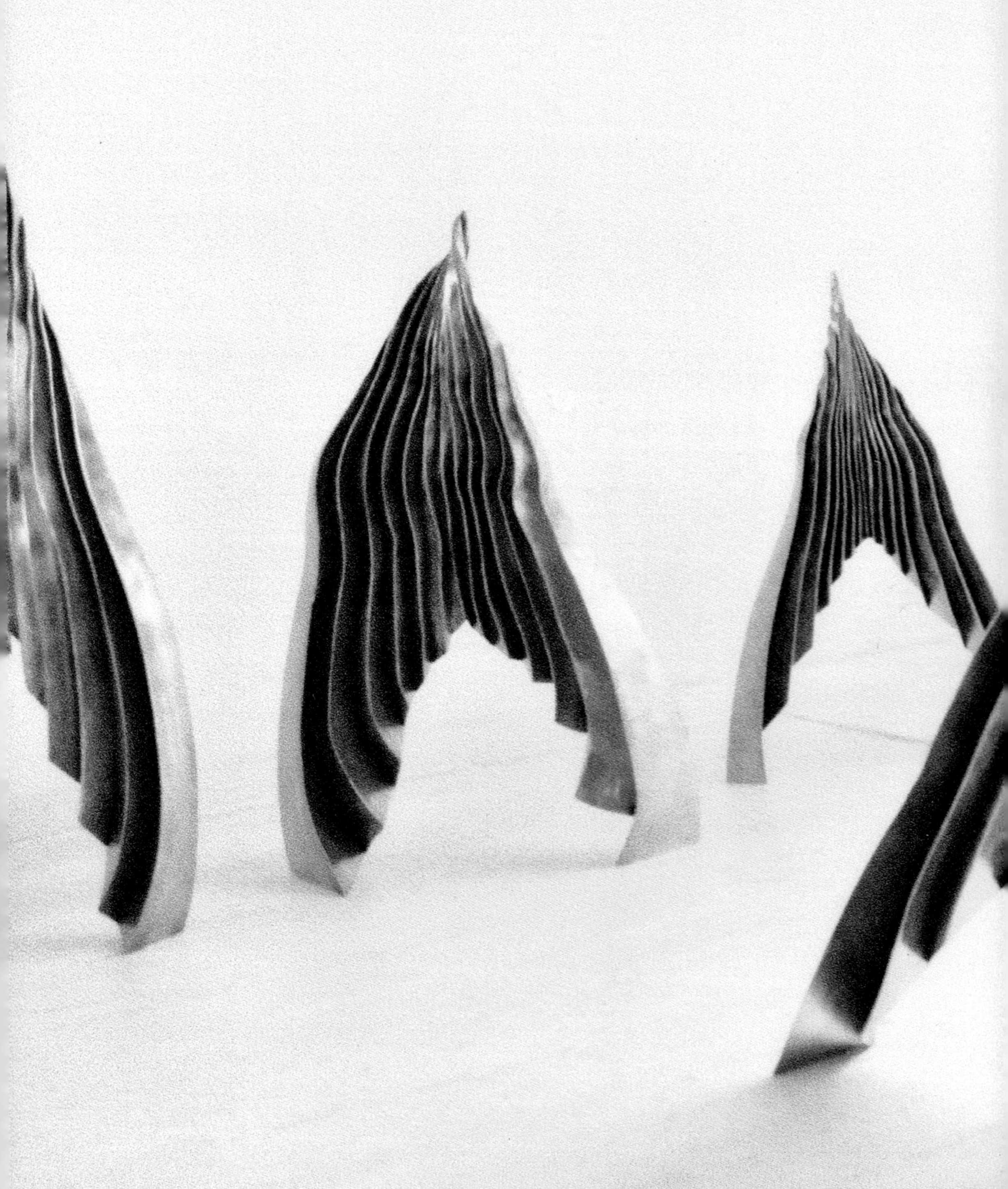

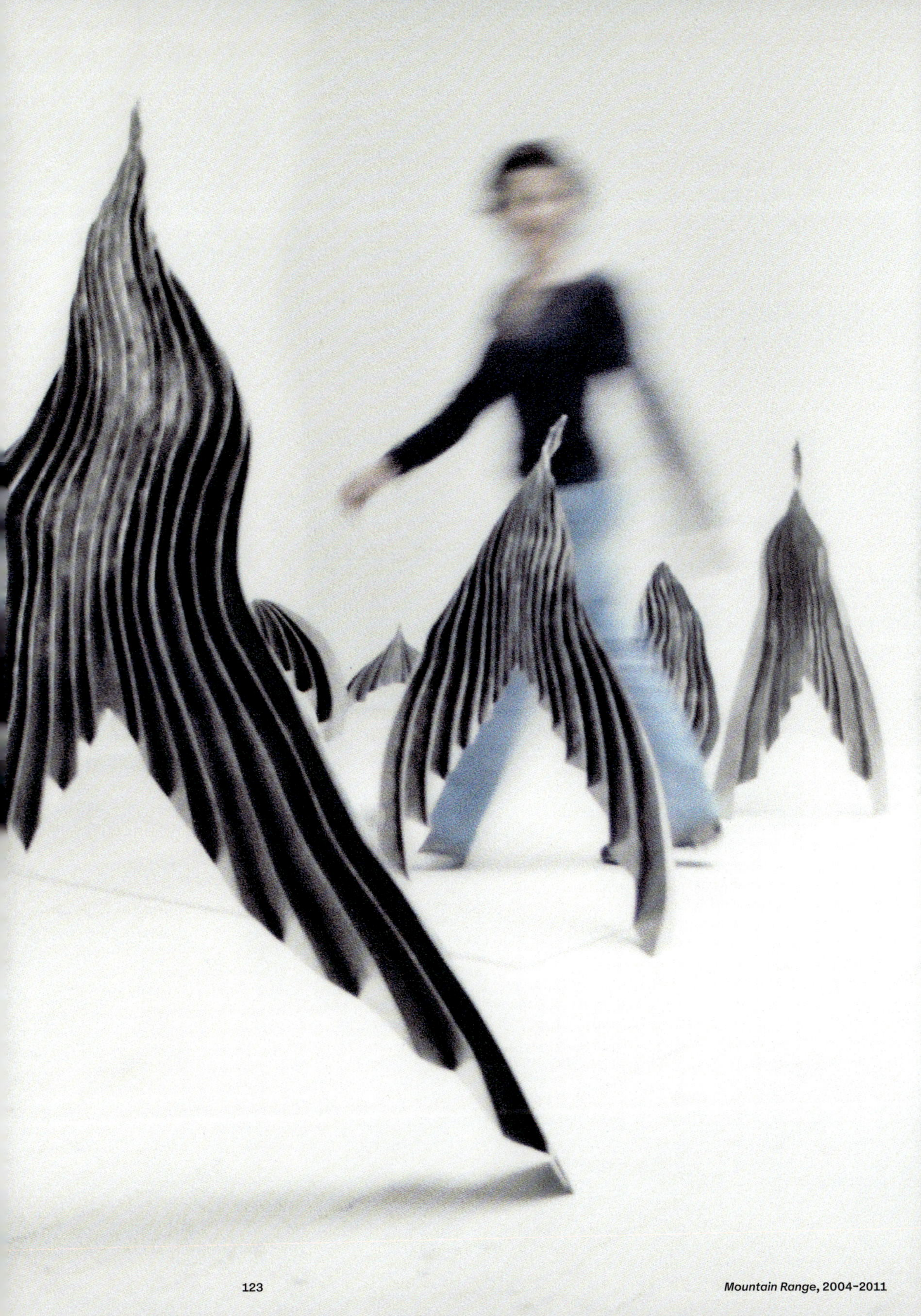

Mountain Range, 2004–2011

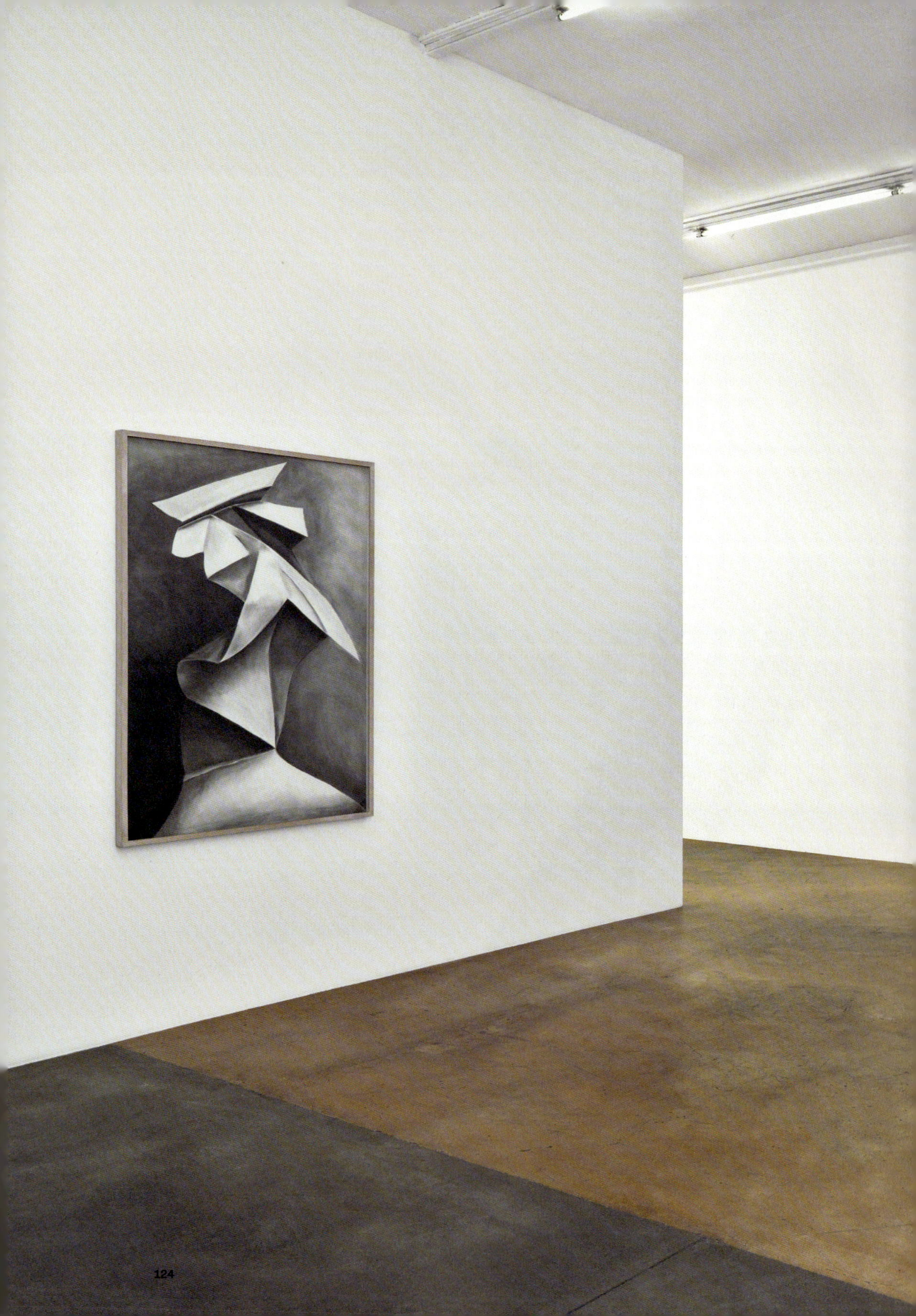

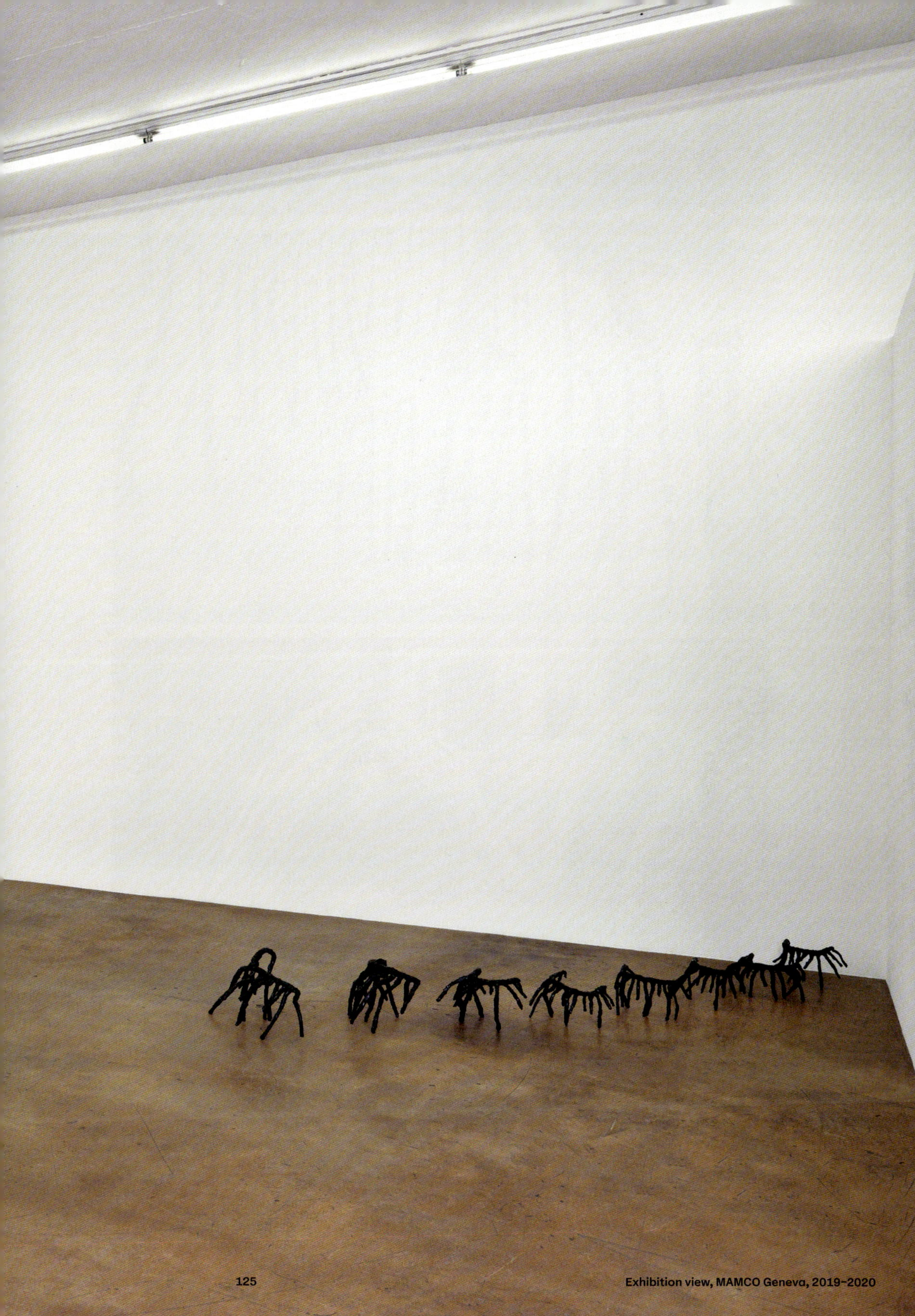

Exhibition view, MAMCO Geneva, 2019–2020

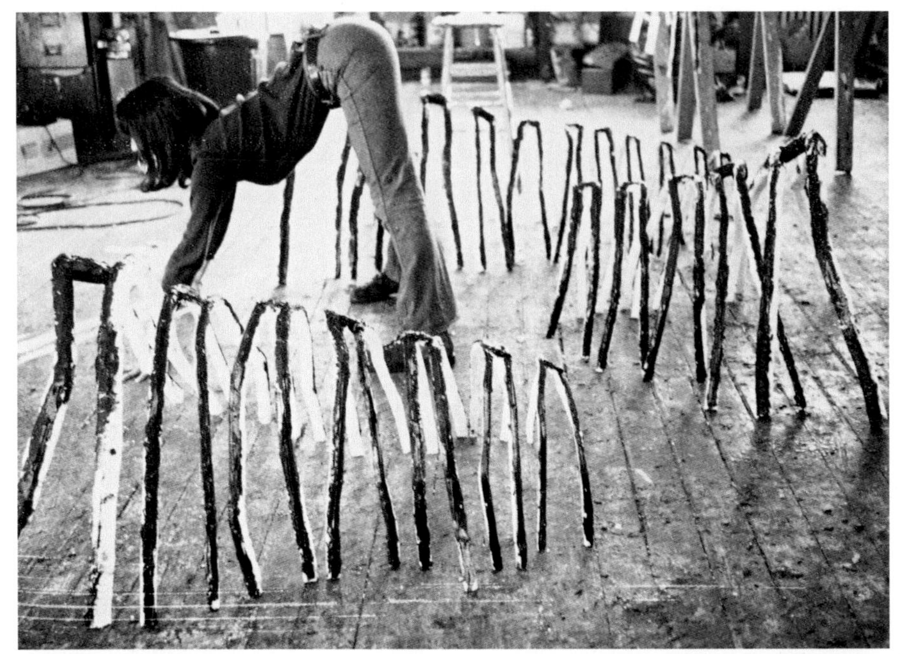

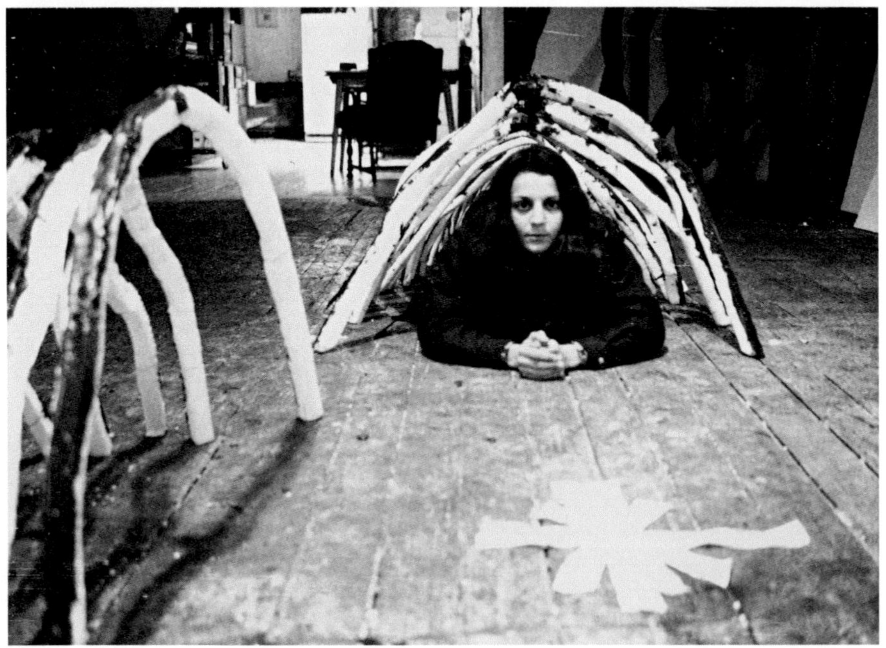

Tunnel, 1974

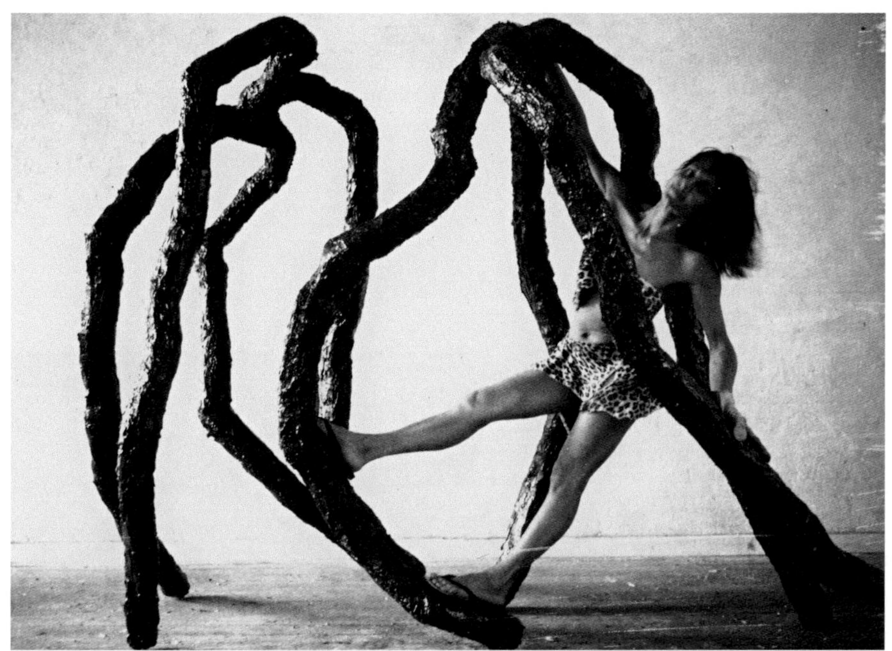

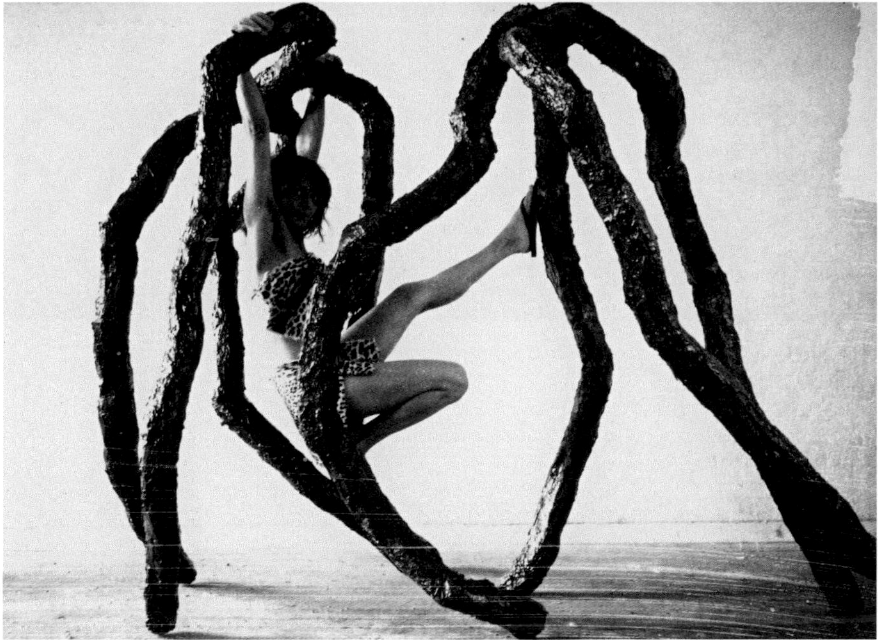

Symphony, 1974

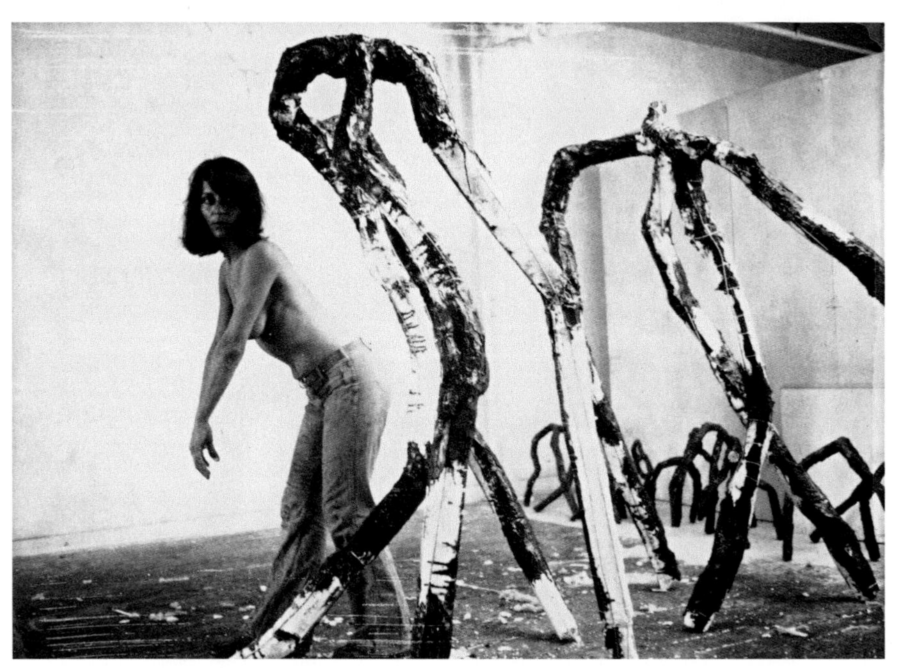

Symphony, 1974

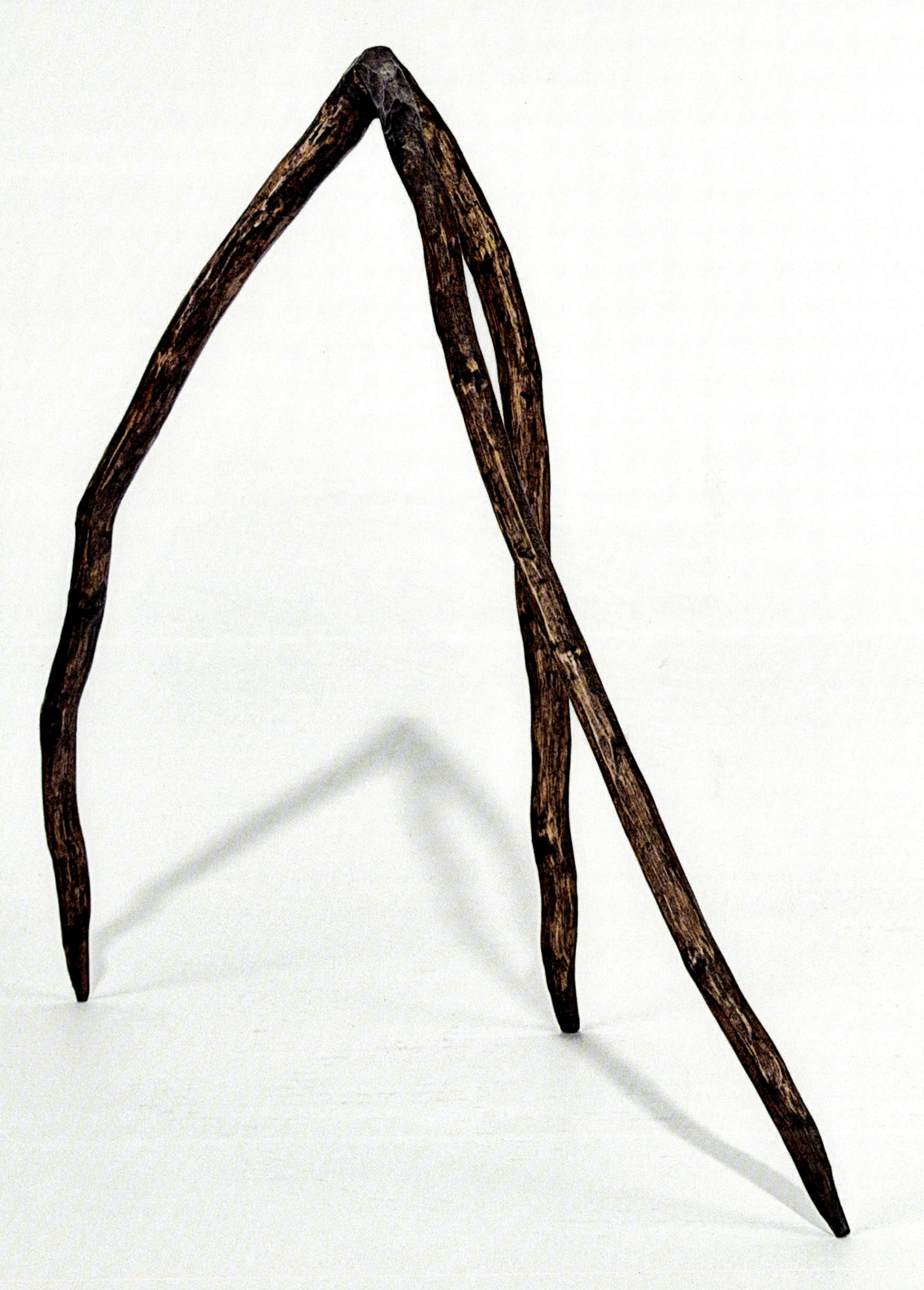

Branch Dance, 1977

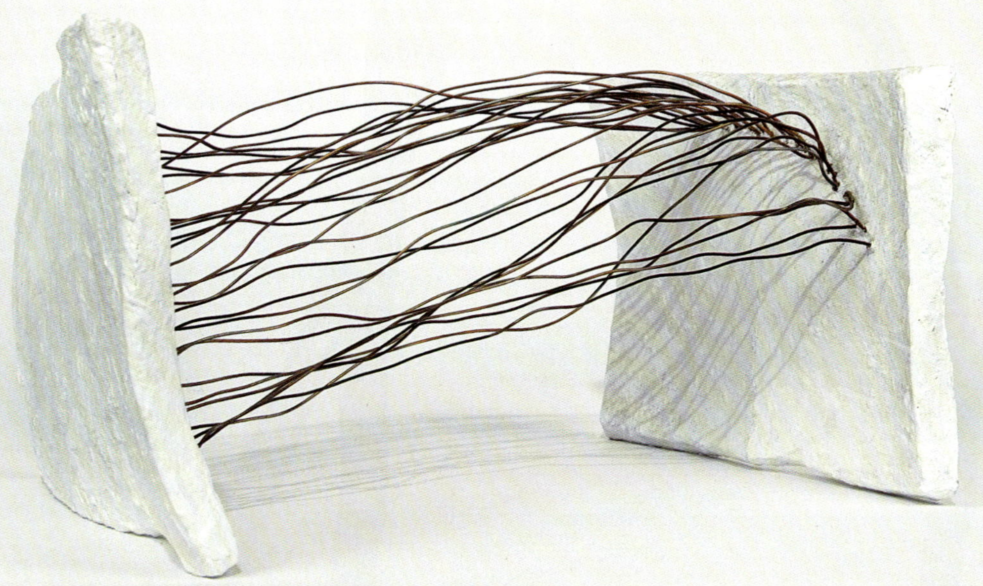

Two Walls Wired, 1976

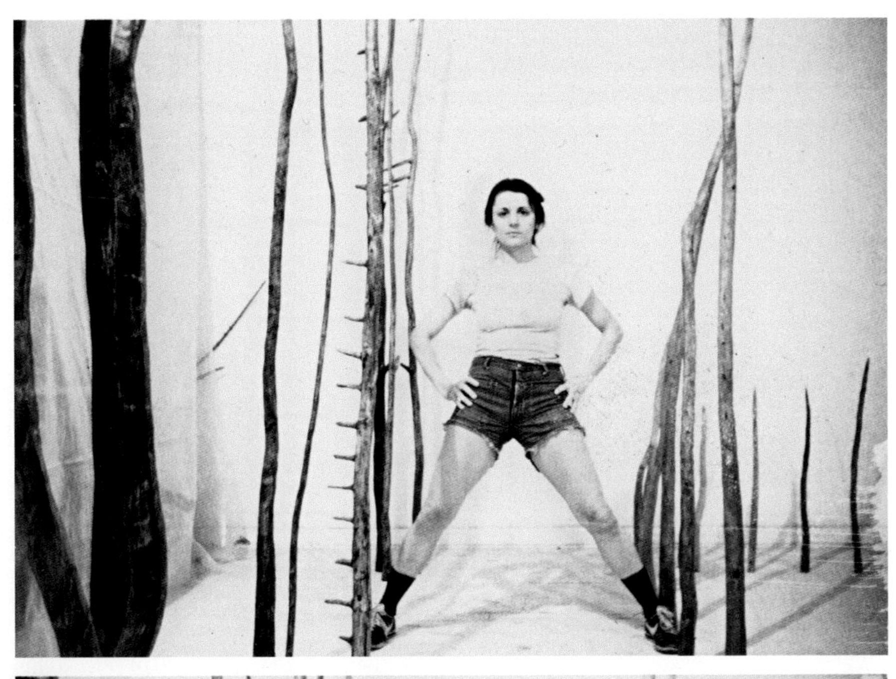

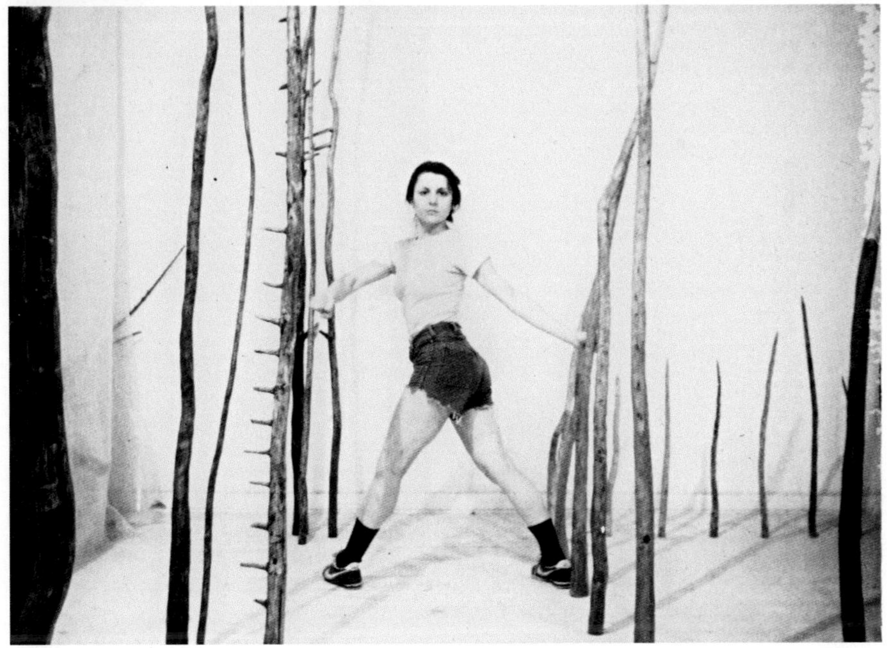

   Beaver's Trap and *Forest of Threes*, 1977–1978

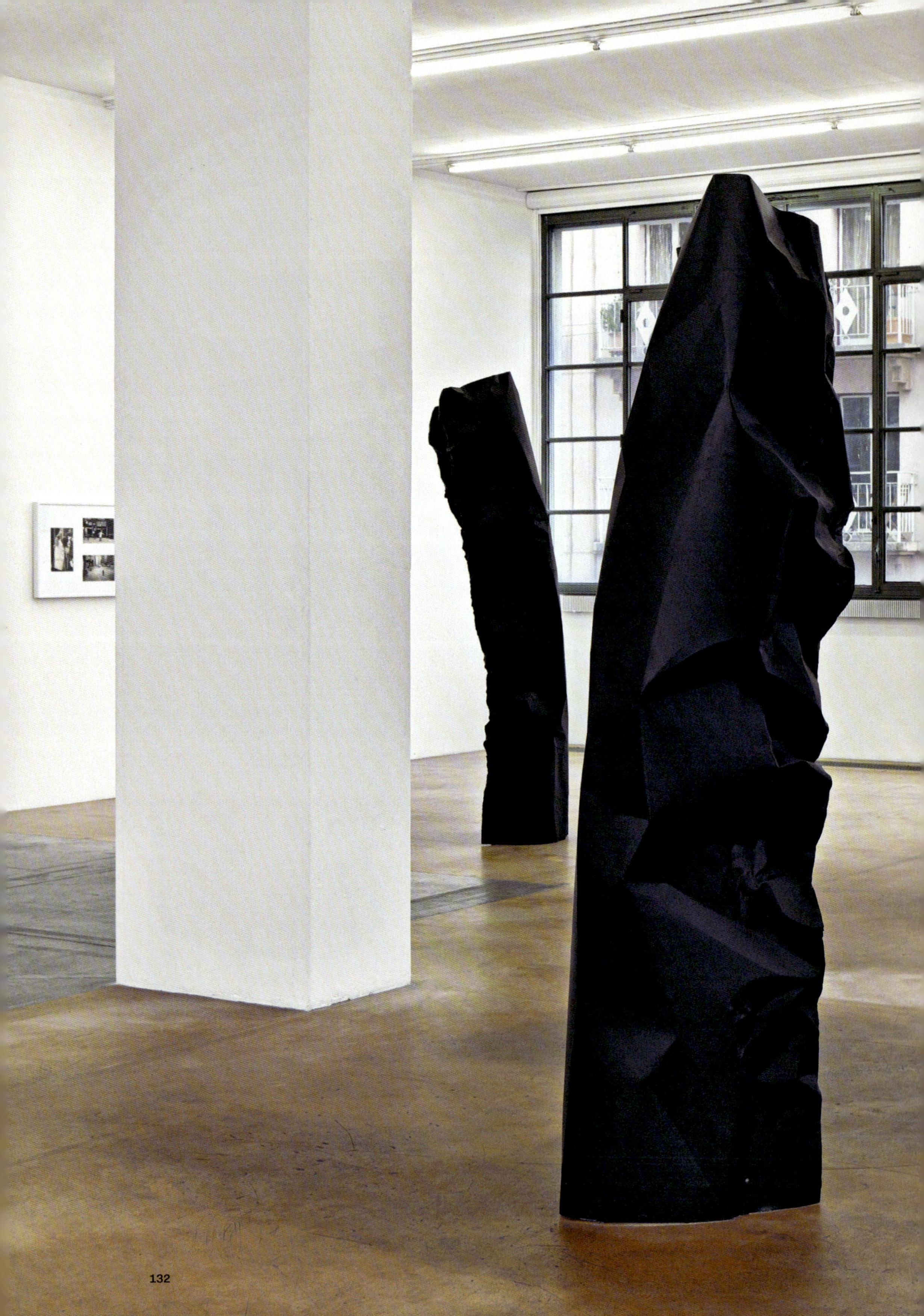

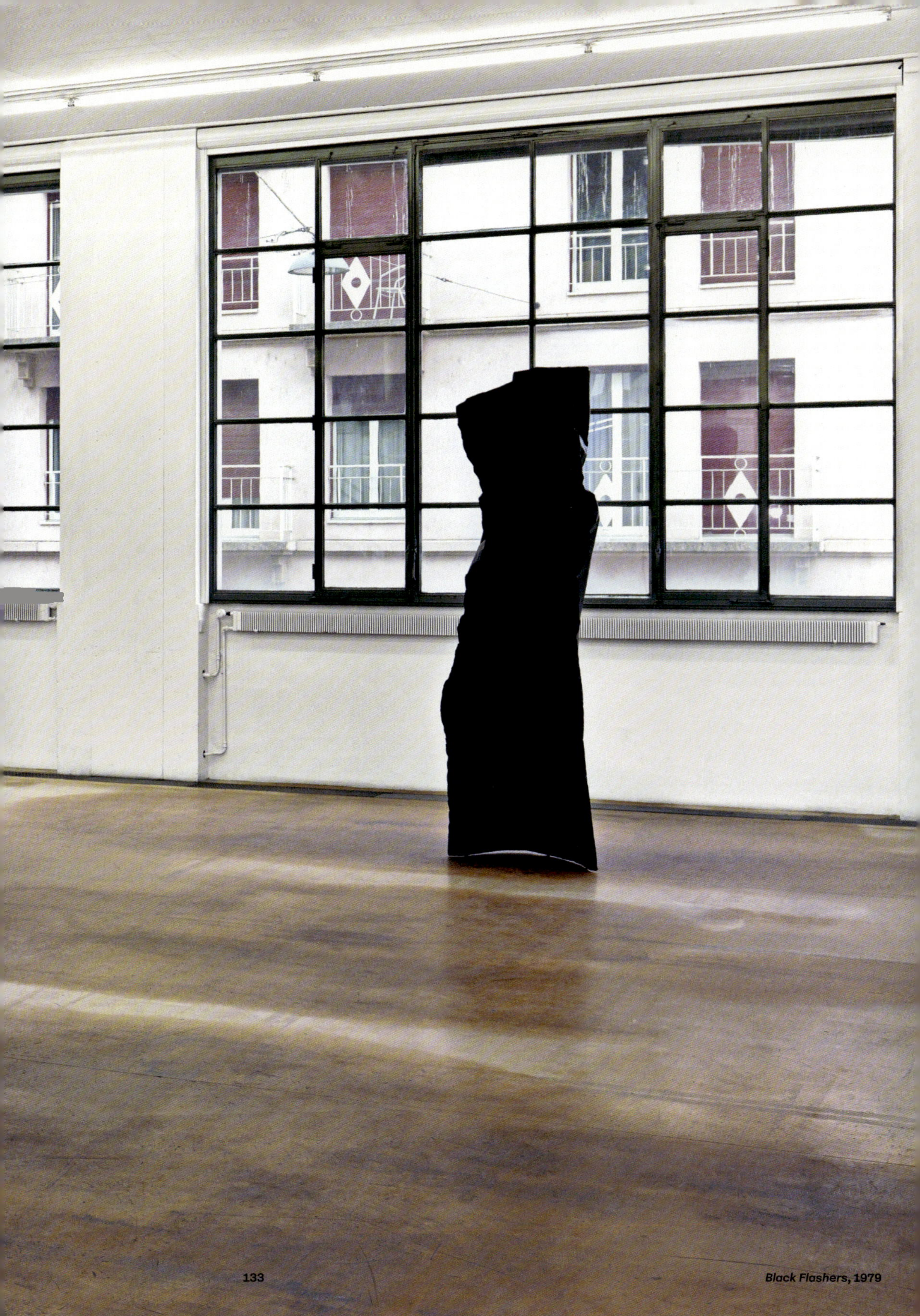

Black Flashers, 1979

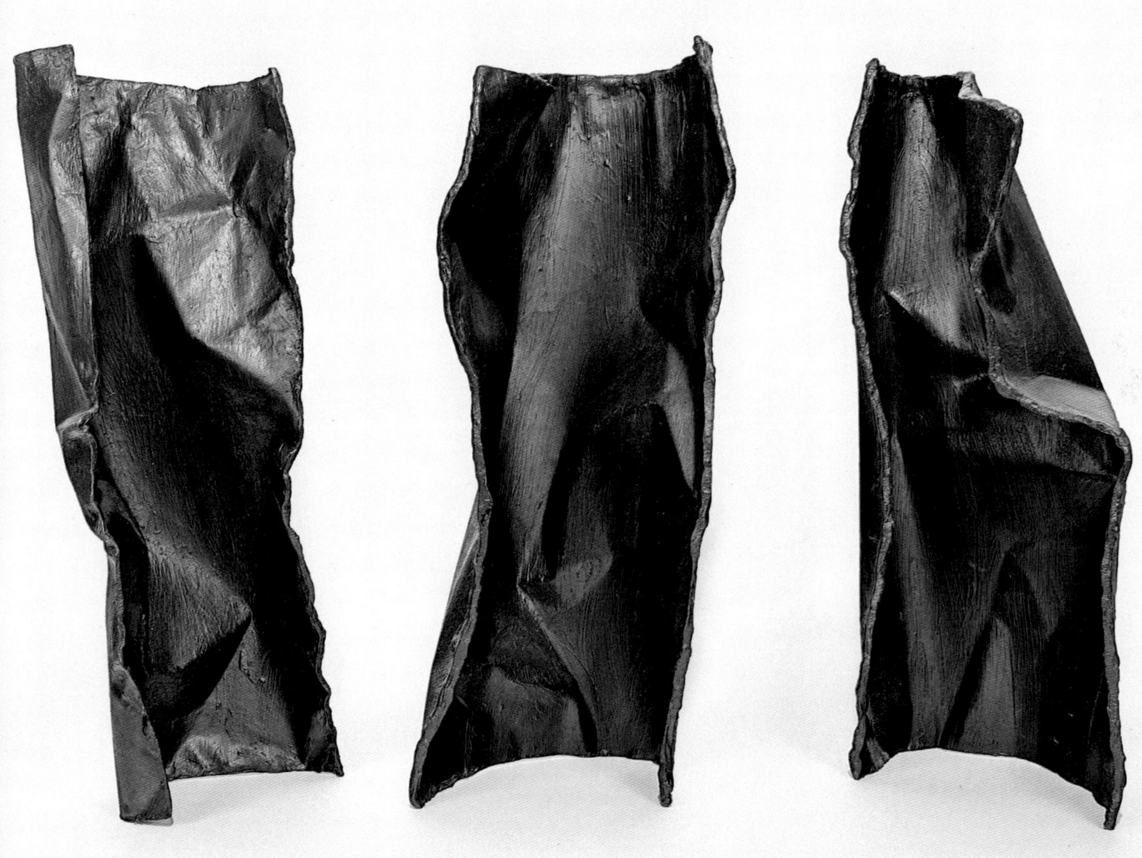

Knee-High Flashers (Triptych), 1979

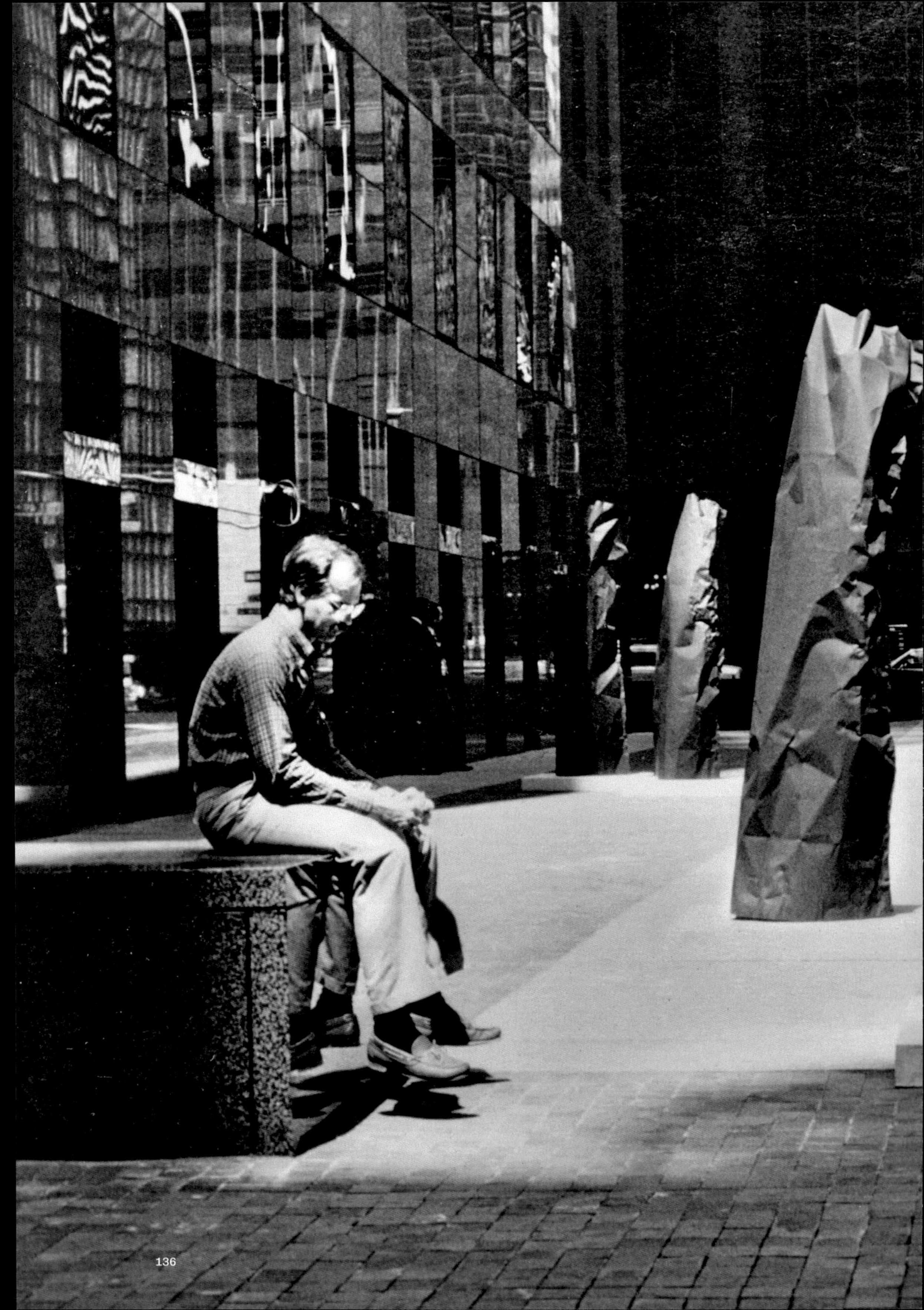

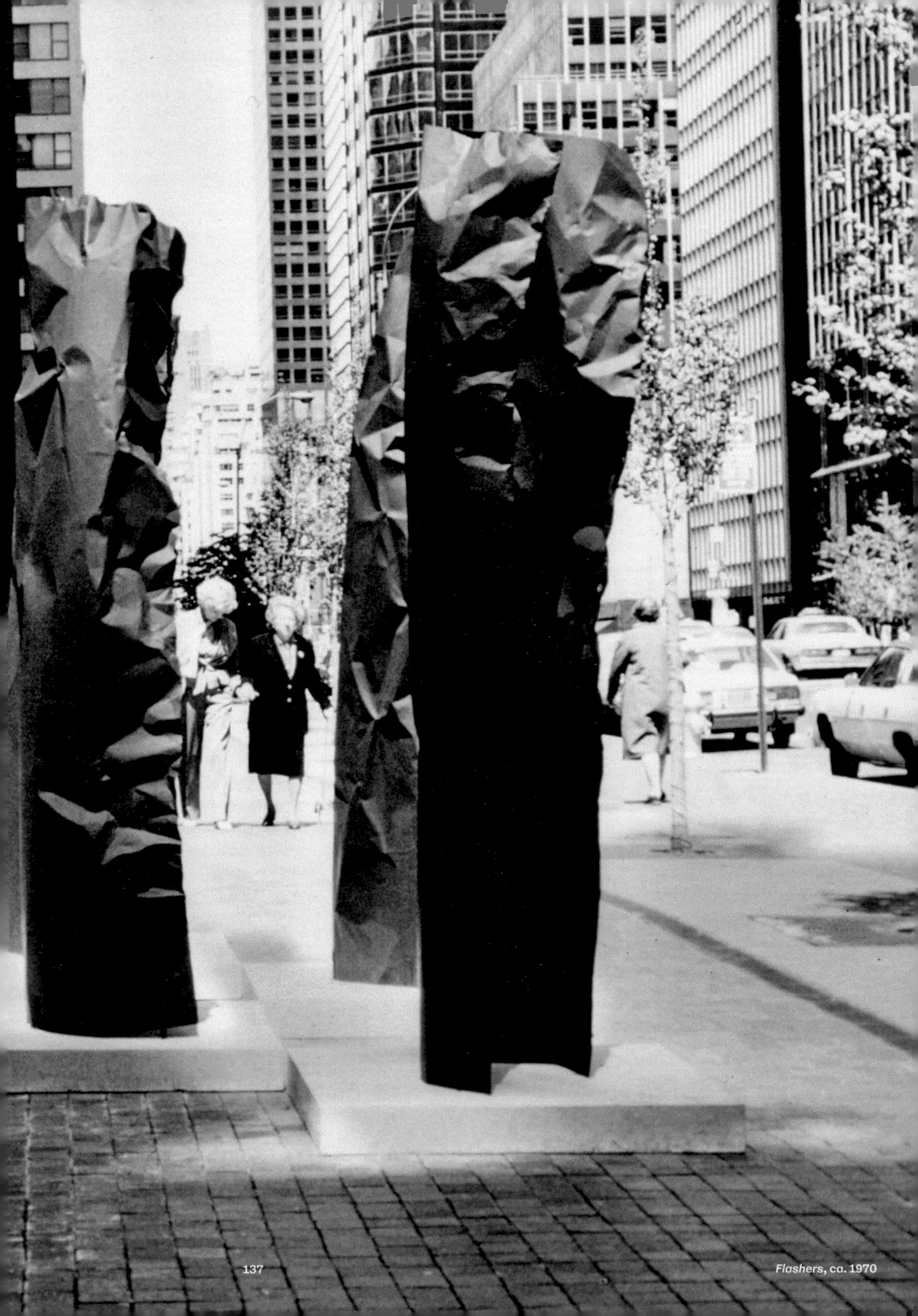

Flashers, ca. 1970

SIX YEARS:

THE EARLY CAREER OF ROSEMARIE CASTORO

FROM 1966 TO 1972

Rachel Stella

WORDS INTO ART

In addition to making word-based works part of her artistic practice, Rosemarie Castoro also wrote statements for publication. A few were political, addressing the artist's role in the *polis*. Some concerned her aesthetic intentions, prefacing a catalog, for instance. Still others were aesthetic resumes, meant to flesh out in narrative prose the bare bones of a professional CV. She penned two such texts, in 2003 and 2008, and called them "narrative biographies." These pithy documents (neither runs to more than 2 pages) provide a boiled down view of her work that the reader must ruminate, elaborate, or unpack. Hereafter, some additional information to dilute Castoro's ultra concentrated self-description for a more fluid reading of her work.

SALAD DAYS

In the "narrative biography" written in 2003 at the age of 64, Rosemarie Castoro situates the beginning of her artistic vocation at the Pratt Institute in Brooklyn, NY, where she obtained a BFA despite her family's disbelief in female higher education. The first paintings she evokes were made right out of school: "In 1963–64, studying my own work, a dominant element emerged, the 'Y,' a question and its own answer. 7' square 'Y' paintings in 1965, the largest size canvas I could stretch and paint in a brownstone parlor apartment were playful color acrylic works, using a same size element to build and articulate a field, finding rhythms in the repeated pattern." This narrative, which aims to summarize the esthetic milestones of a career, offers little biographical information; so we must turn elsewhere to shed light on the personal events that influenced RC's artistic trajectory. In 1961 RC sets up with a young man she thought looked like Richard Burton. She told Calvin Tomkins: "I was standing against a column in Dillon's Bar, and somebody came up to me and said, 'Are you a caryatid?' I said, 'You call this the Erechtheion?' And from then on Carl and I were together."[1] She was referring to Carl Andre, an employee of the Pennsylvania Railroad who, unbeknownst to any public, wrote poetry and made artworks. Andre was living in a Lower East Side tenement, in an unforgettable apartment, described by his friend Hollis Frampton (not yet a maker of Structuralist films) in these terms: "There were a bed and a wardrobe somewhere, but no other furniture ... There were at least five classes of objects, ranging from prodigiously ugly through downright hideous. Collage 'paintings' incorporating whole physical objects (gloves, umbrellas, lettuce), covered entirely in glossy enamel paint in primary colors ... 'Polymorphous perverse carpentry' made by nailing up disheveled scrap wood from the streets ... Polychrome stalagmites of pigmented concrete ... 'Pizza pies,' flat patties of Portland cement ... And a curiously memorable set of pieces made of

1   Calvin Tompkins, "The Materialist: Carl Andre's Eminent Obscurity," *The New Yorker*, December 5, 2011.

'slices' of wet concrete, laid one upon another in collocations reminiscent of the excrement of dogs."[2]

Undaunted by the mess, in 1962 RC handed Carl Andre a set of keys—"being too occupied with school, dance classes and free-lance mechanical paste-ups to actually 'date' … After he gave up his apartment to move in with me, there was very little space for him to work …. I was making paintings, taking up a 7' square space between the living room and kitchen, creating my own brushwork systems. We had a pact not to interfere with each other's art, unless invited. The rhythm of one-fingered typing punctuated the air with the beat of his art. He needed very little storage space for slices of paper. Hollis Frampton visited frequently, both working alternately on their 'Dialogs.' There was an air of art-making in that 13 Willoughby Avenue apartment."[3] Benjamin H. Buchloh clarifies: "According to Carl Andre the set-up was comparable to that of a chess game. While one participant was typing, the other was sitting on the bed reading, waiting for his turn to reply."[4] The dialogue of October 21, 1962, refers to Frampton's *Portrait of an Indifferently Attractive Young Lady*, who is none other than RC. She looks rather spooked, wrapped in a tartan blanket, against a textured textile background. Frampton also photographed Carl Andre against the same burlap surface —was it the wall at 13 Willoughby Avenue? Or perhaps the flat where Andre lived before moving in with Castoro.[5] In any case, the pendant portraits were not a wedding memento, for the couple did not marry until 1963.

SPRING AND ALL

"We moved to a loft on Spring Street, where the one-fingered typing continued. I was able to stretch large canvases on the floor before raising them up to the wall to paint. Carl admired those huge stretches of white canvas on the floor and said I should keep them there."[6] RC presciently suggests that Andre make his own floor-based work. During the *Shape and Structure* show which took place at the Tibor de Nagy Gallery in January 1965, Andre's contribution, consisting of piles of pine beams, was so heavy that the floor of the gallery buckled. To avoid collapse, Andre disassembled the sculpture, displayed it on the floor, and changed its title from *Well* to *Redan*.

From Spring Street it was only two subway stops to Max's Kansas City, a bar/restaurant/nightclub on Park Avenue South, launched by Mickey Ruskin on December 6, 1965. In his persona as critic on wheels, the artist John Perreault recalls: "In general, women were not welcome in the front room, so much so that I remember an all-woman sit-in that tried to claim some space: artists Jackie Winsor, Jackie Ferrara, Brenda Miller, Joan Jonas, Rosemarie Castoro, and maybe one or two others. And they were not going to settle for sitting at the bar and being harassed."[7]

2 Letter to Enno Develing, May 24 1969, in *Carl Andre*, Haags, Gemeentenmuseum, 1969.

3 "Carl Andre's Formation," RC archives.

4 Carl Andre and Hollis Frampton, October 14, 1962 and September 22, 1963, *12 Dialogues: 1962-1963*, edited and annotated by Benjamin H. D. Buchloh—The Press of the Nova Scotia College of Art and Design and New York University Press

5 Frampton, op. cit.

6 "Carl Andre's Formation," RC archives.

7 https://www.artsjournal.com/ artopia/2010/10/praxis_at_maxs.html

The extraordinary décor at Max's was possible because Ruskin let artists exchange work for meals and drinks. Anton Perich, photographer and busboy, reminisces: "Mickey was the top curator of that time. The bar had a hovering sculpture by Forest Myers. The window was by Michael Heizer. At the 'Long Wall' was Donald Judd. The passageway had a crashed car by John Chamberlain; it had sharp ends, so all waitresses had bruises. The 'Back Room' had the legendary bloody neon cross by Dan Flavin as well as Myer's *Laser's End*—probably the most immaterial sculpture ever made. Upstairs had some Warhols."[8]

A YEAR OF LIVING COLLABORATIVELY

RC's narration of the year 1966 highlights her first significant public exposure: "The Tibor de Nagy and Stable Galleries showed seven large canvases in a 5-person show in 1966. Eliminating saturated color in 1966, in search for form, I used a single angle in a monochromatic field, drawing with pencil on painted canvas, investigating undulating space."

Perhaps because she did not consider collaborative experience a form of personal expression, RC doesn't take into account how much of 1966 was devoted to participating in other artists' work.

Between October 15 and 21, 1966, she spent her days at New York City's 25th Street Armory. As one of the youngest artists on the scene, she could be counted on to perform gratis in *9 Evenings: Theater and Engineering*. The poster for the event announced a fusion of high-tech research and avant-garde art with "dance-music-film-technology by Cage-Childs-Fahlström-Hay-Hay-Paxton-Rainer-Rauschenberg-Tudor-Whitman-Executive coordination Kluver." RC performed in Yvonne Rainer's *Carriage Discreteness*, which was staged twice. The first evening, Rainer gave instructions by walkie-talkie to dancers and non-dancers.[9] Robert Morris had his hand on the button for the second performance. The floor was gridded into 20 sections on which various objects, some conceived by Carl Andre, were disposed according to size, material or function. The performers moved the objects as per the instructions they receive by walkie-talkie while slides (some by Hollis Frampton) and films were projected on the wall. Instructions transmitted to Castoro included "Rosemarie, the wooden sewing machine top behind you to section three." "Rosemarie, turn around and take the strip on the floor to section seven." "Rosemarie Castoro, the wooden beam behind you to section eleven."[10]

Hollis Frampton also called upon the kindness of his friends in 1966. He described the short film *Manual of Arms* as a "courtly dances with friends and lovers, in the form of a 14-part drill for the camera, incorporating physiognomic & locomotor evidence related to the lens by 13 artists and an

8   https://www.dazeddigital.com/photography/article/35764/1/max-s-kansas-city-new-york-1970s-anton-perich

9   Carl Andre, Becky Arnold, Rosemarie Castoro, William Davis, Letty Lou Eisenhauer, June Ekman, Ed Iverson, Kathy Iverson, Julie Judd, Michael Kirby, Alfred Kurchin, Benjamin Lloyd, Meredith Monk, Steve Paxton, Carol Summers.

10   *9 Evenings: Theatre & Engineering—Carriage Discreetness*, directed by Barbro Schultz Lundestam, 16 mm film transferred to video, 1966 ©Schultz Förlag AB for E.A.T. 2008

historian." Carl Andre, Barbara Brown, Rosemarie Castoro, Lucinda Childs, Barry Goldensohn, Robert Huot, Eric Lloyd, Lee Lozano, Linda Myer, Larry Poons, Michael Snow, Marcia Steinbrecher, Twyla Tharp, and Joyce Wieland appear on screen in alphabetical order, first in close-up portraits in which only half of the face is lit; then in motion, the camera movements and editing techniques specific to each personality.

1967:
ELIMINATING ALL BUT ONE ANGLE

Nor does RC have much to say, in the narrative biographies, about her activities in 1967 and 1968. It was a time of upheaval in the USA; and in her own life, of withdrawal.

The press used the term "Long Hot Summer" in 1967 to evoke the violent heatwaves, but also the heated riots in Newark, Detroit, Minneapolis, and New York. Norman Mailer recounted a more serene moment of civil discontent in his best-selling "non-fiction novel," *Armies of the Night,* in which he described Abbie Hoffman's attempt to "encircle the Pentagon with twelve hundred men in order to form a ring of exorcism sufficiently powerful to raise the Pentagon three hundred feet. In the air the Pentagon would then, went the presumption, turn orange and vibrate until all evil emissions had fled this levitation. At that point the war in Vietnam would end."

The paintings RC executed in 1967 were restricted to private views that year and until 1976, when they were finally exhib-ited at the Hal Bromm Gallery. Her construction of this coherent series of nearly monochrome canvases is based on limiting the brushstroke action to one angle. Each canvas is thus covered in a field of diagonal strokes. She then drew parallel pencil lines on the surface. In a laudatory review in *Artnews*, Ann Sargent Wooster describes the effect as "a simulacrum of pin-stripe fabric."

1968

April 4, 1968: assassination of Martin Luther King
June 5, 1968: assassination of Robert F. Kennedy
On the walls from May 25 to June 22 *Language II* was the Dwan Gallery's second end of season group show featuring words as visual phenomena. RC is tapped for a piece, title unknown, the checklist in the Dwan Gallery archives being incomplete. On June 3 the show received a long review by John Perreault in the *Village Voice,* the same day that "Valerie Solanas shoots Andy Warhol" was on the front cover of the *New York Post.*

For its September 1968 issue, *Artforum* runs RC's photograph on the cover. It depicts *Lever* by Carl Andre.

In summarizing her career, Castoro accords only two sentences to the year 1969: "Interacting with the world outside my studio, I attended Art Workers Coalition meetings in 1969. In 'Street Works,' I taped an aluminum strip in the middle of the sidewalk around a city block to 'make an atoll out of Manhattan Island'."

Yet if we are to look closely, at a single day for instance, the intensity of her activity is staggering. On April 10, 1969, the first public meeting of the Art Workers' Coalition is convened. Castoro attends. Discussion is spirited and contradictory. Nonetheless, participants agree to publish a document bringing each artist's opinion on museum reform and artistic property rights to the attention of all.[11] Many argued for a system of residual and resale rights; but Castoro was alone in proposing that these rights be mutualized for reasons of artistic solidarity: "Making art is the artist's responsibility; its care and exposure should be by command of its maker. To free those energies that are otherwise diverted, the artist should be entitled to life's basic necessities: food, shelter and clothing. We can get this money from the profits of dead artists. We should demand, from exorbitantly priced works sold by institutions, a cut for the living." Her suggestions for institution reform reflect some of her own concerns, for she was already a maker of cumbersome objects: "Functional Institutions are great warehouses. We should encourage them to store our works for us. But neither do we want a dumping ground. Facilities should be available to those who wish to store large works."

On the evening of April 10, 1969, RC was at the Unit Playhouse on West 22nd Street to participate in *Aleph-70*, "a live magazine of performing poetry" directed by Joachim Neugroschel. Projecting slides of her hand-drawn texts and declaiming the words, she performed *24 Hours in the Life of a Conscientious Objector*. The original text of colored markers on graph paper would be exhibited a few weeks later in *Language III* at the Dwan Gallery (May 24–June 18, 1969). This show also included slides for another text-based work, *Sharp Changes*. Both slide sets could be purchased as multiples.

POLITICS/
ART/
CONCEPTS

Castoro's narrative biography eschews chronological precision with the aim of consolidating her conceptual credentials. "'Cracking' the Paula Cooper Gallery and 'Moving Ceilings' with casters, the art critic Lucy Lippard invited me into museum shows, such as *555,087*, Seattle Center, Washington. I wrote articles in *Artforum* and *Arts Magazines* in 1970 and 1971 about

11   RC's statement appeared in a long but revealing list of art world personalities: Carl Andre, Robert Barry, Gregory Battcock, Jon Bauch, Ernst Benkert, Don Bernshouse, Gloria Greenberg Bressler, Selma Brody, Bruce Brown, Bob Carter, Frederick Castle, Michael Chapman, Iris Crump, John Denmark, Joseph Di Donato, Mark Di Suvero, George Dworzan, Farman, Hollis Frampton, Dan Graham, Chuck Ginnever, Bill Gordy, Alex Gross, Hans Haacke, Clarence Hagin, Harvey, Gerry Herman, Frank Hewitt, D. Holmes, Robert Huot, Ken Jacobs, Joseph Kosuth, David Lee, Naomi Levine, Sol LeWitt, Lucy Lippard, Tom Lloyd, Lee Lozano, Len Lye, James McDonald, Edwin Mieczkowski, Minority A, Vernita Nemec, Barnett Newman, John Perreault, Stephen Phillips, Lil Picard, Peter Pinchbeck, Joanna Pousette-Dart, Barbara Reise, Faith Ringgold, Steve Rosenthal, Theresa Schwarz, Seth Siegelaub, Gary Smith, Michael Snow, Anita Steckel, Carl Strueckland, Gene Swenson, Julius Tobias, Jean Toche, Ruth Vollmer, Iain Whitecross, Jay Wholly, Ann Wilson, and Wilbur Woods.

STREET WORKS II

FRIDAY, APRIL 18, 1969
5 to 6 PM

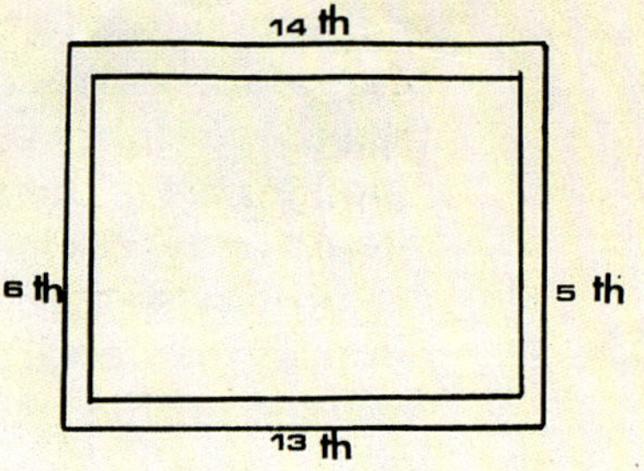

VITO HANNIBAL ACCONCI
TERENCE ANDERSON
ARAKAWA
GREGORY BATTCOCK
MICHAEL BENEDICT
MICHAEL BROWNSTEIN
SCOTT BURTON
JAMES LEE BYARS
ROSEMARIE CASTORO
EDUARDO COSTA
BILL CRESTON
LARRY FAGIN
MADELINE GINS
JOHN GIORNO
BOBBI GORMLEY
TOM GORMLEY
DAN GRAHAM
KATHERINE GREEF
STEPHEN KALTENBACH
JOSEPH KOSSUTH

LEANDRO KATZ
ALCIDES LANZA
LUCY LIPPARD
BERNADETTE MAYER
ROSEMARY MAYER
BEN PATTERSON
JOHN PERREAULT
LIL PICARD
ADRIAN PIPER
H ALEXANDER ROBERTS
MARJORIE STRIDER
MR. T.
BERNAR VENET
FRANK LINCOLN VINER
ANNE WALDMAN
LEWIS WARSH
LUIS WELLS
HANNAH WEINER
LARRY WEINER

Poster for *Street Works II*, 1969

art and politics. Ursula Meyer's book *Conceptual Art* included my stopwatch works, such as *Eclipse* and *Love's Time*."

In fact, RC's contribution to the art magazines of record were themed statements in answer to an editorial call. The September 1970 issue of *Artforum* published a symposium of texts by members of the Art Workers Coalition to accompany the actions they initiated. Castoro's contribution emphasizes the distinction she makes between art and political action: "I have been involved and will still be involved in: peace benefit shows, weekly group encounter Art Workers Coalition meetings, my own studio, and wherever I happen to be. I have been called upon to donate paintings. I have been asked to tax my half of sales, which, during this recession, doesn't mean very much, but when money starts flowing, I have stipulated that the art-changers take upon themselves the tax burden—that dead artists support live artists through trust funds collected by taxing the profits from the auction block ... It's all a matter of economics, not politics ... The artist does battle on his own field, and resents being forced into combat with strangers, by a government that does not nourish him."

In January 1971, *Artnews* published a special issue on "Women's Liberation, Women Artists and Art History." Castoro was invited to contribute her point of view—decidedly untouched by 'Consciousness Raising.' Linda Nochlin's article "Why Have There Been No Great Women Artists?" remains famous to this day.

Reacting against the spate of recent exhibitions in which the spectator suffers "to absorb new complex thoughts by standing in front of a wall covered with endless typed or hand-scribbled pages," the curator Athena Spear followed the example of Seth Siegelaub, who advocated that the most appropriate space for the exhibition of "idea art" was the catalog. Spear organized *Art in the Mind* for the Allen Art Museum in Oberlin, OH (April 17–May 12, 1970). Spear's catalog included two of Castoro's "stopwatch" pieces, *Love's Time* and *Eclipse*. *Eclipse* was written on March 7, 1970, the day a total solar eclipse was visible across most of North and Central America. It was republished in 1972, in the anthology edited by Ursula Meyer, *Conceptual Art*, along with a reproduction of the Seattle "room-cracking."

ALL IT'S CRACKED UP TO BE

It was in March of 1969 that Lucy Lippard sent invitations to participate in an expansive traveling exhibition. She described the project: "There is no theme as such; the title will be different in each city; there is no limitation to conception except financial. What I'd like is several propositions so I can choose the one that seems most feasible. I won't know exactly where I stand on expenses until all the projects are in, but I do know they won't pay the artists' expenses to Seattle, etc., so it has to be something I can execute with the help of friends and volunteers ... The catalog will be typed on loose 5×8 index cards and projects can be changed for each city."[12] Although there is no evidence as to how Castoro's trip was funded, photograph showing her "cracking" the former Fine Arts Pavilion of the 1962 World's fair prove that she made the trip to Seattle.

The same year, Lippard also organized *Number 7*, an exhibition at the Paula Cooper Gallery (May 18–June 15, 1969). An enthusiastic review in the *Village Voice* by John Perreault notes a Castoro "wall-cracking" in the room with Bollinger, Bochner, Smithson, Serra, and De Maria. Looking back on this event in her book *Six Years: The Dematerialization of the Art Object from 1966 to 1972,* Lippard reproduces just two images from this show, making a striking visual comparison between RC's *Room Cracking#7* and Carl Andre's *Cut Cable Wires.*

THE WALLS GO TUMBLING UP

"I built walls with Masonite, gave up the straight edge and drew with graphite, striking blackness, recalling the shadows of people on my walls of Vancouver's 'Room Revelations.' I quit doing paste-ups, receiving the Woodard Foundation Grant (Art in Embassies) and the 1971 Guggenheim Fellowship Award for painting. Instead of cradling Masonite, I hinged doors together to form free-standing walls, parts of rooms, corners, foyers, and shower stalls."

In this narrative, Castoro barely mentions that her first solo show was with Tibor de Nagy in 1971, showing free-standing walls. On view from February 20 to March 11, the panels made of wood and Masonite, their front surface treated with gesso, modeling paste, graphite stick, and fixative received mixed reviews. *Artforum* covered the show at length, but without enthusiasm; the reviewer found it objectionable that the panels were not treated on both sides. *Arts Magazine* expressed more appreciation, and Lawrence Alloway penned a descriptive paragraph for *Artnews.*

Reflecting on her career in 2010, RC evokes with hindsight the social tensions of the era and writes less cryptically about her walls: "I was a painter of multi-hued monochromes before the world turned upside down in 1969; in the wake of the transformation, borders were transgressed. I cracked rooms, moved ceilings, and built rooms. Out of room building, I began cradling panels on which to draw. In priming the panels, the gessoed brush-stroke became visible, despite my diligent sanding of the Masonite panel, so I thickened the paint with marble dust. If it wanted to exist, I would help it. In handling large expanses of panels by myself, I bolted the edges together and discovered that by curving the 15' and 25' walls, they would freestand. Instead of hanging them on an existing wall, they became free-standing."[13]

12   Form letter inviting artists to participate in the *955,000* exhibition, March 14, 1969. Lucy R. Lippard papers, Archives of American Art, Smithsonian Institution.

13   Statement January 21, 2010, RC archives.

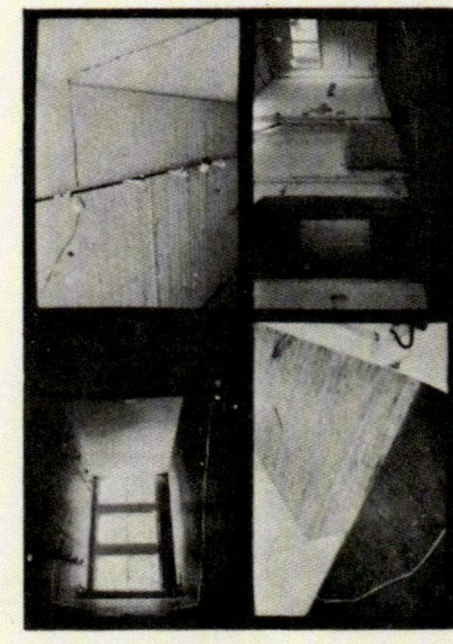

R. CASTORO
3/1/39
NEW YORK

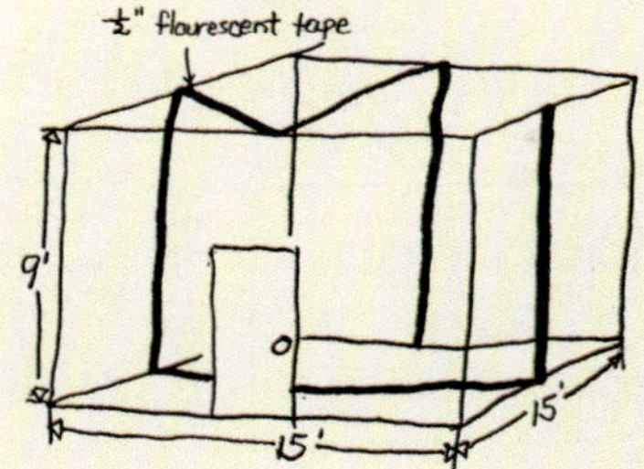

THE DOOR OPENS ONTO DARKNESS. THE DOOR CLOSES
BEHIND YOU. A SWITCH CONNECTED TO THE DOOR
STARTS A REOSTATED LIGHT BULB PLACED IN THE
MIDDLE OF THE CEILING TO BRIGHTEN TO ITS 250 W.
INTENSITY WITHIN FIVE MINUTES.

Galleries

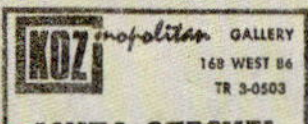

"ORBLITTS'"
SPECTRUM
1043 MADISON

WELLIVER
TIBOR DE NAGY 29 W 57

Thru March 31
LASSITER
Fantastic Tableaux & Drawings
NEWSWEEK GALLERY 10
444 Madison Ave. (10th floor)
9 to 5 · Monday - Friday only

CLAIRE thru April 12
VAN VLIET
watercolors
GREEN MOUNTAIN GALLERY
17 PERRY ST. (cor. 7 Ave.)

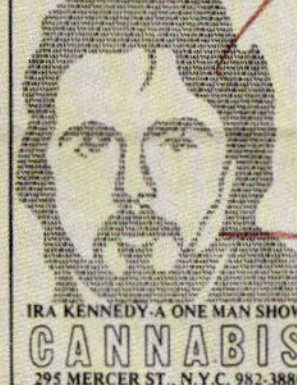

Marlborough
41 East 57th Street, N.Y. PL 2-5353

...ckson Pollock

...k & White

...tant 19th and 20th
...ry Paintings and
... avai...ble

...ARLBOROUGH GRAPHICS GALLERY
...fifth floor

...y
...Dor...zio, G...lieb,
...oko...hka, L...pchitz,
...Relli, Moore,
...on, Pasmore, Tilson

...rough-Gerse...Gallery, Inc.
...y through Saturday, 10-5.

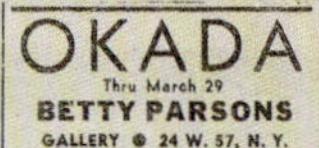

KENNETH EVETT
Paintings—Watercolors
Thru March 29
Kraushaar Galleries
1055 Madison Ave. (ent. 80 St.)

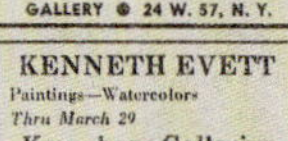

THRU MARCH 22
SAMUEL BEHAR
DILYS EVANS
RUTH JACOBSEN
LYNN KOTTLER GALLERY
3 EAST 65 ST.

FIOL   GORMAN
FRANCIS   GWATHMEY
PAINTINGS
MARCH 8TH THROUGH APRIL 5TH
43 EAST 20 STREET, 5TH FLOOR
SATURDAY AND SUNDAY, 12 - 6 PM
MONDAY - FRIDAY BY APPOINTMENT
673-2903 or 765-3051

R. CASTORO
Mover of Ceilings
is
Dropping a Line
March 15 from 42nd to 52nd Sts
between 5th and Madison Aves.

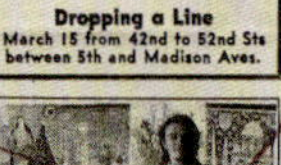

PAUL MOGENSEN
BYKERT
24 E 81

Jason
Seley
at Kornblee
58 e 79

Thru March 29
Paintings and Ceramics by
Henry Varnum POOR
Frank Rehn Gallery
655 Madison (at 60th St.)
2nd floor

MAY STEVENS
Big Daddy Drawings
Queens College
Klapper Art Center

AGOSTINI
DRAWINGS
RADICH GALLERY
818 MADISON AVE.

ADRIAN PIPER
from March on

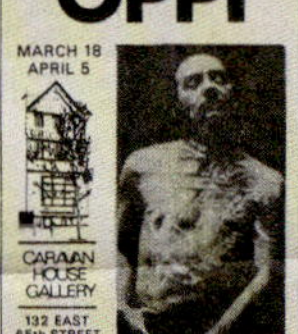
DANIELE
OPPI
MARCH 18
APRIL 5
CARAVAN HOUSE GALLERY
132 EAST
65th STREET
NEW YORK

AT
COLUMBUS
CIRCLE
The Gallery of Modern Art
incl. the Huntington Hartford Collection
Open Tuesday thru Sunday 11-8

Grandma MOSES

LAURENCE   Opens
SISSON   March 18

20th Cent. American Art
Alfredo Valente Collection

CINEMATHEQUE   2 and 6 PM Daily

Willy   Lectures on
Ley   "Astronomy from Space"
March 13, 20, at 4 P.M.

Gallery   Tuesday thru
Talks   Friday 2 P.M.

GAUGUIN   open until 8
restaurant   Tues. thru Sun.

CAESAR
Weyhe Gallery
794 Lexington Ave

March 14 to 29
Sherwood
OHLENDORF
Oils, Lacquers, Lithos
GALERIE PAULA INSEL
987 Third Avenue (59th)

DORSKY 867 MADISON
Drawings & Gouaches
11 MARCH — 4 APRIL

JOAN   THRU MARCH 29
REMY
OPENING MARCH 9 — 4 to 6 PM
LINCOLN INSTITUTE OF
PSYCHOTHERAPY
340 WEST 58 ST.

ATTENTION
ARTISTS
Paintings & Sculpture wanted for exhibitions. All Media. Well-known Gallery. Est. 1949. Call or write.
LYNN KOTTLER GALLERIES
3 E. 65th St., N.Y.C. RE 4-3491

The ORR—
HIS BAG
PAPER BAG SCULPTURE
His Studio
219 Seventh Ave. at 23rd
MARCH 8 thru 24
2 to 8 PM   691-3790

Collect art where the artists
live and work
THE LOFT
gallery
IMPRESSIONS OF
THE HUMAN FORM
1 pm - 6 pm - 691-5074
154 W. 27 St., 5th flr. Sat. & Sun.

Art Auction
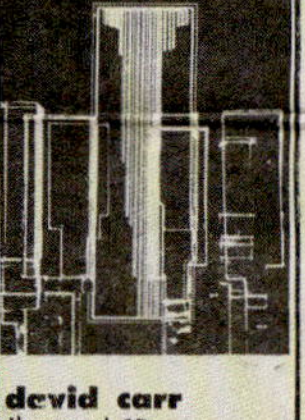
To Benefit SCEF   SOUTHERN CONFERENCE
EDUCATIONAL FUND INC.
SUNDAY, MARCH 16, 1969
2 W. 64th Street
Dali, Picasso, Levine, Soyer, Shahn, Baskin, Friedlander,
Lebadang, Buffet, Alvar, Papart, Daumier
original graphics donated by collectors, artists, institutions and dealers
Viewing 2 to 4 P.M. / Auction 4 P.M.   Contribution $2.00

THRU MARCH 22
MANDAKINI KULKARNI
BATIK PAINTINGS
THE ART IMAGE
232 East 64 St.

RICHARD A.
MILLER
PERIDOT 820 Madison (68)

WEEKENDS
MOSER
123 MADISON

Recent Paintings
R. BARANIK
channel 31   Friday March 14, 9 pm
Sun. Mar. 16, 3:30pm

M SACHS
29 W. 57
TAD
MIYASHITA

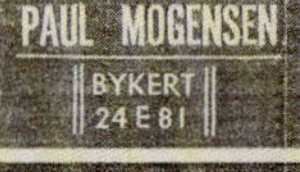

david carr
thru march 27
bertha schaefer
41 east 57

A CONTENDER IN NEW YORK

Shortly after the show at the well-respected uptown Tibor de Nagy Gallery, RC participates in a three-person exhibition at 112 Greene Street. This venue, a few blocks from her loft in Soho, became an exhibition space when its owner, the artist Jeffrey Lew, responded to Gordon Matta-Clark's suggestion to invite other sculptors, painters, dancers, filmmakers, and performance artists to make the most of the space. "We created a platform of complete freedom and without any direction and supervision. It was not bound by curators, either. The gallery provided a space where, unlike in commercial galleries, the artist was allowed to dig, cut, and sometimes destroy some of the architecture. The doors of this gallery were never locked, so artists had access 24 hours a day, seven days a week. It created a spirit; the spirit of complete and total freedom. Gallery owners took notice and curators took notice, and often these artists were provided with a more mainstream art gallery. If you walked into 112 Greene Street at any time, there were always people engaged in conversation and debauchery, and you could feel the spirit of delight."[14]

From April 10 to May 8, 1971, people walking in could see RC's *Cold Sake,* composed of two curved, free-standing walls made with textured gesso and graphite on Masonite. The two other artists participating in the exhibition were Carl Andre and Marjorie Strider.

At the end of 1970, the Tibor de Nagy Gallery compiled a list of collectors of RC's work. It includes Lynda Benglis, John Chamberlain, Mark Di Suvero, Michael Heizer, Sol LeWitt, Lucy Lippard, Vera List, Janie C. Lee, John Weber, Marjorie Strider, Holly Solomon, the University of Connecticut Art Museum, and the Woodward Foundation.[15]

DIFFERENT STROKES FOR DIFFERENT FOLKS

"In 1972 I received the CAPS grant. In my second show, 'Rotating Corners' turned in my mind, I released the brushstroke. Out came Pitman shorthand, the basis for drawing symbols of people's names, words, and body parts."

RC's concise account might better be grasped with some expansion. On December 15, 1971, she wrote in her diary: "Pitman shorthand has returned in the form of brushstrokes spelling people's names." Where Pitman returned from is not specified, but its allure is undeniable: RC relished the simplified and easy-to-draw characters, which she manipulated to evoke names and words with her own secret system of metonymy. In an album published in Pretto's memory, Castoro explained: "Julian changed his name from Leonard in 1972 after I made a cut-out graphite Masonite work called Pray Do, based on the short-hand symbol for Leonard Pretto."

14　*112 Greene Street A Nexus of Ideas in the Early 70s*, organized by Ned Smyth, January 12–March 6, 2011, Salomon Contemporary Project Room, New York.

15　Tibor de Nagy Gallery records, Box 15, Folder 5, Archives of American Art, Smithsonian Institution.

The Creative Artists Public Service program (CAPS) was operated between 1970 and 1980 by the New York State Council on the Arts to support individual artists' work. *Rotating Corners* was not exhibited in Castoro's second solo show, but was included in *Painting and Sculpture 1972* at the Storm King Art Gallery in Mountainville, NY, while RC's second solo show at Tibor de Nagy (February 5–24, 1972) received consequential press. Kenneth Baker reviewing for *Artforum* found the new free-standing pieces more successful than those of 1971. He remarked: "One gets most clearly the sense of a double movement, making a sculptural element pictorial and a pictorial element sculptural ... What Castoro still hasn't dealt with is an aspect of the work that hangs on from the early folded screen setups, namely, the sense that the panels are screening something from us." Unlike Baker, who did not appreciate the new wall pieces, Denise Wolmer, writing for *Arts* magazine, finds that RC "combines a lyrical seductiveness of form with a determined and compelling use of materials in her cut-out mock-ups of gigantic brushstrokes." *Artnews* again limits coverage to a descriptive paragraph. John Perreault gives an appreciative mention in the *Village Voice;* and *Vogue* sends Duane Michaels to photograph RC at work for an article about "Living the Loft Life".

August 20, 1972, a photograph of RC's *Party of Nine* is reproduced in the *New York Times* to illustrate Peter Schjeldahl's review of *Oversized Drawings* at NYU's Loeb Student Center. He describes the work as "what looks like giant vertical brushstrokes, roughly modeled in thick gesso on Masonite and streaked with graphite. The strokes, each different, curl at the top, which gives them a vaguely anthropomorphic air. It's hard to decide quite how to take these things—as ironic depictions of 'gestural' energy, say, or as actors in a kind of abstract psychological drama—but undeniably they do pack a punch."

Should we read anything into the interstices between RC's accounting and other documents? Perhaps her interest in forms of experimental writing incited her to a form of pithy prose that leaves much about her artistic intentions to the reader's imagination. In 2010, she compiled a hefty 976 pages presentation of Powerpoint slides. Sisyphean or Quixotic, it was a determined attempt to influence the reception of her oeuvre. Scholars can only try to be so valiant.

Clockwise

3-1 3 panels 1 panel
4-1 more than five but
     steel post
0-1 more than five but of
     negative account
2-1 2 chairs stuffed
     and one not
2-1 2 lamps 1 TV set
2-5 2 circles + lots
     of paint
4-1 2+2 circles 1 machine
4-2 4 individual
     articles 1 brick
     with 2 holes
4-1 4 articles 1 canvas
2-3 2 sprinkler
     pipes 3 surfaces

3-1 3 brown 1 bed
5-2 lots of book
     2 things
0-2 lots of things
     2 things
3-1 3 light brown
     chairs 1 dark
     brown chair

colors of pencils

3-4 3 green 4 yellow
3-2 3 dark green
     2 blue
3-2 3 gold 2 Red
3-1 3 lt brown
     2 purple
4-2 4 Red 2 gray
0-2 all the pencils
     1 stool plus 1 glass
3-2 1 box 1 slat + 1
     stool to 1 box
     plus 1 glass

2-0 2 long and
     orange
     cancellation
3-2 plant water
     brush
     and glass and
     box
5-2 most of the
     above and 1
     brush + 1 shovel
2-1 2 black objects
     + 1 tape work

2-3 2 large cans 3 small
2-3 2 lights 3
     brown rolls
3-1 3 lamps
     1 gas meter
5-1 5 visable
     canvasses 1 back
     of painting
2-0 2 chairs one
     exercise pad

left and right hand
walk around my studio

R. Castoro
1968-69

Left and right hand walk around my studio, 1968–1969

EXHIBITION HISTORY

Rosemarie Castoro's last biographical narrative, dated February 26, 2013, differs from all the previous versions in that it is written in the third person. Hence, we did not mine it in order to produce our own telling of her early career. Instead, we present it here to introduce a chronology of her exhibitions.

Rosemarie Castoro, user of tools and technology to manifest ideas and desires in the physical world, began her career drawing desert islands and empty city streets as a child in a chaotic household. Winning a painting scholarship to MoMA as a high school student introduced possibilities. After graduating Pratt Institute, she became a painter, transitioning to sculpture through performance and dance. Called out of the studio by peers to participate in "Street Works," an atoll out of Manhattan Island was created by "cracking" a city block with aluminum tape and later, dripping paint using a bicycle as an instrument. Examining time, a stop-watch-accompanied writing logged a day, weekend and week. A room in Vancouver was built experiencing compressed time. The three-minute rheostated single light bulb placed in the center of the floor revealed people through their shadows.
    Flying back to the studio, in the desire to make perma-nent the shadowy experience, wall panels were built and graphite drawn onto the white painted surfaces. Bolting together many panels, the walls became free-standing, turning into parts of rooms, foyers, and corners. The corners gathered together to become rotating doors which imaginatively turned and out came the brushstroke, sawed from Masonite; initially a made-up shorthand for people's names. Groups of people ensued, going somewhere, waiting on line, relating to one another. Teaching in Fresno, the people groups were buried, their roots emerging from the ceiling, then suspended, finally landing on the ground, made from epoxy and steel: resembling tree tops after a hurricane. The tunnel straightened and became a ladder, perspective built into the works. Teaching sculpture in Boulder without a studio, "traps" were carved from tree branches. With 200 tree trunks gathered from Central Park, *Trap A Zoid* was laid into the sand on a rope grid. The bark of the tree became *Flashers*: eighteen 8' tall wres-tled steel and paint carapaces. Structuring the *Flasher* by weld-ing stainless steeled in creating *Mountain Range*, of *Arched Waves*… making the transitory permanent.

Editor's Note: The chronology ends on 2015, the year of Rosemarie Castoro's death. Since then, two posthumous career retrospectives have been held at MAMCO Geneva (2019) and MACBA Barcelona (2017). Rosemarie Castoro's Estate is now rep-resented by Thaddaeus Ropac (London/Paris/Salzburg/Seoul).

SOLO EXHIBITIONS

1971 Tibor de Nagy Gallery, New York
1972 Tibor de Nagy Gallery, New York
1973 Tibor de Nagy Gallery, New York
Suspensions, Lubin House Gallery,
    Syracuse University, NY
1975 Tibor de Nagy Gallery, New York
Painting 1967–68, Hal Bromm Gallery,
    New York
1977 University of Colorado, Boulder, CO
1978 Tibor de Nagy Gallery, New York
P.S. 1, Long Island City, NY
Beaver's Trap, Hal Bromm Gallery,
    New York
Sculpture, 1970–78 and *Drawings,
    1964–78*, Julian Pretto, New York
Galerie Farideh Cadot, Paris
1979 Hal Bromm Gallery, New York
Dirty Old Men, Julian Pretto, New York
24 Flashers, ArtPark, Lewiston, NY
1980 *Knee-High Flashers*, Tibor de Nagy
    Gallery, New York
Selected Major Works,
    Hal Bromm Gallery, New York
1981 Tibor de Nagy Gallery, New York
Marion Deson, Chicago
*Making the Transitory Permanent:
    A Decade of Black & White Sculpture*,
    Hal Bromm Gallery, New York
1983 Tibor De Nagy Gallery, New York
The American Center, Paris, France
Hal Bromm Gallery, New York
Seven Flashers, Duane Park, New York
1984 Eaton/Shoen Gallery, San Francisco
Flashers on Third Avenue, New York
1985 Tibor de Nagy Gallery, New York
1986 Hal Bromm Gallery, New York
Eaton/Shoen Gallery, San Francisco
1987 Saint Peter's Church, Citicorp Center,
    New York
New Sculpture, Hal Bromm Gallery,
    New York
1989 *Rosemarie Castoro: A Retrospective of
    Selected Works*, 127 Grand St,
    New York
Tibor de Nagy Gallery, New York
1990 Blue Hill Cultural Center, Pearl River, NY
1991 *Brush Stroke Series*, Newark Museum,
    Newark, NJ
Hal Bromm Gallery, New York
1993 *Knee-High Flashers*,
    Galerie Arnaud Lefebvre, Paris
1972–76 Drawings, Stella R Graphics,
    Paris
1995 *1964–1994 (small) works*,
    Galerie Arnaud Lefebvre, Paris
1997 *Short Stories*, Hal Bromm Gallery,
    New York
Underconsciousness,
    Galerie Arnaud Lefebvre, Paris
1998 *Syncope*, Galerie Arnaud Lefebvre, Paris
1999 *Gallery Floating*,
    Galerie Arnaud Lefebvre, Paris
2000 *Black & White & Steel*, Eaton Fine Art,
    West Palm Beach, FL
2002 *Archetypes*, Hal Bromm Gallery,
    New York
2003 *Arches and Tunnels, 1974–75*,
    Galerie Arnaud Lefebvre, Paris
2004 *Mosquito Net Works*, Eaton Fine Art,
    West Palm Beach, FL
Écrits/Writings, Galerie Arnaud Lefebvre,
    Paris
2006 *The Dimension of Line*,
    Hal Bromm Gallery, New York
2007 *Armpit Hair Coming from the Corner
    of a Room* and *Party of Nine*,
    150 East 52 Street, New York
2009 *Straight Sided & Knee-High Flashers*,
    Galerie Arnaud Lefebvre, Paris

2011 *The Forest*, Hal Bromm Gallery, New York
Snow Jobs, Galerie Ivana de Gavardie,
    Paris
2015 *SP Arte*, Cicillo Matarazzo Pavilion,
    Sao Paulo, Brazil
Loft Show, Broadway 1602,
    Rosemarie Castoro Studio, New York

SELECTED GROUP EXHIBITIONS

1963   *Prints*, Brooklyn Museum, New York
1966   *Invitational*, Park Place Gallery, New York
       Distillation, Tibor de Nagy & Stable
          Galleries, New York
       E.A.T. Benefit, Castelli Gallery, New York
1967   *Invitational*, Park Place Gallery, New York
1968   Richard Feigen Gallery, New York
       Language II, Dwan Gallery, New York
1969   *Number 7*, Paula Cooper Gallery, New York
       Street Works, 13th & 14th Streets, New York
       Language III, Dwan Gallery, New York
       555,087, Seattle Art Museum, Seattle, WA
       Drawing Show, Paula Cooper Gallery,
          New York
       Richard Feigen Gallery, New York
1970   *995,000*, Vancouver Art Gallery,
          British Columbia, Canada
       Between 4, Städtische Kunsthalle,
          Dusseldorf, Germany
       Drawing Show, Bard College,
          Proctor Art Center,
          Annandale-on-Hudson, NY
       Art in the Mind, Allen Art Museum,
          Oberlin, OH
       Young Artists for Young Collectors,
          Reese Palley, New York
       High Class Drawings, Hundred Acres
          Gallery, New York
1971   *Drawings*, Paula Cooper Gallery,
          New York
       Erasable Structures, School of Visual
          Arts Gallery, New York
       Projected Art: Artists at Work,
          Finch College, New York
       The Drawn Line, Parker 470 Gallery,
          Boston, MA
       Three Persons, 112 Greene Street
          Gallery, New York
       Auction for Max's, Lo Guidice Gallery,
          New York
       Highlights of the Season, Aldrich
          Museum of Contemporary Art,
          Ridgefield, CT
       Drawings, Weatherspoon Gallery,
          Greensboro, NC
       Changing Terms, School of the Museum
          of Fine Arts, Boston, MA
1972   *New York*, Richard Gray Gallery,
          Chicago, IL
       Paintings and Sculpture, Storm King Art
          Gallery, Mountainville, NY
       Oversized Drawings, Loeb Student
          Center, New York University
       Armpit Hair, 112 Greene Street Gallery,
          New York
1974   *Art Acquisitions, 1973*, University of
          Massachusetts, Amherst, MA
       Storm King Art Gallery, Mountainville, NY
1975   *New Drawings*, Grapestake Gallery,
          San Francisco
       Arches and Bridges, Storm King Gallery,
          Mountainville, NY
1976   *Ladders*, Grapestake Gallery,
          San Francisco
       Artists '76, McNay Art Institute,
          San Antonio, TX
       Thinking Drawings, Womencenter,
          Boulder, CO
       Sculptor's Drawings, Fine Arts Building,
          New York
       Five Artists, Otis Art Institute, Los Angeles
1977   *Collection in Progress*, Moore College
          of Art, Philadelphia, PA
       Invitational, Tyler Gallery of Art, SUNY,
          Oswego, NY
       Video and Performance, UMC Center,
          University of Colorado, Boulder, CO
       Art in Public Places, OIA,
          26 Federal Plaza, New York

Drawings for Outdoor Sculpture,
    John Weber Gallery, New York
Forms in Focus, Co-op City, New York
Moving, Hal Bromm Gallery, New York
$100 Gallery, New York
Shelf of Grass, Hal Bromm Gallery,
    New York
…Trap, Julian Pretto Gallery, New York
1978   *Indoor–Outdoor*, P.S.1,
          Long Island City, NY
       Armpit Hair, Auditorium, U.S. Mission
          to the United Nations, New York
       Painting and Sculpture Today,
          Indianapolis Museum of Art, IN
       Art on the Beach, Creative Time, Inc.,
          Battery Park, NY
       Sculpture Library: Part One, OIA,
          Ward's Island Sculpture Garden,
          New York
       The Presence of Nature, Whitney
          Museum of American Art, New York
       Adams and Castoro, Rush Rhees
          Gallery, University of Rochester, NY
       Review and Preview, Nancy Lurie
          Gallery, Chicago
       Rotating Corners, II, Hal Bromm Gallery,
          New York
       Arches and Bridges, Walt Whitman
          Poetry Center, Rutgers University,
          Camden, NJ
       Black and White on Paper,
          Nobe Gallery, NJ
1979   *Art on Paper*, Weatherspoon Art
       Gallery, Greensboro, NC
       A Great Big Drawing Show, P.S. 1, Long
       Island City, NY
       Julian Pretto & Co, New York
1980   *Fine Art for Federal Buildings
          1972–79*, Smithsonian Institute,
          Washington, D.C.
       Hunter Museum of American Art,
          Chattanooga, TN
       Painting and Sculpture Today, 1980,
          Indianapolis Museum of Art, IN
       Arte Americana Contemporanea,
          Udine, Italy
       OIA, Ward's Island Sculpture Garden,
          New York
       All in Line, Lowe Art Gallery,
          Syracuse University, NY
       Banco Galleria, Brescia, Italy
       Hirschl & Adler Gallery, New York
       Painting & Sculpture, Leah Levy Gallery,
          San Francisco
       Breaking In, Old Islip Station,
          Creative Time, New York
       Apokalypsis, Nardin Gallery, New York
1981   *Inside Spaces*, MOMA Art Lending
          Service, New York
       Direction 1981, Hirshhorn Museum and
          Sculpture Garden, Washington, D.C.
       New Dimensions in Drawing, Aldrich
          Museum Contemporary Art,
          Ridgefield, CT
       OIA, Ward's Island Sculpture Garden,
          New York
       Art on Paper, Weatherspoon Art
          Gallery, Greensboro, NC
       Drawings, Hal Bromm Gallery, New York
       Selections from Hal Bromm, New York,
          Eaton/Shoen Gallery, San Francisco
       Drawings, Watercolors and Prints,
          Leah Levy Gallery, San Francisco
       Creative Arts Program Winners,
          Pratt Institute Gallery, Brooklyn, NY
       New Art II: Surfaces/Textures,
          MOMA Art Lending Service, New York
       U.S. Art Now, Jan Eric Lowenadler,
          Stockholm, Sweden
       Heresies Second Annual Benefit Show,
          Grey Art Gallery, NYU, New York

Arches and Bridges, Snug Harbor
    Cultural Center, Staten Island, NY
The Summer Show, Hal Bromm Gallery,
    New York
Sculptor's Work on Paper, Quay Gallery,
    San Francisco
1982   *Drawing/New Directions*, Summit Art
          Center, NJ
       Selections from the First Year,
          Eaton/Shoen Gallery, San Francisco
       Artists in a Frank Lloyd Wright House,
          courtesy of Eaton/Shoen,
          Scottsdale, AZ
       On Ward's Island, Organization
          of Independent Artists, New York
       Sweet Art Sale, Benefit for Franklin
          Furnace, Ronald Feldman Gallery,
          New York
       Collector's Choice, Hal Bromm Gallery,
          New York
       The Destroyed Print, Pratt Manhattan
          Center Gallery, New York
       *Sculpture on the Lawn and in the
          Gallery*, Eaton/Shoen Gallery,
          San Francisco
       *Anti-Apocalypse: Artists Respond to
          the Nuclear Peril*, William Paterson
          College, NJ
       American Abstraction Now, Institute
          of Contemporary Art, Richmond, VA
1983   *Connections: Bridges/Ladders/Ramps/
          Staircases/Tunnels*, ICA, Philadelphia, PA
1984   *On an Intimate Dimension*,
          Tibor de Nagy Gallery, New York
       Celebration of Italian Americans,
          Passaic County Community College
          Art Gallery, Patterson, NJ
       Art on Paper, Weatherspoon Art
          Gallery, Greensboro, NC
       Noho, Soho, Tribeca, Maier Museum
          of Art, Lynchburg, VA
       Intoxication, Monique Knowlton Gallery,
          New York
       Pratt Invitational Alumni Exhibition,
          Brooklyn, NY
       A Public Works Project, Auction
          at Limbo Lounge, New York
1985   *Figure It Out: Exploring the Figure
          in Contemporary Art*, Laguna
          Gloria Art Museum, Austin, TX
       The Governor's Art Show,
          57th Fl. World Trade Center II,
          New York
       Not Just Black and White, City Gallery,
          New York
       New Sculpture, Hal Bromm Gallery,
          New York
       Drawing the Figure, Hal Bromm Gallery,
          New York
       Side by Side, MoMA, New York
       Contemporary Triptychs,
          Edith C. Blum Art Institute,
          Annandale-on-Hudson, NY
       The Destroyed Print, University
          of Colorado, Boulder, CO
       Highlights from the Collection, Bank of
          America Headquarters, San Francisco
       City Streets, Hal Bromm Gallery,
          New York
       American Women Artists, Stamford, CT
       San Jose State University, San Jose, CA
       5 Galvanized Portraits, Itokin Plaza,
          Madison Ave. & 53rd Street, New York
1986   *TEN*, Hal Bromm Gallery, New York
       Non-Objective, Hal Bromm Gallery, New York
       Home Sweet Home, Hal Bromm Gallery,
          New York
       From the Collection, Citicorp,
          St. Peter's Sanctuary, New York
       Socrates Sculpture Space/Park,
          Long Island City, NY

1987 *From the Collection*, Museum of Modern
     Art Lending Service, New York
     Castoro/Sharon, Hal Bromm Gallery,
     New York
     Socrates Sculpture Space/Park,
     Long Island City, NY
     Realism and Abstraction, 20th Century
     Art, Newark Museum, NJ
1990 *Old Friends... New Friends,*
     Marvin Seline Gallery, Houston, TX
     Annual Exhibition, Maier Museum of Art,
     Lynchburg, VA
     Season's Best, Tibor de Nagy Gallery,
     New York
     Works from the Seventies,
     Hal Bromm Gallery, New York
     Sculptors Working, Jan Baum Gallery,
     Los Angeles
1992 *La boîte à malices,* Stella R Graphics, Paris
     Points of View: 10 New York Artists,
     Northcutt Gallery, Eastern Montana
     College, Billings, MT
     Visions of Angels, Nancy Driscoll Gallery,
     New York
1993 *Rosemarie Castoro, Daniel Dezeuze,*
     Simon Hantaï, Galerie Arnaud
     Lefebvre, Paris
     2×1000, Galerie Arnaud Lefebvre, Paris
     Two Kings, Boca Raton Museum,
     Boca Raton, FL
     Double Muse, Henry Street Settlement,
     New York
1994 *1969. A Year Revisited,* Grey Art Gallery,
     NYU, New York
     FIAC, Galerie Arnaud Lefebvre, Paris
     Woodstock 94, mural, New York
1995 *The Art of the Opera,* Athenaeum
     Music & Arts Library, La Jolla, CA
     Une Constellation, Galerie Arnaud
     Lefebvre, Paris
     Phallic Symbols, 24 Hours for Life Gallery,
     New York
     Américains dans les collections françaises,
     1960–70, Beaumanoir, Le Leslay, France
1996 *Benefit in memory of Max's Kansas City,*
     165 Thompson St. Gallery, New York
     Julian Pretto Collection,
     Wadsworth Athenaeum, CT
     Eric Satie..., Galerie Arnaud Lefebvre,
     Paris
     Chelsea Walk, I.C.E. Gallery, New York
1997 *Les Moments de Lieu Propre Qui*
     Rythment Le Silence,
     Galerie Arnaud Lefebvre, Paris
     Small & Beautiful, Eaton Fine Art,
     West Palm Beach, FL
1998 *Director's Choice,* Boca Raton
     Museum of Art, Boca Raton, FL
2000 *Go Figure,* Eaton Fine Art,
     West Palm Beach, FL
2001 *Mosquito Net Works,*
     Galerie Arnaud Lefebvre, Paris
     Ironic Column, Side Show Gallery,
     Brooklyn, NY
2002 *Art in the Park,* Ft. Taylor, Key West, FL
2003 *Art in the Park,* Ft. Taylor, Key West, FL
     America Drill, Galerie Arnaud Lefebvre,
     Paris
     Metal and Paper, Eaton Fine Art,
     West Palm Beach, FL
     Site/Insight, P.S. 1|MoMA, New York
     Poetry/Prose, Galerie Arnaud Lefebvre,
     Paris
2005 *Gesture,* Eaton Fine Art,
     West Palm Beach, FL
     Configurations, MAMCO, Geneva
     Galerie Arnaud Lefebvre, Paris
     After Minimalism, Boca Raton Museum
     of Art, Boca Raton, FL
     Black and White, Hal Bromm Gallery,
     New York

Summer Sculpture, Eaton Fine Art,
     West Palm Beach, FL
     Inside Out, Byrdcliffe, Woodstock, NY
2007 *War is Over, Again,* Side Show Gallery,
     Brooklyn, NY
     It Takes a Lifetime, Paula Barr, New York
     A Day in the Life of a Gallerist,
     Galerie Arnaud Lefebvre, Paris
     Contemporary Selections, Eaton Fine Art,
     West Palm Beach, FL
2008 *Peace,* Side Show Gallery, Brooklyn, NY
     Volume I, Eaton Fine Art,
     West Palm Beach, FL
     Summer Show, Eaton Fine Art,
     West Palm Beach, FL
     Grids, Galerie Arnaud Lefebvre, Paris
     EKG of the ALGallery, Galerie
     Arnaud Lefebvre, Paris
2009 *It's a Wonderful Life,* Side Show Gallery,
     Brooklyn, NY
     Subversive Spaces: Surrealism &
     Contemporary Art, Whitworth Art
     Gallery, Manchester, UK and
     Compton Verney, Warwickshire, UK
     and Sainsbury Centre, Norwich, UK
     Galerie Arnaud Lefebvre, Paris
     The Paper Fool Gallery, Provincetown, MA
2010 *It's a Wonderful 10th,* Side Show Gallery,
     Brooklyn, NY
     Galerie Ivana de Gavardie, Paris
     Anti-Icon, Eaton Fine Arts,
     West Palm Beach, FL
     New Works/Small Scale,
     Art 612 Gallery, Key West, FL
     Neo-Vitruvian, Hal Bromm Gallery,
     New York
     ArtPark 1974–1984, University of
     Buffalo, Art Gallery, Buffalo, NY
2011 *Turtle,* Galerie Arnaud Lefebvre, Paris
     Gallery Floating, Galerie Ivana de
     Gavardie, Paris
     Architectures/Dessins/Utopies,
     Muzeul National de Arta
     Contemporana, Romania
     It's All Good!! Apocalypse Now,
     Side Show Gallery, Brooklyn, NY
     Four Sculptors, Leslie Heller
     Workspace, New York
     Galerie Ivana de Gavardie, Paris
2012 *Shem, PO(M) and Poem 2,* Galerie
     Ivana de Gavardie, Paris
     Wish You Were Here, 70s Avant Garde,
     Albright-Knox Art Gallery, Buffalo, NY
2013 *Enact,* Cleveland Performance Art
     Festival, including *River of Street*
     on YouTube
     The First 10 Years, ArtPark, Lewiston, NY
2014 *Ultrapassado,* Broadway 1602,
     New York
     Artevida, Fundação Casa França-Brasil
     Rio de Janeiro, Brazil

LIST OF WORKS

All works are courtesy of the Estate of Rosemarie
Castoro and Galerie Thaddeus Ropac (London,
Paris, Salzburg) unless otherwise mentioned.
Works exhibited at MAMCO Geneva in
2019–2020 are marked by an asterisk.

4–5 Exhibition view, MAMCO Geneva,
2019–2020
Clockwise: *Dioxomine Cerulean*, 1965;
Orange Ochre Purple Yellow Y, 1965;
Blue Blue Y, 1965; *Red Blue Purple
Green Gold*, 1965

6 *Blue Blue Y*, 1965*
Acrylic on canvas, 212×212 cm

7 *Orange Ochre Purple Yellow Y*, 1965*
Acrylic on canvas, 212×210 cm

9 *Red Pink Green Gray Blue Tan*, 1964
Acrylic on canvas, 213×213 cm

10 *Red Yellow Blue Pink Brown*, 1964*
Acrylic on canvas, 201×211 cm

11 *Yellow Pink Brown Blue*, 1964*
Acrylic on canvas, 213×213 cm

12 *Red Pink Green Gray*, 1965*
Acrylic on canvas, 213×213 cm

13 *Green Black*, 1964*
Acrylic on canvas, 182×180 cm

14–15 *Blue Red Gold Pink Green Yellow Y Bar*,
1965*
Acrylic on canvas, 181×360 cm

16–17 *Multi Raw Bar*, 1965*
Acrylic on canvas, 181×360 cm

18 *Orange Green Blue Interference*, 1965*
Acrylic on canvas, 201×200 cm

19 *Purple Orange Bar Interference*, 1965*
Acrylic on canvas, 209×213 cm

20–21 *Dioxomine Cerulean*, 1965*
Acrylic on canvas, 146×247 cm

22 Rosemarie Castoro painting *Arm Swing
Blues*, studio Polaroids, 1967

23 *Arm Swing Blues (Pencil Paintings)*, 1967
Acrylic and graphite on canvas,
211×314 cm

24 *Orange China Marker (Pencil Paintings)*,
1967*
Acrylic, Prismacolor pencils,
China marker, and graphite on canvas;
212×210 cm

25 *Pencil Painting Blues
(Pencil Paintings)*, 1967*
Acrylic, Prismacolor pencils,
China marker, and graphite on canvas;
209×212 cm

26–27 Exhibition view, MAMCO Geneva,
2019–2020
Clockwise: *Grey, Prismacolor Pencil
(Pencil Paintings)*, 1967; *Orange
China Marker (Pencil Paintings)*, 1967;
Purple Rose (Pencil Paintings),
1967–1968; *Pencil Painting Blues
(Pencil Paintings)*, 1967

28–29 Studio Polaroids from Castoro's
journals, 1970

40–41 *July Interference*, 1966*
Graphite on paper, 25×38 cm

42 *January Interference 2*, 1966*
Acrylic and graphite on paper,
25×38 cm

43 *January Interference*, 1966*
Acrylic and graphite on paper,
25×38 cm

44 *Inventory Series White and Brown*, 1968*
Acrylic, Prismacolor pencils, and
graphite on canvas; 152×250 cm

45 *Walking Hair Brain*, 2005
Artist's hair, inscription
"January 8, 2005"

46 *Split Inventory*, 1968*
Graphite on paper, 58×58 cm

47 *In Celebration of Part Time Work.
The Spaces Between the Objects
Oct 28 1968, April, 1969*, 1968–1969*
Graphite and color pencil on paper,
48×61 cm

48 *Oct 25, 1968/Jan 24, 1969*, 1968–69*
Graphite on paper, 48×62 cm

49 *Controlled Arbitrary Statements*, 1968*
Graphite on paper, 30×48 cm

50–51 Exhibition view, MAMCO Geneva,
2019–2020
Clockwise: *Owl Glasses: To See or
Not to See, That Is the Option*, 1993
(coll. Michel Bernheim); *Paula Cooper
Gallery Cracking*, 1969–2003
(coll. MAMCO); *Paula Cooper Gallery
Cracking*, 1969 (reprography);
What Is there anyway anywhere, 1969

52 *Paula Cooper Gallery Cracking*,
1969–2003*
Photo-collage, aluminum tape on
black and white print, coll. MAMCO*

53 *Seattle Cracking Outside*, 1969*
Pencil and aluminum tape on paper,
22.8×33 cm

55 *Cracking #7*, Paula Cooper Gallery,
1969*
Aluminum tape
Exhibition view: *Number 7*,
curated by Lucy Lippard

56 *Seattle Cracking*, Seattle Art Museum,
Washington, 1969
Aluminum tape
Exhibition view: *557,087*,
curated by Lucy Lippard

57 *Seattle Cracking*, Seattle Art Museum,
Washington, 1969
Aluminum tape
Exhibition view: *557,087*,
curated by Lucy Lippard

58 *Ariadne's Trail*, 1969*
Offset print, reproduced in *0 TO 9* n.6,
edited by Vito Acconci and Bernardette
Mayer, July 1969
Performance, 52nd Street and Fifth
Avenue, New York City, March 21, 1969
Contribution to *Street Works I*

59 *Ariadne's Trail*, 1969*
Black and white photograph
Performance around the artist's
studio at Spring Street, New York City,
March 15, 1969
Contribution to *Street Works I*

60 *Ariadne's Trail*, 1969*
Black and white photograph
Performance around the artist's
studio at Spring Street, New York City,
March 15, 1969
Contribution to *Street Works I*

61 *Atoll*, 1969*
Offset print, reproduced in *0 TO 9* n.6,
edited by Vito Acconci and Bernardette
Mayer, July 1969
Performance, 14th Street, 5th & 6th
Avenues, New York City, April 18, 1969
Contribution to *Street Works II*

62 *Atoll*, 1969*
Black and white photograph
Performance

63 *Atoll*, 1969*
Black and white photograph
Performance

64 *Atoll*, 1969*
Black and white photograph
Performance

65 *Atoll*, 1969*
Black and white photograph
Performance

66 *Gates of Troy*, 1969*
Black and white photograph
Performance

67 *Gates of Troy*, 1969*
Black and white photograph
Performance

68 *Gates of Troy*, 1969*
Black and white photograph
Performance

69 *Gates of Troy*, 1969*
Black and white photograph
Performance

77 *Running*,
1968–1970*
Color felt and pencil on paper,
27.9×21.5 cm

78 *A Day in the Life of a Conscientious
Objector, February 23, 1969, Hour #1*,
1969
Color felt and pencil on paper, leather
binder, 29.5×26 cm

79 *A Day in the Life of a Conscientious
Objector, March 21, 1969, Hour #20*, 1969
Color felt and pencil on paper, leather
binder, 29.5×26 cm

80 *A Day in the Life of a Conscientious
Objector, February 24, 1969, Hour #2A*,
1969
Color felt and pencil on paper, leather
binder, 29.5×26 cm

81 *A Day in the Life of a Conscientious
Objector, February 25, 1969, Hour #3*,
1969
Color felt and pencil on paper, leather
binder, 29.5×26 cm

82   *A Day in the Life of a Conscientious
        Objector, March 16, 1969, Hour #16,*
        1969
        Color felt and pencil on paper, leather
        binder, 29.5×26 cm

83   *A Day in the Life of a Conscientious
        Objector, March 18, 1969, Hour #18,*
        1969
        Color felt and pencil on paper, leather
        binder, 29.5×26 cm

84-88   *Love's Time, February 26, 1970 6:15
        P.M.–March 1, 1970 3:30 P.M.,* 1970
        Typewritten text on paper,
        27.9×21.5 cm

89   *Running,* 1970
        Typewritten text on paper,
        27.9×21.5 cm

99   *Room Revelation,* 1969*
        Installation, MAMCO Geneva,
        2019-2020: casters, hinges, door
        knob, sheetrock, plaster, light bulb,
        Rheostat mechanism;
        460×460×275 cm

100   *Room Revelation,* 1969*
        Installation, MAMCO Geneva,
        2019-2020: casters, hinges, door
        knob, sheetrock, plaster, light bulb,
        Rheostat mechanism;
        460×460×275 cm

        Ceiling Movement, 1969*
        Installation, MAMCO Geneva,
        2019-2020: casters attached
        to ceiling

101   *Room Revelation,* 1970*
        Pencil on paper, 43.8×55.8 cm

102-103 *8 Corners,* 1971*
        Installation, MAMCO Geneva,
        2019-2020: graphite, marble dust,
        gesso, hollow core doors;
        213×292×762 cm

104   *Rotating Corners,* 1971*
        Graphite on paper, 27.9×35.5 cm

        Cold Sake, 1971*
        Graphite on paper, 33×43.1 cm

105   *Cold Sake Deep Reflection,* 1971*
        Graphite on paper, 33×43.1 cm

106   *Foyer,* 1971*
        Graphite, marble dust, gesso, hollow
        core doors; 213.3×208.2×370.8 cm

107   *Spine on its Side,* 1970
        Graphite, gesso, marble dust,
        Masonite; 213×457×117 cm

        Two Curves, 1970*
        Graphite, gesso, marble dust,
        Masonite; 213.3×640×60.9 cm

109   *Corners,* 1971*
        Graphite on paper,
        25.4×35.5 cm (each)

110-111 *Guinness Martin,* 1972*
        Masonite, marble dust, gesso,
        graphite; 91×457 cm

113   *St.,* 1972
        Masonite, marble dust, gesso,
        graphite; 238×106 cm

114-115 Exhibition view, MAMCO Geneva,
        2019-2020
        Guinness Martin, 1972
        Corner Cut, 1972

116   *Sitting,* 1972*
        Gesso and graphite on paper,
        28×38 cm

        Up and Down, 1972*
        Gesso and graphite on paper,
        56.5×76.2 cm

117   *About C,* 1972*
        Gesso and graphite on paper,
        56.5×76.2 cm

118-119 *Land of Lads,* 1975*
        Epoxy, steel, pigments, Styrofoam;
        274×457×53 cm
        Collection Museum für
        Angewandte Kunst, Wien

120   *Land of Lads,* 1975*
        Ink on paper, 29.9×28.1 cm

121   *Untitled,* 1975*
        Graphite on paper, 29.9×28.1 cm
        coll. Cabinet des estampes,
        Musée d'art et d'histoire, Genève

122-123 *Mountain Range,* 2004-2011*
        Welded stainless steel,
        152×396×243 cm

124-125 Exhibition view, MAMCO Geneva,
        2019-2020

        Pressure, 1984
        Charcoal on museum boards,
        152×101 cm

        Land of Lashes, 1976
        Epoxy, steel, pigments, Styrofoam,
        28×322×122 cm

126   *Tunnel,* 1974
        Black and white Polaroids
        from Castoro's journal,
        August 1974-January 1975

127   *Symphony,* 1974
        Black and white Polaroids
        from Castoro's journal,
        August 1974-January 1975

128   *Symphony,* 1974
        Black and white Polaroid
        from Castoro's journal,
        August 1974-January 1975

129   *Branch Dance,* 1977*
        Whittled wood, 24.7×30.4×7.6 cm

130   *Two Walls Wired,* 1976*
        Gesso, marble dust, museum board,
        and wire; 13.3×23.5×21.5 cm

131   *Beaver's Trap* and *Forest of Threes,*
        1977-1978
        Black and white Polaroids
        from Castoro's journal

132-133 Exhibition view, MAMCO Geneva,
        2019-2020
        Black Flashers, 1979*
        Galvanized steel and paint;
        243×91 cm/250×70 cm/250×84 cm

135   *Knee-High Flashers (Triptych),* 1979*
        Steel, acrylic, and graphite;
        52.3×17.7×14.2 cm/
        53.3×23.5×17.7 cm/
        53.3×16.8×19 cm

136-137 *Flashers,* ca. 1970
        Installation view at 780 3rd Avenue,
        New York, 1984

144   Poster for *Street Works II,* 1969*
        Offset print, in *0 TO 9* n.6, July 1969

147   *Seattle Land Cracking/
        Room Revelation,* 1969*
        From the catalog of *557,087,*
        Seattle Art Museum, 1969

148   *Mover of Ceilings* insert in
        The Village Voice, March 13, 1969

151   *Left and right hand walk around
        my studio,* 1968-1969*
        Pencil on paper, 43×33 cm

160   Group portrait in Castoro's studio,
        ca. 1969

This book is published following the exhibition *Rosemarie Castoro. Time = space between appointment and meeting*, MAMCO Geneva, October 9, 2019–February 2, 2020. The exhibition was curated by Julien Fronsacq and received a donation by the Soros Fund Charitable Foundation.

MAMCO GENEVE

MAMCO Geneva
10, rue des Vieux-Grenadiers
CH–1205 Geneva
T +41 22 320 61 22
F + 41 22 781 56 81
E info@mamco.ch

MAMCO opened in 1994 thanks to the perseverance of AMAM (Association for a Modern Art Museum, now Friends of MAMCO) and the generosity of eight patrons, who created the FONDATION MAMCO. Pooling together the support of its founders and, later, its co-founders, the foundation was the main source of funding and the sole governing body of the museum up until 2005, when it joined forces with the State and City of Geneva to create a public foundation, known as FONDAMCO.

MAMCO is overseen today by FONDAMCO, which is made up of FONDATION MAMCO, the Canton, and City of Geneva. FONDAMCO would like to thank all its partners, both public and private, and in particular: JTI, Fondation Leenaards, and Fondation VRM, as well as Fondation Bru, Fondation Coromandel, Fondation du Groupe Pictet, Fondation Jan Michalski, Fondation Lombard Odier, Fondation Philnor, Lenz & Staehelin, Mirabaud & Cie SA, Christie's, and Sotheby's.

FONDAMCO

Philippe Bertherat, President
Ronald Asmar, Vice President
Anne Laure Bandle
Patrick Fuchs
Emmanuelle Maillard
Jérôme Massard
Carole Rigaut
Veronica Tracchia
Lada Umstätter

FONDATION MAMCO

Council
Philippe Bertherat, President
Luis Freitas de Oliveira, Vice-President
Jean Marc Annicchiarico, Treasurer
Karma Liess-Shakarchi, Secretary
Charles Beer
Jean-Pierre Greff
Emmanuelle Maillard
Shelby du Pasquier
Simon Studer

Founders
Claude Barbey
Jean-Paul Croisier
Pierre Darier
André L'Huillier
Philippe Nordmann
Pierre Mirabaud
Bernard Sabrier
—as well as the Friends Association, represented by its President, Patrick Fuchs

Co-founders
Anne-Shelton and Jean-Michel Aaron
Antonie and Philippe Bertherat
Marc Blondeau
Maryse Bory
Nicole Ghez de Castelnuovo
Bénédict Hentsch
Christina and Pierre de Labouchere
Aimery Langlois-Meurinne
Jean-Léonard de Meuron
Nadine and Edmond de Rothschild
Lily and Edmond Safra

Patrons
Jean Marc Annicchiarico
Antonie and Philippe Bertherat
Association des Amis du MAMCO
Verena and Rémy Best
Marc Blondeau
Bach-Nga Croisier
Darier Family
Angela and Luis Freitas de Oliveira
Christina de Labouchere
Karma Liess-Shakarchi
Emmanuelle Maillard
Jean-Léonard de Meuron
Pierre Mirabaud
Jacqueline Nordmann
Shelby du Pasquier
Marine and Claude Robert
Bernard Sabrier
Safra Foundation, represented by Samuel Elia
Sophie Sallès de Meuron
Simon Studer

TEAM

Lionel Bovier, Director

Museum Management and Development
Valérie Mallet, Administrator
Damien Grimm, Development Manager
Chloë Gouédard, Library, Archives, and Museum Resources
Julien Gremaud, Digital Communication
Viviane Reybier, Press and Communication

Exhibitions and Collection
Julien Fronsacq, Chief Curator
Françoise Ninghetto, Honorary Curator
Elisabeth Jobin, Curator
Charlotte Schaer, Collection Curator
Cyrille Maillot, Chief Exhibition Productions
Filipe Dos Santos, Exhibition Productions and Collection Registrar
Benoît Charron, Transport Registrar
Pierre-Antoine Héritier and Caroline Dick, Associate Restorers
Annik Wetter, Associate Photographer

Public and Education Services
Yann Abrecht, Public Services Manager
Virginie Keller, Public Services Coordinator
Franco Osses Vidal, Public Services Coordinator
Charlotte Morel, Education Services Manager
Julie Cudet, Education Services Coordinator

Facility Management and Surveillance
Antonio Magalhaes, Chief of Facility Management
Joana Gomes Da Silva, Facility Management
Carlos Martins Fonseca, Surveillance

PUBLICATION

Edited by
Lionel Bovier, with Chloë Gouédard

Translations from the French
Christophe Scala (Scala Wells)

Design
Gavillet & Cie/Devaud

Typeface
Tiny Gothic (www.optimo.ch)

Color Separation & Print
Musumeci S.p.A., Quart (Aosta)

Photo Credits
Estate Rosemarie Castoro, except Annik Wetter: p. 4–5, 24–27, 50–52, 99–100, 102–103, 110–111, 114–115, 118–119, 124–125, 132–133

ACKNOWLEDGMENTS

The book has received the support of the Estate Rosemarie Castoro and the gallery Thaddaeus Ropac London/Paris/Salzburg/Seoul. Special thanks go to Suzann Giugliano, Lori Maines, Werner Pichler, and Polly Robinson Gaer.

Printed in Europe

Published by
JRP|Editions
39, rue des Bains
1205 Geneva—Switzerland
www.jrp-editions.com

ISBN 978-3-03764-621-2

JRP|Editions books are available internationally at selected bookstores and from the following distribution partners:

Switzerland
AVA Verlagsauslieferung AG
www.ava.ch

Germany and Austria
JRP|Editions
books@jrp-editions.com

France
Les presses du réel
www.lespressesdureel.com

USA, UK and other European countries, Canada, Asia, and Australia
ARTBOOK | D.A.P.
www.artbook.com

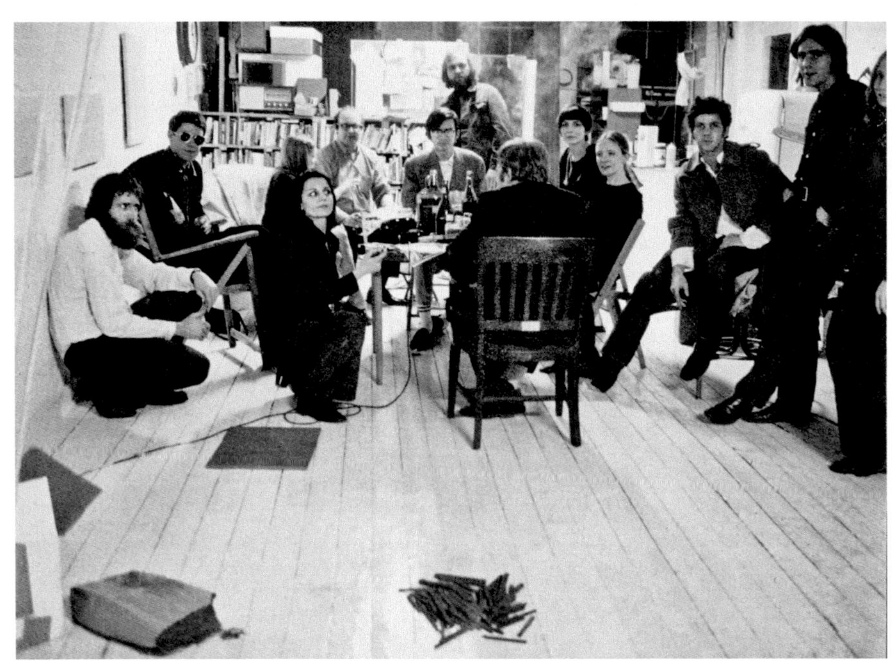

Group portrait in Castoro's studio, ca. 1969

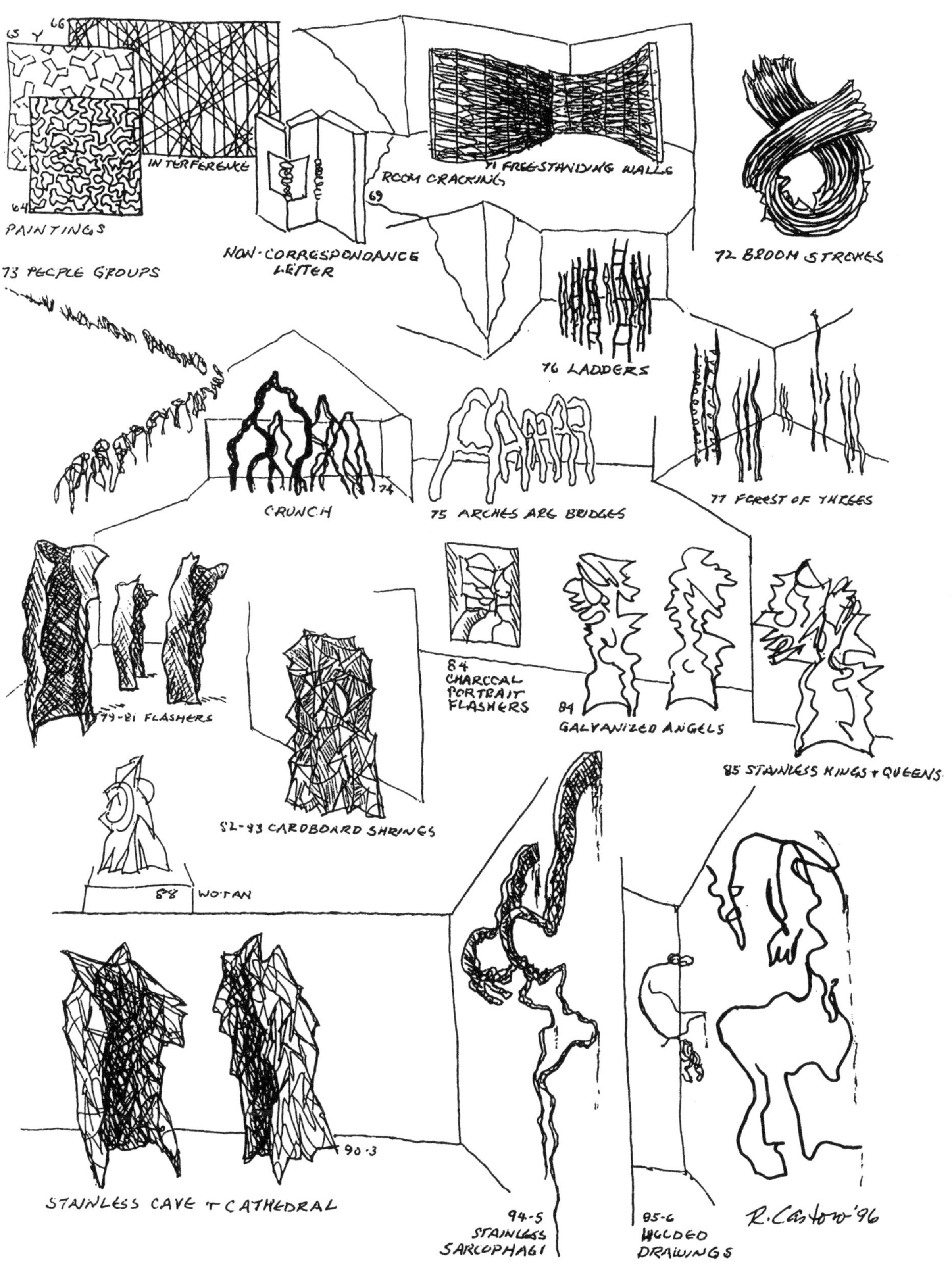

PAINTINGS
INTERFERENCE
NON-CORRESPONDANCE LETTER
ROOM CRACKING
71 FREESTANDING WALLS
72 BROOM STROKES
73 PEOPLE GROUPS
76 LADDERS
CRUNCH
75 ARCHES ARE BRIDGES
77 FOREST OF THREES
79-81 FLASHERS
82-83 CARDBOARD SHRINES
84 CHARCOAL PORTRAIT FLASHERS
84 GALVANIZED ANGELS
85 STAINLESS KINGS & QUEENS
88 WOTAN
STAINLESS CAVE & CATHEDRAL
94-5 STAINLESS SARCOPHAGI
95-6 WELDED DRAWINGS
R. Castoro '96